U0073626

China's International Military-Civilian Virology Fusion

High-Risk Pathogen Research,

Global Linkages and Strategic Implications

Dr. Ryan Clarke, Dr. Xiaoxu Sean Lin and LJ Eads

FIRST ENGLISH-LANGUAGE EDITION

Cover design by Tsao Xiurong

Published by Broad Press International Co., Ltd.
Printed in Taiwan
https://www.broadpressinc.com/
Tel: 886-2-2769-0599

For distribution and order inquiries:
Tel: 886-2-8245-8786
Fax: 886-2-2331-1073
silkbook.com Inc.

ISBN: 978-986-97774-8-3

First Printed April, 2023
Printed in Taiwan

Contents

Disclaimer

This book has been produced via utilizing exclusively open-source materials in order to ensure factual objectivity, independent verifiability and replicability. Through this strategic approach and set of methods, it has surfaced multiple transnational networks that are clearly engaging or have the potentials to engage in high-risk Gain-of-Function research in Chinese Communist Party-controlled facilities. However, this book does not impute specific intent to any individual or entity to engage in bioweapons research. We leave it to the reader to make their own determination and judgement. This book is not associated with any accusation of any individual or institution regarding the risks of their studies. This book is written based on the fundamental fact patterns, network structures and other direct or indirect evidence provided in this book.

About the Authors

Ryan Clarke is a Senior Fellow at the East Asian Institute, National University of Singapore. He has held leadership positions in defense and intelligence technology companies (full spectrum), investment banking, biodefense, strategic think tanks, emergency response organizations, and Tier 1 national security units. He is the author of four books and over 70 journal articles. He holds a PhD from the University of Cambridge where he was awarded the Salje Medal for the most innovative research. He can be contacted at eairjc@nus.edu.sg.

Xiaoxu Sean Lin is an Assistant Professor at Feitian College Middletown New York. He is a former U.S. Army Officer and Microbiologist. He obtained his Ph.D. degree in Microbiology and Immunology at University of Alabama at Birmingham, and a Master Degree in International Relations from the Maxwell School at Syracuse University. He is a frequent commentator for the Epoch Times Media Group, Radio Free Asia and Voice of America. He is also a member of the Committee of Present Danger: China.

LJ Eads is a retired U.S. Air Force Intelligence Officer, Signals Intelligence Analyst, and the Founder of Data Abyss. He has developed artificial intelligence capabilities in the domains of Space, Cyber, and Open-Source Intelligence for the Intelligence Community. He currently develops capabilities that are directly improving capabilities to collect, analyze, and provide intelligence products in the areas of China's strategic science and technology development using multi-lingual open sources.

The CCP BioThreats Initiative

Dr. Ryan Clarke, Dr. Xiaoxu Sean Lin and Mr. LJ Eads are the Founding Members of the CCP BioThreat Initiative. This book represents a foundational output of this Initiative. This has been produced to surface fundamental fact patterns, network structures and other targeting-relevant information pertaining to the CCP's multi-pathogen, multi-site bioweapons programs inside China and internationally. The CCP BioThreat Initiative is directly vectored against the full spectrum of bioweapons, neurobiological warfare, and human-computer interface-driven information warfare programs under the control of the Chinese Communist Party and its People's Liberation Army, United Front, and Ministry of State Security (國 家 安 全 部) . This Initiative leads multi-domain strategic net assessment exercises, specialized investigations and provides domain-specific augmentation and force multiplier enablement to government and private sector leaders in the United States and across the entire American Alliance structure globally.

Introduction and Strategic Rationale

This book is a must read for anyone concerned about national security, international security, health security and biosecurity, and next-generation asymmetric warfare.

The world has been dealing with nuclear threats for decades, both during and after the Cold War period. During the Cuban Missile Crisis in 1962, the world was on the brink of nuclear war. When the USSR collapsed, fourteen of the fifteen successor states to the Soviet Union chose to be nuclear weapons-free. Out of the roughly 3,200 strategic nuclear warheads that were once in Ukraine, Kazakhstan, and Belarus, most of them were intercontinental ballistic missiles (ICBMs). These were deactivated and returned to Russia where they were dismantled and the nuclear material in the warheads was blended down to produce fuel for civilian reactors. However, the former USSR also had 22,000 tactical nuclear weapons with smaller yields and shorter ranges[1] . It is surely an unrealistic assumption that all of these have also been returned to Russia thereby leaving zero nuclear weapons in any other state of the former Soviet Union or in the hands of non-state entities or hostile regimes. As such, it

---

1. Graham Allison, 'What Happened to the Soviet Superpower's Nuclear Arsenal? Clues for the Nuclear Security Summit', Faculty Research Working Paper Series RWP12-038, Harvard Kennedy School of Government, August 2012.

can be attributed to pure luck that no nuclear weapons were used following the collapse of the USSR.

Will the world be this lucky again if the Chinese Communist Party (CCP) regime collapses? As the CCP has become increasingly unstable, especially after the harsh economic conditions triggered by extreme 'zero-covid' policies and the intense power struggle surrounding Xi Jinping's third tenure fight, many people have realized that the collapse of the CCP is not an unrealistic scenario. Many people worried about the security of the nuclear arsenals under the control of People's Liberation Army (PLA) during this period of CCP destabilization or a transition period before complete collapse. Considering the CCP's long time support to the nuclear programs in Iran, Pakistan and North Korea, will the PLA's nuclear weapons be 'transferred' to them at a faster pace then? Will any of the PLA nuclear weapons end up in the hands of the Taliban? It could be a period that everything is for sale in the eyes of PLA military commanders.

However, while the national and global security experts are counting the nuclear arsenals under the PLA's Rocket Force, what about the other imminent threats and danger of biological weapons? China possesses an advanced biotechnology infrastructure as well as the requisite munitions production capabilities necessary to develop, produce and weaponize biological agents. Although China has consistently claimed that it has never researched or produced biological weapons, it is nonetheless believed likely that it retains a biological warfare capability that begun before acceding to the Biological Weapon Convention.

The PLA is ambitious in developing biological weapons as it is regarded as one core approach under the Unrestricted Warfare Doctrine. In 2015, then-president of the Academy of Military Medical Sciences He Fuchu (賀浮初) argued that biotechnology will become the new 'strategic commanding heights' of national defense, from biomaterials to 'brain control' weapons.[2] In addition, the 2017 edition of Science of Military Strategy (戰略學), a textbook published by the PLA's National Defense University that is considered to be authoritative, debuted a section about biology as a domain of military struggle, mentioning the potential for new kinds of biological warfare to include 'specific ethnic genetic attacks.'[3]

Going as far back as 2002, Eric Croddy at the Center of Nonproliferation Studies under the Monterey Institute of International Studies was able to identify multiple research, cultivation, and productions sites of biological warfare agents (BWA) in China :[4]

- Four unnamed biological warfare agents (BWA) production facilities in Lanzhou, Shenyang, Shanghai and Guangzhou.

2. Elsa Kania and Wilson Vorndick, Weaponizing Biotech: How China's Military Is Preparing for a 'New Domain of Warfare', Defense One, 14 August 2019.
   The Science of Military Strategy 2017, National Defense University, People's Liberation Army, Beijing, 2017.
3. Elsa Kania and Wilson Vorndick, Weaponizing Biotech: How China's Military Is Preparing for a 'New Domain of Warfare', Defense One, 14 August 2019.
   The Science of Military Strategy 2017, National Defense University, People's Liberation Army, Beijing, 2017.
4. Eric Croddy, 'China's Role in the Chemical and Biological Disarmament Regimes', The Nonproliferation Review. Spring 2002.

- Four named BWA production facilities (mentioned as 'factories'), affiliated, in general, with the 'Institutes for Biological Products'
- BWA productions systems in Kunming (dealing with research and cultivation of BWA), Chongqing (research and cultivation of BWA), Wuhan/Wuchang (cultivation of BWA) and Changchun (cultivation and experimentation of BWA)
- One named facility, Yan'an Bacteriological Factory, which produces warheads containing bacterial BWA, such as smoke type (probably aerosol) bombs as well as paper canister-type containers. [5]

According to assessments made by former Israeli Intelligence Officer Dany Shoham, China's Biological Weapon Program has a total of 32 institutes that are involved in the research, development, production, testing or storage of BWA. He states that:

> 'China is capable of developing, producing and weaponizing, on the whole, some 40 anti-human pathogens and toxins (P&T), either intact or genetically upgraded, if not largely engineered. Presumably, it comprises a first generation of BWA (for example, plague and brucellosis germs) in an operational state; a second generation of BWA (for example, Hantan and Japanese Encephalitis viruses) in an operational state; plus a third generation of BWA (for example, SARS, Ebola and Influenza viruses) still under development, in part or

---

5. Eric Croddy, 'China's Role in the Chemical and Biological Disarmament Regimes', The Nonproliferation Review. Spring 2002, Table 1, page 28.

entirely. Included are a considerable variety of P&T, both classic BWA and emergent P&T. Anti-livestock and anti-crop BWA are included as well in the Chinese BW inventory. A spectrum of toxins has been weaponized and others are under development.'[6]

Indeed, since the outbreak of COVID-19, the Gain-of-Function (GoF)[7] studies conducted on dangerous pathogens in the Wuhan Institute of Virology (WIV) have caught global attention. As a lab leak potential is no longer regarded as a conspiracy theory, WIV has become a potential origin of the SARS-CoV-2 virus and more and more people are questioning the connection between WIV and PLA operations. For example, WIV had a Military Management Division outlined on its own webpage prior to the COVID-19 outbreak.

Meanwhile, the impacts of WIV are not confined within China's borders either. WIV has launched a joint laboratory facility with the Defense Science and Technology Organization (DESTO),

---

6. Dany Shoham, 'China's Biological Warfare Programme: An Integrative Study with Special
Reference to Biological Weapons Capabilities', Journal of Defence Studies, Vol. 9, No. 2, April-June 2015.
7. Gain-of-Function (GoF) experiments are a controversial domain within biomedical science, defense and security fields. They are distinct from other scientific methods and approaches. These experiments are deliberately designed to enable pathogens to acquire and develop new properties including increased transmissibility, increased lethality, and resistance to drugs. It can also involve modifying pathogens to enable them to be transmitted between humans asymptomatically and/or to evade the human immune system response. Such lab-made chimera viruses are potentially more dangerous than viruses found in nature. GoF research has been subjected to episodic bans in the West while it has continued uninterrupted and virtually unregulated in China. During these prohibition periods in the West, some Western scientists have continued their GoF research with partners in China.

which is under the direct control of the Pakistan Army. This laboratory is a Biosafety Level 4 (BSL4) facility located in Rawalpindi, Pakistan.

The joint WIV-DESTO operation in Pakistan is not a bilateral biomedical research partnership between two civilian institutes focused on advancing human and animal health. It represents a dangerous platform for WIV and multiple other CCP-run institutions, including those with PLA links, to conduct bioweapons research under Pakistan Army cover. This structural reality combines with Pakistan's decades-long proven track record of utilizing home-grown terrorist groups, such as Lashkar-e-Taiba (LeT), to carry out terrorist operations in India. The net result is an extraordinarily high-risk geostrategic situation that has been virtually ignored by most analysts.

If the joint WIV-DESTO bioweapons program is left unchecked, China will further expand this kind of joint collaboration in other countries that might have fallen into the Belt-Road-Initiative Debt Trap. That is to say, China has been building a biological weapons network beyond China's territory, not just a conventional weapons arsenal.

The benefits of this strategy also include the diversion of risks as well as global attention on core facilities like the BSL4 at WIV. Indeed, Xi Jinping has ordered every province in China to build at least one BSL-3 lab. And China now has a total of four BSL4 labs[8] , which include one such facility built in Kunming. This BSL4 lab in Kunming has gone almost entirely undetected by the international community and is primarily tasked for experiments on large animals like non-human primates. This lab is officially managed by the Chinese Academy of Medical Sciences (CAMS).

So even after the CCP collapses, the world might find that the CCP has placed biological weapon mines in multiple locations in China and across the world. Are we ready to contain or neutralize the unprecedented risks posed by this transnational network of dangerous pathogen research? Moreover, this strategy of biological weapons development might be further obfuscated when military research projects could be integrated with or transferred entirely to civilian projects, which could be funded through nominally civilian national science or health agencies.

There is no such thing as a purely civilian virology lab in China under the CCP. The Civil-Military Fusion Law, which was exercised by the PLA during the COVID-19 pandemic, renders any institution, private company, or non-governmental organization vulnerable to forcible takeover by the state at any time. In addition, high-risk pathogen research that is being conducted at various Chinese virology institutes is under the direction of the CCP and, in some cases, the PLA. This represents a fundamental difference in the system between China under the CCP and the select few other nations that have the demonstrated capability to work with dangerous pathogens. It should also be noted that while the PLA continues to lag far behind the United

---

8. Gilles Demaneuf, 'BSL-4 laboratories in China: Kunming, Wuhan, Harbin', Medium, 27 April 2022.
   This report confirmed three BSL-4 labs (in Kunming, Wuhan and Harbin respectively) have been established. This report also made reference to a fourth BSL4 lab at Chinese CDC Beijing Headquarters, although the lab is not references in the World Health Organization Consultative Meeting on High/Maximum Containment (Biosafety Level 4) Laboratories Networking. For additional details, please see:
   WHO Consultative Meeting on High/Maximum Containment (Biosafety Level 4) Laboratories Networking, Meeting Report, World Health Organization, Lyon, France, 13-15 December 2017.

States and its Allies in the Indo-Pacific, the bioweapons domain is the one key area where China is currently 'upstream' and has clearly assessed that this provides the CCP with asymmetric options.

The WIV's experimentation with the Nipah virus (which has an 80-85% lethality rate in nature) is a clear case in point. Another clear example is WIV's demonstrated track record of enabling bat coronaviruses to directly infect human beings for the first time and to also enable these bat coronaviruses to evade the human immune system and to pass asymptomatically between people, all of which are clear indications of bioweapons research. No bioweapons development would be possible at WIV without the direct approval and control of the CCP and the PLA. However, the CCP's program extends well beyond WIV and also involves extensive transnational linkages outside of China.

Much of the contemporary focus regarding the current COVID-19 outbreak has centered on a relatively limited number of scientists at only one research institution in China, WIV, and, to a much lesser extent, the Harbin Veterinary Research Institute (HVRI). This overly narrow approach has resulted in a substantial gap in awareness regarding the broader Chinese network of high-risk pathogen research institutes that their international partners that are involved in very similar, if not outright identical, GoF experiments like those that have been conducted at the WIV.

This book provides unique primary data sources and forensic analysis related to WIV and HVRI while clearly demonstrating that the high-risk pathogen research that occurs within them can be traced back to transnational linkages with the West. This book also specifically focuses on the poorly understood Chinese Academy of Medical Sciences and Peking Union Medical College (CAMS/PUMC) and its specific constituent research units of the Institute of Medical Biology (IMB), Institute of Pathogen Biology (IPB), Christophe Merieux Laboratory (CML), and the Institute of Laboratory Animal Sciences (ILAS).

In addition, this study is the first extensive investigation and assessment of the Guangzhou Institute of Respiratory Health/ Huyan Institute (GIRH) and unique linkages with the CCP at the Guangzhou municipal level. Lastly, this study provides an in-depth description of the Academy of Military Medical Sciences (AMMS) and the Chinese Center for Disease Control and Prevention (Chinese CDC), their key personnel, high-risk experiments, and ongoing transnational linkages in the West and elsewhere.

There is an apparent pattern in our case studies: while these leading Chinese virology labs have benefited from extensive transnational links in the past, they have now reached 'criticality' in which they are domestically self-sustaining in their research capabilities. This will likely remain the case even if Western virology labs and universities were to decouple from their Chinese counterparts in joint collaboration due to intensifying geostrategic competition between their countries.

This work utilizes primary sources (both in English and Chinese) to fundamentally enumerate, characterize, map, and determine various strategic implications of the domestic linkages of these Chinese virology research labs. Some have been demonstrated to be conducting potential high-risk experiments on SARS-CoV-2, Nipah (80% lethality rate), African Swine Flu Virus, Zika, and

H5N1/H1N1/H7N9 while also internationally sourcing specific viral samples, such as Nipah virus, under unclear circumstances. The same analytical exercise is also executed regarding the international linkages of these Chinese labs to other partner labs in countries such as the United States, Canada, Australia, Holland, France, and Japan. The experiments that have been done by Dr Shi Zhengli and her team at the WIV are indeed high-risk and deserving of scrutiny. However, this research clearly demonstrates that this represents only one node of a much more domestically diversified and ambitious high-risk pathogen research network that extends throughout China and internationally, often across nominally civilian labs.

This study highlights the previously sparsely analyzed activities of WIV, HVRI, CAMS/PUMC, IMB, IPB, CML, ILAS, GIRH, AMMS, and Chinese CDC and places them into an international context. This research is the first concrete step to enumerate this international network in a fundamental manner. The intent is to more fully inform a range of strategic decision-making processes. All of the fundamental information in this assessment is derived from open and publicly-available sources in order to ensure technical objectivity and to establish a consistent, replicable foundation upon which future research can be conducted. This fundamental analysis fills a currently acute unmet gap in understanding for a range of strategic decisions that are currently being made and/or will be made over the near-term. This assessment is designed to serve as an analytical baseline 'reference map' for decision-makers and other related stakeholders in this critical domain.

CHAPTER ONE

Pathogen Research Networks in China: Origins and Steady Development

- Origins: Chinese Students Abroad
- How Do BSL4 Labs Operate?
- Wuhan Institute of Virology (WIV) –China's First BSL4 Lab: Past and Present
- WIV: Western-Trained Founding Fathers
- Management Structure of WIV: Party and State (National and Provincial)
- WIV Scientists: Domestic and International Networks
- Harbin Veterinary Research Institute (HVRI): BSL4 for Avian and Swine Flu
- Summary

CHAPTER 1 [9]

Pathogen Research Networks in China: Origins and Steady Development

Origins: Chinese Students Abroad

Chinese virologists and other related biomedical scientists began receiving training in advanced techniques and establishing subsequent scientific partnerships with Western institutions as early as the 1930s. For example, Professor Gao Shangyin, who is widely considered to be a founder of modern virology in China, went to the Rollins College in US for his undergraduate education in 1930 and earned his PhD from Yale in 1935. Professor Gao also founded the Wuhan Microbiology Laboratory in 1956 which then became the South China Institute of Microbiology CAS (Chinese Academy of Sciences) before

---

9. Segments of this chapter have previously appeared in Ryan Clarke and Lam Peng Er, 'Coronavirus Research Networks in China: Origins, International Linkages and Consequences', Centre for Non-Traditional Security Studies, May 2021, Singapore. They have been published with the consent of the Centre for Non-Traditional Security Studies.

https://rsis-ntsasia.org/wp-content/uploads/2021/06/NTS-Asia-Monograph-Coronavirus-Research-in-China-by-Ryan-Clarke-and-Lam-Peng-Er-May2021-1.pdf

becoming the Wuhan Microbiology Institute CAS in 1962. In 1970, control of this institution was transferred to the Hubei Commission of Science & Technology and it was renamed as Microbiology Institute of Hubei Province. In June 1978, administration was returned to CAS and the institution became known as the Wuhan Institute of Virology (WIV). WIV eventually established the first Biosafety Level 4 (BSL4) lab[10] in China in 2015 in cooperation with the French government. [11]

Initial progress in the field was incremental and problematic due to a combination of the loss of Soviet technical assistance and the domestic chaos triggered by the Great Leap Forward (1958-1962) and the Cultural Revolution (1966-1976). There is no record of Chinese publications before 1982 in Biomedical Social Sciences in the Web of Science (WS) database which covers the majority of the publications in this field since 1900.

Following the normalization of Sino-US relations in 1978 and paramount leader Deng Xiaoping's economic reforms from the same year, there was a large wave of Chinese students across

---

10. BSL4 is the highest level of biosafety precautions and facilities are specifically designed for work with pathogens that could easily be transmitted within the laboratory and cause severe to fatal disease in humans for which there are no available vaccines or treatments. Biosafety level 3 is appropriate for work involving microbes which can cause serious and potentially lethal disease via the inhalation route. Many of the protocols and other control measures in BSL4 and BSL3 labs are similar. For a more detailed technical overview, see United States Centers for Disease Control and Prevention, Biosafety in Microbiological and Biomedical Laboratories – 5th Edition, Atlanta, December 2009.
11. Economic Times, 'China flaunts French connection to Wuhan lab; Ambivalent on WHO probe into origin of coronavirus', 7 May 2020.

many disciplines (including virology) sent to the West for scientific training. As a result, the share of Biomedical publications from China over all publications in this field recorded by WS gradually increased since 1982 (Figure 1). The first few batches of Chinese students sent to the United States were mature scholars with families and strong links to China to ensure that they returned home. [12]

Figure 1. Share of Publications from China in the Field of Biomedical Science

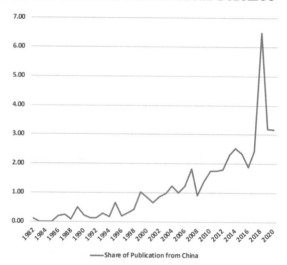

Share of Publication from China

Source: Authors' calculation based on search results from Web of Science.

Between 1978 and 2000 over 200,00 Chinese students went to the US alone. 57,000 of these students were directly funded by

---

12. William Wei, 'China's Brain Drain to the United States: Views of Overseas Chinese Students and Scholars in the 1990s', China Review International, Vol. 4, No. 1, 1997.

the Chinese government while another 102,000 were funded by government-related entities and companies. Some of these students returned upon completion of their studies while others chose to work abroad before returning to China to train the next generation of scientists. The 1989 Tiananmen Square massacre did not significantly impede the outward flow of Chinese students. Indeed, more Chinese students chose to stay in the United States after 1989 for better career progress and living environment and benefits. Then after China joined WTO, more Chinese overseas students chose to return to China as the economic rise in China provides opportunities for them to have high offer jobs in China, or having joint appointments in both China and abroad. [13]

This trend was particularly pronounced in the field of virology, epidemiology, and other related clinical/scientific fields. For example, the head of the Chinese Center for Disease Control and Prevention (Chinese CDC), Dr Gao Fu (also known as George Gao), did his doctoral training at Oxford (1991), spent time at the University of Calgary, and then returned to Oxford as a post-doctoral researcher. Gao then worked at Harvard Medical School in 1999 (funded by the UK's Wellcome Trust) and subsequently became a Lecturer at Oxford (2001-2004). [14]

There were virtually no restrictions on Chinese students studying scientific or technical fields in the United States, such as biological

---

13. Yabin Zhang and Xiaoqing Ma, '65 Years of Study Abroad History: From Soviet Union to the US, From Paid by Government to Paid by Family', Edited by Xiaoyi Wang, Data.163, 28 September 2014.
14. Chinese Academy of Sciences (CAS), 'Gao Fu'.
    http://people.ucas.ac.cn/~GeorgeGao

engineering. The Deng Xiaoping era from 1978 to 1989 has been referred to as a 'golden period' in Sino-US relations where there was a continuous flow of Chinese students into the United States with nearly unrestricted fields of study.[15] This trend continued in the post-Cold War era until the era of the COVID-19 global pandemic amid the sharp deterioration in Sino-US relations.

The 2003 Severe Acute Respiratory System (SARS) pandemic was a catalyst for China to rapidly enhance its biomedical research and BSL4-related domestic capabilities. The Chinese leadership prioritized the country to be adequately prepared for the next major outbreak by building out more domestic infrastructure and enhancing specific transnational scientific partnerships. The term 'biosafety' appeared in China's 10th Five-Year Plan (FYP) for the first time in 2001[16] prior to the 2003 SARS pandemic. In Section 2 (Cultivating the Bio-industry) of the 10th chapter (Accelerating the Development of High-tech Industries) in China's 11th FYP Outline in 2006, the need to 'guarantee biosafety' is also emphasized. [17]

This document mentioned 'biosafety research facilities' for the

---

15. For example, see Ezra Vogel, Deng Xiaoping and the Transformation of China, Belknap Press: 2011.
    Ezra Vogel (ed.), Living with China: U.S./China Relations in the Twenty-first Century, W.W. Norton: 1997.
16. National People's Congress of the People's Republic of China, 'Report on the Outline of the Tenth Five-Year Plan for National Economic and Social Development (2001)', 2001.
17. National People's Congress of the People's Republic of China, 'Report on the Outline of the 11th Five-Year Plan for National Economic and Social Development (2006)', 2006.

first time in an official FYP. In column 14 (Major Science and Technology Special Projects and Major Science and Technology Infrastructures) of Chapter 27 (To Accelerate Science and Technology Innovation), it specifically addresses and identifies major science and technology infrastructure such as the construction of spallation neutron sources, strong magnetic field devices, large-scale astronomical telescopes, and agricultural biosafety research facilities. To achieve these national objectives, China invited leading Western scientists who obtained unique and career-enhancing access to Chinese clinical/scientific networks, viral samples (such as SARS, avian influenza, and swine flu), and datasets. As we can see from Figure 1, the share of biomedical publications from China increased to be above 1% after 2003.

The period of 2008 to 2019 saw a major increase in the number of Chinese students going to the United States. The academic year of 2008/2009 saw 98,235 Chinese students heading to the United States. This figure increased to 369,548 by the academic year of 2018/2019. The most popular course was business management with engineering coming in a near second followed by computer science and mathematics. Interestingly, the majority of these students appeared to be self-funded.[18] This rapid increase in the representation of a specific nationality in American universities and laboratories is unprecedented.

---

18. This data has been derived from, Statista, 'Number of college and university students from China in the United States from academic year 2008/09 to 2018/19'. https://www.statista.com/statistics/372900/number-of-chinese-students-that-study-in-the-us/

The significant increase of self-funded students and scholars provides a great resource of income for colleges and universities in the United States. It also further obscured the differentiation between the self-funded and Chinese government funded.The student or scholar visa types did not indicate their connection with the Chinese government. Neither did visa types provide any information regarding their loyalty degree to the CCP or whether they have denounced CCP.

The efflux of Chinese students and scholars provides a great opportunity for many people to learn western science and technology and have better lives, yet it also provides a great opportunity for CCP to significantly infiltrate into the Western societies, to incubate United Front operations, to steal intellectual properties and technologies, as well as to build large international collaborations on projects that most people do not appreciate the true objectives and related threats.

International collaboration surely has its tremendous value when we enter this information age, as well as when the world is experiencing more and more disease outbreaks and threats that are not endemic to any particular countries only. The covid-19 pandemic has once again shown the value of international cooperation and collaboration. When the World Health Assembly convened in May 2020, member states passed a resolution emphasizing the need for solidarity, resource redistribution, and collective action.

However, do we have established mechanisms to sufficiently monitor and manage the risks associated with international collaboration? Do we have established mechanisms that help defend us from malign intentions or players that take advantage of international collaborations to reach their own objectives?

How Do BSL4 Labs Operate?

BSL4 labs are specifically designed to handle a range of analytical tasks and experiments with the world's most dangerous pathogens. In principle, a BSL4 lab has globally consistent standards, protocols, and training regimes regardless of which specific country the facility is in. The network ecosystems of BSL4 (and some specialized BSL3 labs) have highly dense connections and very frequent interactions with other peer labs within China and across the world. This is due to the finite number of these labs as well as the highly specialized research that occurs within them that only a select group of scientists are even capable of conducting.

Flows between these labs include (but are not limited to) datasets, scientific/clinical opinions, new technological methods and parameters for experiments, personnel themselves ,[19] physical samples, re-agents, and even temporary loaning of spare capacity. For example, one common practice is to divide the tasks based on each lab's expertise, with one lab focused on in vitro studies, another lab on animal studies, and other labs or centers on drug development, etc. Internationally, the overall mode of

---

19. Visiting research positions are common between peer labs.

interaction between BSL4 labs is collegiate with little competitive friction between groups due to a clear strategic preference from international funding bodies for multi-institutional and even multi-country research. As such, barriers to the abovementioned flows are minimal.

In addition, through collaboration, many institutions developed their own unique focus and expertise while sharing related knowledge and techniques are mutually beneficial. Publications from WIV and HVRI show that these two institutions have become more pathogen-specific and specialized, with the WIV being increasingly driven by work on coronaviruses. HVRI appears to do relatively less work on coronaviruses instead focusing heavily on avian influenza viruses, swine flu, and a range of other related zoonotic and exotic viruses.

Many of the international scientific partnerships in coronaviruses (especially bat-borne), avian influenza research (as well as other research on other rare but dangerous pathogens) are driven by a combination of self-interest mixed with pragmatic scientific considerations. This research on bat coronaviruses was previously considered highly obscure. Many working in this field around the world faced challenges such as finding permanent positions, obtaining adequate funding, and peer recognition. Close international partnerships were essential to collectively secure research funds, data, scientific journal editorial board connections, and physical samples required for their field to survive, attract talent, and grow.

A small number of lab groups distributed throughout China

(and a cluster of Western countries) became highly prominent in a manner uncharacteristic of many other branches of science. Chinese scientists who want to work in these fields have a highly constrained set of options within China (and even globally) that involve working under a handful of prominent scientific personalities. This configuration is ideal for the formation of a 'mutual echo chamber' that does not tolerate dissenting views regarding the safety or even the necessity of this research. This is potentially problematic in a scientific field that poses the types of global risks inherent in bat coronavirus, avian influenza, and other dangerous pathogen research. Many other scientific fields are characterized by a more diverse range of lab groups with competing approaches and methods. This has traditionally served the purpose of minimizing the risk of the blind pursuit of a scientific end-goal without adequate consideration being given to potential ethics violation, negative consequences, including catastrophic ones.

Since the advent of its post-Mao reform era, China has made strategic and sustained investments in higher education. This included scholarships for Chinese students to study in top international universities (especially in the United States), domestic scientific training (to seed the next generation), and laboratory/other related facility construction. China also established many programs (such as the Thousand Talents Program) for international scientists to serve as advisors and/or visiting research scientists in China. China has also frequently hosted high-profile international conferences (including a pipeline of 2021 conferences)[20] and funded spin-off companies in China to inspire scientists by demonstrating the 'real world impact' of the research they do in partnership with Chinese researchers.

WIV –China's First BSL4 Lab: Past and Present

While China has over 800 civilian virology labs across the country [21], China's three official BSL4 labs [22] are among the best known globally in terms of research output, international partnerships, and deep integration into China's larger public health ecosystem (civilian and military). The WIV was established in 1956 as a Microbiology Laboratory of CAS and it is one of the earliest national-level research institutes established after the founding of the People's Republic of China in 1949.[23] In 1961, the Microbiology Laboratory of CAS was upgraded to CAS Central South Institute of Microbiology and then renamed as CAS Wuhan Institute of Microbiology in 1962. In 1970, during the Cultural Revolution, it separated from CAS and was

20. For example, please see: Bioexpo – China 2021, 'The 4th China International BioPharma Conference & Exhibition', 19-21 September 2021.
http://www.cajc-china.com/?_l=en

21. George Gao, 'For a better world: Biosafety strategies to protect global health', Biosafety and Health, Vol. 1, No. 1, June 2019.

22. The other BSL4 labs are located in Harbin and Kunming and will be discussed in subsequent sections.

23. For more details, refer to Wuhan Institute of Virology (WIV), '中國科學院武漢病毒研究所喜迎建所五十周年華誕' (Wuhan Institute of Virology, Chinese Academy of Sciences celebrates its 50th anniversary; Zhong Guo Ke Xue Yuan Wu Han Bing Du Yan Jiu Suo Xi Yin Jian Suo Wu Shi Zhou Nian Hua Dan), 11 January 2006.
http://www.whiov.cas.cn/xwdt_160278/zhxw2019/201911/t20191111_5428884.html

renamed as Hubei Institute of Microbiology. In June 1978, it returned to the CAS and was named the Wuhan Institute of Virology of CAS with research disciplines adjusted accordingly.

After the SARS outbreak, the Chinese government initiated the construction of the BSL4 laboratory. WIV's BSL4 lab is jointly constructed by the CAS and the Wuhan local government. The technology and equipment of the BSL4 laboratory in Lyon, France were used. Chinese and French architects and scientists jointly designed the laboratory, and the Chinese construction unit completed the construction of the laboratory and the installation of its main facilities and equipment. After more than a decade, the major construction work of WIV's BSL4 lab was finished in 2015.

Since the COVID-19 outbreak in Wuhan in December 2019 (some estimates claim it was earlier)[24] , the WIV has attracted global attention because the WIV is China's first BSL4 lab and is located in the epicenter of this global epidemic. Despite the disruption and the lockdown of Wuhan city, the WIV worked round the clock to conduct a series of tasks including sequencing the RNA of this mysterious coronavirus, developing antivirals

---

24. For example, see Steven Quay, 'A Bayesian analysis concludes beyond a reasonable doubt that SARS-CoV-2 is not a natural zoonosis but instead is laboratory derived', Zenodo, 29 January 2021.
Steven Quay and Angus Dalgleish, The Origin of the Virus: The hidden truths behind the microbe that killed millions of people, Clinical Press Ltd., September 2021.
Steven Quay and Richard Muller, 'The Science Suggests a Wuhan Lab Leak: The Covid-19 pathogen has a genetic footprint that has never been observed in a natural coronavirus', Wall Street Journal, 6 June 2021.

and vaccines. The People's Liberation Army (PLA), led by Major General Dr Chen Wei, also inspected the WIV.[25] She was a key scientist that tackled SARS in 2003. The PLA is led by the Central Military Commission and headed by the CCP General Secretary and President Xi Jinping. The WIV is managed by the CAS under the State Council headed by Chinese Premier Li Keqiang. Notwithstanding this parallel system of governance (party and state) in China, Major General Chen investigated the WIV amidst a national crisis.

WIV: Western-Trained Founding Fathers

The three most important founders of WIV are Dr Gao Shangyin, Dr Chen Huagui, and Dr Jian Haoran. They obtained their PhDs abroad before the founding of the People's Republic of China in 1949. Dr Chen received his PhD in microbiology from the School of Bacteria and Tropical Diseases, University of London in 1939.[26] Dr Jian received his PhD in soil microbiology from the University of Wisconsin in 1948. [27]

All three founding fathers were active political party members. Gao Shangyin was a member of the Central Committee of the

---

25. For example, see Chan, Minnie and Zheng, William, 'Meet the major general on China's coronavirus scientific front line', South China Morning Post, 3 March 2020.

26. Xinhua,' 在 ' 土地上 ' 默默耕耘的陳華癸 ' (Chen Huagui who works silently on the 'land'; Zai Tu Di Shang Mo Mo Geng Yun De Chen Hua Gui), 6 November 2018.

27. Institute of Microbiology - Guangdong Academy of Sciences, ' 简 浩 然 教 授 ' (Professor Jian Haoran; Jian Hao Ran Jiao Shou), 26 August 2013. http://www.gdim.cn/jggk/lrld/201308/t20130826_121604.html

Democratic League and a member of the Central Senate Committee of the Democratic League.[28] Chen Huagui joined the CCP in 1956 and was a representative of the 3rd, 4th and 6th National People's Congress.[29] According to the official website of the Institute of Microbiology at the Guangdong Academy of Sciences (where Jian Haoran retired from), he was the alternate member of the 5th and the member of the 6th Central Committee of the Chinese Kuomintang Revolutionary Committee, member of the Standing Committee of the 5th Hubei Provincial People's Congress, and representative of the 2nd Guangzhou Municipal People's Congress. He was also a member of the CCP. [30]

Management Structure of WIV: Party and State (National and Provincial)

The WIV has formal organizational ties to CAS, CCP (party represented on the WIV Board of Directors as well as the CAS Leadership), provincial and city governments, and various other bodies. CAS is the peak scientific academy of China in Beijing under the State Council led by Premier Li Keqiang. CAS sets the strategic direction to the country's broader national technology

---

28. For more details, refer to the Wuhan Digital Local Chronicles Museum at ' 武漢 市志 - 第八卷 社會人物大事記 : 高尚蔭 ' (Wuhan City Chronicles-Volume 8 Memorabilia of Social Figures: Gao Shangyin; Wu Han Shi Zhi – Di Ba Juan She Hui Ren Wu Da Shi Ji: Gao Shang Yin).
http://szfzg.wuhan.gov.cn/book/dfz/bookread/id/273/category_id/58160.html

29. Huanchun Chen, et. al, The 100th Anniversary of Mr. Chen Huakui's Birth Anthology, China Science Publishing & Media Ltd. Beijing, 2014.

30. Institute of Microbiology - Guangdong Academy of Sciences, ' 簡 浩 然 教 授 ' (Professor Jian Haoran; Jian Hao Ran Jiao Shou), 26 August 2013.
http://www.gdim.cn/jggk/lrld/201308/t20130826_121604.html

development. It has more than 71,000 staff and has direct official oversight of WIV.[31] The President of CAS is Dr Hou Jianguo. He is also the CCP secretary of CAS and an Academician of Chinese Academy of Sciences (ACAS). Among the seven Deputy Presidents of CAS, only Gao Hong Jun is nonpartisan and not the member of CAS CCP Leader Group. However, Gao Hong Jun is a Member of the Standing Committee of the 12th and 13th National Committee of the Chinese People's Political Consultative Conference and also has the ACAS title. Four other Deputy Presidents of CAS also hold the ACAS title: Zhang Ya Ping, Zhang Tao, Li Shu Shen and Zhou Qi.

Dr Wang Yanyi is the current Director General of WIV while also holding the position of Deputy Chair of a United Front political party in Wuhan. She is married to Dr Shu Hongbin, a fellow immunologist who has held several senior positions at Wuhan University College of Life Sciences (Dean) and Wuhan University (Vice President). The power couple of Wang and Shu has a track record of joint publications.[32] They represent an established formal and informal relationship between the WIV,

---

31. For more details, refer to Chinese Academy of Sciences (CAS),' 中國科學院簡介 ' (Introduction to Chinese Academy of Sciences; Zhong Guo Ke Xue Yuan Jian Jie), 20 December 2020.
   https://www.cas.cn/zz/yk/201410/t20141016_4225142.shtml
   Chinese Academy of Sciences (CAS) ' 侯建國 '(Hou Jianguo; Hou Jian Guo).
   https://www.cas.cn/houjianguo/
32. For example, see YY Wang, HB Shu, et. al., 'VISA is an adapter protein required for virus-triggered IFN-beta signaling', Molecular Cell, Vol. 19, No. 6, 16 September 2005.
   YY Wang, HB Shu, et. al., 'A20 is a potent inhibitor of TLR3- and Sendai virus-induced activation of NF-kappa B and ISRE and IFN-beta promoter', FEBS Letters, Vol. 576, No. 1-2, 8 October 2004.

CAS, CCP, as well as other research institutes in Wuhan working in key areas of virology.

The apex of the WIV leadership structure is a CCP oversight team led by Party Secretary Xiao Gengfu. Another CCP member within WIV is Deputy Secretary of the Party Committee and Secretary of the Disciplinary Committee He Changcai. There are several other official CCP personnel within WIV, namely Guan Wuxiang, Sun Xiaolian, Li Liping, Cui Zongqiang, and Tong Xiao. However, they are simply listed as Party Committee members but with no descriptions of their respective roles. He Changcai's official mandate is presiding over the overall work of the Disciplinary Committee, assist the Party Committee in ensuring clean governance and anti-corruption work, and ensure the implementation of the CCP's official policy, party discipline, relevant laws and regulations, as well as WIV's own rules and regulations. [33]

WIV Scientists: Domestic and International Networks

WIV has established itself as a center of excellence across pathogens ranging from the Middle East Respiratory Syndrome (MERS), Zika, SARS and SARS-like viruses, Nipah, Ebola, HIV, and various insect-borne viruses such as Malaria.[34] There are 65

---

33. Wuhan Institute of Virology (WIV), 'Party Committee – Wuhan Institute of Virology, Chinese Academy of Sciences'.
   http://www.whiov.cas.cn
34. For example, Shi Zhengli's bat coronavirus bioengineering team at WIV and Chen Hualan's avian influenza bioengineering team at HVRI.

in-house scholars listed on WIV's official website, including 36 senior research fellows, five junior research fellows and 24 associate research fellows. Among them, there are 28 senior research fellows, one junior research fellow and six associate research fellows who have education, working or academic visiting experience abroad. The domestic and education experiences of the WIV scholars are related to 44 universities and institutions over 17 provinces and municipalities. Some scholars are not listed on WIV's official website but claim affiliation with WIV. For example, there are four scholars listed on the official website of the State Key Laboratory of Virology at Wuhan University (WHUKLV). But their names do not appear on WIV's official website. However, the WHUKLV's official website indicates that that they are also affiliated with WIV.

Perhaps the best-known researcher at WIV is Dr Shi Zhengli, a French-trained and internationally recognized bat coronavirus expert with expertise in virus zoonosis and genetic engineering. Shi and several colleagues (both domestically and internationally based) have several landmark publications in leading scientific journals such as Nature and Archives of Virology. Shi's International scientific collaborators include Dr Ralph Baric (University of North Carolina at Chapel Hill), Dr Jonna Mazet (University of California at Davis) and Dr Peter Dazsak (EcoHealth Alliance). [35]

Their studies used novel methods to enable a bat coronavirus to directly infect human beings without the need for an intermediate mammalian host. For example, the 2003 SARS coronavirus might have originated in bats and then infected humans via another mammal species, possibly pigs or civet cats. Additional experiments enabled these researchers to make this new chimera bat coronavirus more transmissible than even the most dangerous bat coronaviruses found in nature.[36] WIV has capabilities across a range of 'wet lab' environments that deal with physical biological materials as well as 'dry lab' environments that utilize advanced computational methods, including artificial intelligence and machine learning. This 'end-to-end' capability enables WIV to conduct state-of-the-art experiments across multiple domains within the field of virology including bat coronaviruses. [37]

---

35. See Shi Zhengli, Ralph Baric, et. al., 'A SARS-like cluster of circulating bat coronaviruses shows potential for human emergence', Nature Medicine, Vol. 21, No. 12, December 2015.
    Joana Mazet, Peter Daszak, Shi Zhengli, et. al., 'Isolation and characterization of a bat SARS-like coronavirus that uses the ACE2 receptor', Nature, Vol. 503, No. 28, November 2013.
    Fang Li, Linfa Wang, Shi Zhengli, et. al, 'Angiotensin-converting enzyme 2 (ACE2) proteins of different bat species confer variable susceptibility to SARS-CoV entry', Archive of Virology, Vol. 155, 22 June 2010.
36. See, Shi Zhengli, Ralph Baric, et. al., 'A SARS-like cluster of circulating bat coronaviruses
    shows potential for human emergence', Nature Medicine, Vol. 21, No. 12, December 2015. See also Joana Mazet, Peter Daszak, Shi Zhengli, et. al., 'Isolation and characterization of a bat SARS-like coronavirus that uses the ACE2 receptor', Nature, Vol. 503, No. 28, November 2013.
    Fang Li, Linfa Wang, and Shi Zhengli, et. al, 'Angiotensin-converting enzyme 2 (ACE2) proteins of different bat species confer variable susceptibility to SARS-CoV entry', Archive of Virology, Vol. 155, 22 June 2010.
    Lei-Ping Zheng, Peter Daszak, Shi Zhengli, et. al. 'Bat Severe Acute Respiratory Syndrome-Like Coronavirus WIV1 Encodes an Extra Accessory Protein, ORFX, Involved in Modulation of the Host Immune Response', Journal of Virology, Vol. 90, No. 14, July 2016.
    Ning Wang, Peter Daszak, Shi Zhengli, et. al. 'Serological Evidence of Bat SARS-Related Coronavirus Infection in Humans, China', Virologica Sinica, 2 March 2018.

WIV previously acknowledged housing a Military Management Division (MMD). This arrangement generated some concern around the potential dual-use nature of some of the research being done at WIV.[38] There are now no direct references to the MMD on the WIV website. Information regarding previous official US State Department visits to WIV has also been removed.[39] WIV also has dense connections with other institutions in Wuhan, such as the Wuhan Institute of Technology, Wuhan University (specifically the Medical School), Wuhan University of Science and Technology, and the Wuhan branch of the China CDC (located near the Huanan Seafood Market, possibly the initial point of origin of the COVID-19 pandemic in Wuhan).

From 1981 to 2020, WIV produced 2,288 publications co-authored with scientists from 1,728 institutions across 80 countries (including China). Before 1981, there had been no record. According to this publication record, scientific cooperation between WIV is particularly consistent with 138 institutions across 23 countries (measured by a track record of at

---

37. For a full organizational chart, see Wuhan Institute of Virology (WIV), 'Administration, Wuhan Institute of Virology – Chinese Academy of Sciences'. http://english.whiov.cas.cn/About_Us2016/Administration2016/
38. Glen Owen, 'Wuhan virus lab was signed off by EU Brexit chief Michel Barnier in 2004 – despite French intelligence warnings that China's poor bio-security reputation could lead to a catastrophic leak', The Guardian, 23 May 2020.
39. Josh Rogin, 'State Department cables warned of safety issues at Wuhan lab studying bat coronaviruses', New York Times, 14 April 2020.
40. Information retrieved from Web of Science by authors.
   Web of Science is a leading automated scientific literature review software tool that enables researchers to query international scientific publications across specific scientific domains, including those directly related to the field of virology.

least 5 joint publications). [40] Domestically, WIV researchers have relatively more active cooperation with colleagues from 119 other institutions (have 5 or more joint publications). WIV has the most productive scientific partnerships with the University of Chinese Academy of Sciences (709 joint publication), the Wuhan University (358 joint publication), the Institute of Biophysics Chinese Academy of Sciences (162 joint publication). It also has very active cooperation with the Academy of Military Medical Sciences China (24 joint publications) and the Second Military Medical University (8 joint publications).[41] These joint publications show WIV's close relationship with both China's academy and military.

Besides the WIV's domestic networks and partnership with the West, it also has links to the Third World. This BSL4 lab in Wuhan appears to be a mentor to some developing countries. For example, the Gates Foundation has sponsored visits from multiple African countries to visit WIV and learn about its BSL4 lab. [42]

41. Information retrieved from Web of Science by authors. See, for example, Wuhan Institute of Virology and the Center for Biosafety Mega-Science, CAS, 'The research team of Wuhan Institute of Virology/ Biosafety Science Center and the Academy of Military Sciences found that calcium channel inhibitors can treat fever with thrombocytopenia syndrome (SFTS)', 30 August 2019.
42. Wuhan Institute of Virology (WIV). 'Experts of public health from 10 African countries visited WIV, CAS', 21 November 2018.
http://english.whiov.cas.cn/Exchange2016/Foreign_Visits/201811/t20181121_201447.html

HVRI: BSL4 for Avian and Swine Flu

The HVRI was established in 1948, a year before the People's Republic of China.[43] The Institute's first director and CCP representative was Professor Chen Lingfeng.[44] Located in Harbin (Heilongjiang Province), the HVRI has been the 'go-to' institute for various animal viruses which are zoonotic and pathogenic to livestock and/or humans. The HVRI has internationally recognized expertise in avian influenza viruses, namely the H5N1 and H7N9 viruses. HVRI is under the Chinese Academy of Agricultural Sciences (CAAS) and can award doctoral degrees. HVRI was established as the PRC's second BSL4 lab in 2018. In addition to avian influenza viruses, HVRI also researches swine flu and other influenza viruses that infect other animal species.

CAAS is a peak scientific academy in Beijing responsible for the national development in agricultural science and related areas. CAAS is led by CCP members and also reports to the State Council. The HVRI has 566 staff with 76 senior researchers. HVRI is physically large (covering more than 69,600 square

---

43. The modern study of virology in Harbin, and arguably China as a whole, traces its origins to Dr. Wu Lien Teh, a Cambridge-educated infectious disease physician from Penang Island, Malaya (present day Malaysia). Dr Wu spearheaded a successful campaign to contain the 1910-1911 Manchurian epidemic that resulted in 60,000 fatalities. Harbin today is home to a museum dedicated to Dr Wu. See Zhongliang Ma and Yanli Li, 'Dr. Wu Lien Teh, plague fighter and father of the Chinese public health system', Protein Cell, 7:3 (March 2016).
44. Ping Yuan, 'The Chinese Society of Animal Husbandry and Veterinary Medicine held an academic annual meeting to show the appearance of experts. Animal husbandry and veterinary experts highlight the role of science and technology to promote animal husbandry. Experts at the meeting wish Chen Lingfeng 90th birthday', China Animal Husbandry, Vol. 19, 2003.

meters) and also has a laboratory animal breeding farm covering 1,532,900 square meters in suburban Harbin. HVRI will relocate to a new site that covers 271,800 square meters. Given the scale of this physical expansion, HVRI is likely to hire more staff. [45]

While it is likely that the CCP exerts similar WIV-style governance and ideological control over HVRI, information regarding specific CCP personnel and their functions at HVRI itself is more opaque. However, the CAAS does provide information on CCP personnel within its governance structure and it appears that CCP personnel occupy more prominent leadership positions than the CAAS's scientific leadership team. For example, Tang Huajun serves both as President of CAAS and as an official Member of the Leading Party Group, Ministry of Agriculture.[46] Other prominent CCP members are Zheng Hecheng (Secretary of the Leading Party Group – CAAS), Li Jieren (Head of Discipline Inspection Group – CAAS), Liu Daqun (Member of Leading Party Group – CAAS), and Jia Guangdong (Director General, Department of Personnel – CAAS). [47]

From the period of 1987 to 2020, HVRI produced 1814 publications co-authored with scientists from 809 institutions across 52 countries, including China. Before 1987, there was no

45. For more information, see Chinese Academy of Agricultural Sciences (CAAS) 'About Us - Harbin Veterinary Research Institute'.
   http://www.hvri.ac.cn/en/aboutus/athvri/index.htm
46. While many scientific personnel within CAAS, HVRI, and/or WIV are members of the CCP, it is not typically officially declared.
47. Chinese Academy of Agricultural Sciences (CAAS), 'Leadership – Chinese Academy of Agricultural Sciences'.
   http://www.caas.cn/en/administration/Leadership/index.html

record. According to these publication records, the cooperation between HVRI and 50 international institutions across 12 countries are especially active (as measured by 5 or more than 5 joint publications). [48]

Domestically, HVRI researchers have relatively more active cooperation with colleagues from 74 other institutions (as measured by 5 or more joint publications). HVRI has the most productive scientific partnerships with the Northeast Agricultural University China (232 joint publication), the Harbin Medical University (80 joint publication), and the Northeast Forestry University China (70 joint publication). It also has very active cooperation with the Academy of Military Medical Sciences China (42 joint publications), Air Force Military Medical University (7 joint publications), China Ministry of Agriculture (18 joint publications), and WIV (10 joint publications). [49] These joint publications show HVRI'S close relationship with both China's academia and military.

HVRI has many international partnerships, including an industry collaboration with leading animal health company Boehringer Ingelheim. The 'industry-academia-research' exchange platform was established in May 2019 and is the first of its kind in China. This partnership encompasses training (classroom and lab-based), joint research and development, and student exchanges that enable HVRI postgraduate students to conduct research within the broader Boehringer Ingelheim corporate scientific

---

48. Information retrieved from Web of Science by authors.
49. Ibid.

infrastructure. [50]

One of the most well-known researchers at HVRI is Dr Chen Hualan, a leading veterinary virologist who worked at the US Centers for Disease Control and Prevention from 1999 to 2002. Chen's recent work focuses on avian influenza viruses. Some of her experiments have generated controversy, especially bioengineering avian influenza viruses. [51]

One of Chen's most controversial studies was published in June 2013 on experimental methods that enabled the H5N1 avian influenza virus to develop pandemic potential by picking up entire genes from H1N1. This H1N1 is the highly virulent influenza virus that caused a global epidemic in 2009. By combining segments of H5N1 and H1N1 viruses in her lab, Chen developed a new hybrid virus that can transmit airborne between mammals. Such a chimera virus is not found in nature. [52]

50. Boehringer Ingelheim, 'Boehringer Ingelheim and Harbin Veterinary Research Institute set up 'industry-academia-research' exchange platform', 10 May 2019.
https://www.boehringer-ingelheim.com/press-release/new-exchange-platform-harbin-research-institute

51. Martin Enserink, 'Single Gene Swap Helps Bird Flu Virus Switch Hosts', Science, 2 May 2013.
https://www.sciencemag.org/news/2013/05/single-gene-swap-helps-bird-flu-virus-switch-hosts

52. Ibid.
Also see Hualan Chen, et. al., 'H5N1 Hybrid Viruses Bearing 2009/H1N1 Virus Genes Transmit in Guinea Pigs by Respiratory Droplet', Science, Vol. 340, No. 6139, 21 June 2013.

Summary

In the critical early developmental period, Chinese scientists benefitted from open and unrestricted access to Western education, mentorship, datasets, and other key scientific inputs. Subsequently, a small core of both Chinese and international scientists emerged and collaborated on risky pathogen research. Many international scientists saw unique opportunities in China often not present in their home countries, such as substantial research funding, strong investment in core scientific infrastructure for novel experiments, and a relatively permissive operating environment. This has boosted China's capability in virology research to the extent where the country is now leading in this domain. It is now capable of autonomous research and development in this field and less dependent on its erstwhile Western pathogen mentors.

CHAPTER TWO

Biosafety Level 4 Laboratories at WIV and HVRI and Their Key International Linkages

- Global Virology Partnerships: Key Drivers
- Are GoF Experiments Necessary for Major Scientific Advances?
- WIV's International GoF Links
- Bat Coronavirus GoF 'Breakthroughs' in 2010-2016: International Cooperation in Bioweapons Research
- GoF Research on Nipah Virus: High-Probability Bioweapons Research With (At Least) International Awareness
- Summary

CHAPTER 2 [53]

Biosafety Level 4 Laboratories at WIV and HVRI and Their Key International Linkages

Global Virology Partnerships: Key Drivers

The origins and diffusion of risky pathogen research are clear and unambiguous. This research began in key Western countries and then diffused to China. Indeed, the most high-risk components were 'outsourced' to a few key Chinese labs.[54] Apparently, some Western lab groups engaging in these scientific activities believed that they could influence and guide these experiments in China. However, this has not occurred.

The network of advanced BSL3 labs and BSL4 labs have highly

---

53. Segments of this chapter have previously appeared in Ryan Clarke and Lam Peng Er, 'Coronavirus Research Networks in China: Origins, International Linkages and Consequences', Centre for Non-Traditional Security Studies, May 2021, Singapore. They have been published with the consent of the Centre for Non-Traditional Security Studies.
https://rsis-ntsasia.org/wp-content/uploads/2021/06/NTS-Asia-Monograph-Coronavirus-Research-in-China-by-Ryan-Clarke-and-Lam-Peng-Er-May2021-1.pdf
54. For example, see Christina Lin, 'Why US outsourced bat virus research to Wuhan', Asia Times, 22 April 2020.

dense connections and almost daily interactions within China and across the world. This is due to the finite number of these labs as well as the highly specialized research that occurs within them that only a select group of scientists are even capable of conducting. Many of the international scientific partnerships in coronaviruses (especially bat-borne), avian influenza research, swine flu, as well as other research on other rare but dangerous zoonotic pathogens are driven by a combination of self-interest mixed with pragmatic scientific considerations.

Many working in the field around the world faced challenges such as finding tenured positions for themselves, obtaining adequate funding, and attaining scientific recognition. Close international partnerships were essential to collectively secure research funds, data, scientific journal editorial board connections, and physical samples required for their field to thrive.[55] A small number of virology lab groups in China and a few Western countries became highly prominent in a manner uncharacteristic of many other branches of science.[56] Scientists who work in these fields have a highly constrained set of options that involve working under a handful of prominent scientific personalities. This characteristic is particularly pronounced in China.

---

55. This is based upon the professional experience of Ryan Clarke when he worked in the fields of biodefense and public health in the Asia-Pacific, United States, and United Kingdom.
56. Ibid.

Are GoF Experiments Necessary for Major Scientific Advances?

GoF experiments are a controversial domain within biomedical science, defense and security fields. They are distinct from other scientific methods and approaches. These experiments are deliberately designed to enable pathogens to acquire and develop new properties including increased transmissibility, increased lethality, and resistance to drugs. Such lab-made chimera viruses are potentially more dangerous than viruses found in nature.

These 'Frankenstein' experiments are supposed to generate predictive knowledge and insight for scientists to anticipate how viruses could leap from one species to another host, and then trigger the next lethal pandemic. Armed with such lab-based knowledge, the global health community can then prepare for early and swift detection, containment and prevention of the next deadly pandemic. As evidenced by the COVID-19 outbreak as well as other coronavirus outbreaks such as the Middle East Respiratory Syndrome (MERS), the track record of these research is dubious. First reported in Saudi Arabia in 2012, MERS spread to many countries including Thailand and South Korea. Avian flu viruses such as H5N1 (2003) and H7N9 (2013), both of which originated in China, have broken out. Simply put, GoF experiments thus far have not prevented any pandemics.

GoF experiments have also been conducted on many highly dangerous pathogens including the Highly Pathogenic Avian Influenza H5N1 (HPAI H5N1)– often referred to as simply H5N1. Before the COVID-19 outbreak, GoF research on H5N1 was considered to be the most high-risk and controversial. Many scientists have voiced outright opposition to these experiments.[57] Some skeptics have pointed out that no major vaccine has been developed despite GoF research on H5N1, SARS, MERS, or any other highly dangerous pathogens.

Funding streams, data sharing, joint publications, and other related outputs on GoF research on H5N1 have taken place with Western scientists working in partnership with their Chinese counterparts. GoF transnational research on bat coronaviruses have gained prominence in recent years. Given the potential risks posed by GoF bat coronavirus research, it is critical that the transnational research network is mapped, characterized, and accurately described for a more comprehensive assessment of risks and benefits.

HVRI and the Doherty Institute at the University of Melbourne: Combining Human and Avian Influenza Viruses

The former mentor and long-time scientific collaborator of HVRI's Chen Hualan is Dr. Kanta Subbarao of the Doherty Institute at the University of Melbourne. Subbarao has a well-established track record of high-risk research on avian influenza viruses and has jointly produced multiple such studies with Chen. Chen and Subbarao have a particular demonstrated focus on

---

57. For example, see Felix Rey, Olivier Schwartz, and Simon Wain-Hobson, 'Gain-of-function research: unknown risks', Science, Vol. 342, No. 6156:311, 18 October 2013.

combining elements of different avian influenza and human influenza viruses to produce new chimeric viruses. For example, in 2003 they conducted an experiment where they combined H1N1 and H3N2 human influenza viruses with genes from the H9N2 avian influenza virus, an event that would have been highly unlikely to have occurred in nature. Chen and Subbarao claimed that combining the genes of human and avian influenza viruses would help to develop a human vaccine. No such vaccine has been developed to date. [58]

Chen and Subbarao went on in 2006 to conduct additional experiments with H3N2 human influenza viruses to make them more transmissible between ferrets via respiratory droplets. They also combined H5N1 (the most lethal known avian influenza virus) genes with H3N2 and noted that this reassortment greatly enhanced H5N1 viral transmissibility. Chen and Subbarao had demonstrated how to make the world's most dangerous avian influenza virus much more transmissible between humans via

---

58. Kanta Subbarao, Hualan Chen, et. al., 'Generation and Characterization of an H9N2 Cold-Adapted Reassortant as a Vaccine Candidate', Avian Diseases, Vol. 47, No. s3, September 2003.
    Please also see Kanta Subbarao, Hualan Chen, et. al., 'Generation and characterization of a cold-adapted influenza A H9N2 reassortant as a live pandemic influenza virus vaccine candidate', Virology, Vol. 305, Iss. 1, 5 January 2003.
    Kanta Subbarao, Hualan Chen, et. al., 'Evaluation of a Genetically Modified Reassortant H5N1 Influenza A Virus Vaccine Candidate Generated by Plasmid-Based Reverse Genetics', Virology, Vol. 305, Iss. 1, February 2003.
    Kanta Subbarao, Hualan Chen, et. al, 'Generation and characterization of a cold-adapted influenza A H9N2 reassortant as a live pandemic influenza virus vaccine candidate', Vaccine, Vol. 21, November 2003.
59. Kanta Subbarao, Hualan Chen, et. al., 'Lack of transmission of H5N1 avian– human reassortant influenza viruses in a ferret model', PNAS, Vol. 103, No. 32, 8 August 2006.

reverse engineering techniques. [59]

WIV's International GoF Links [60]

The WIV bat coronavirus research group led by Dr Shi Zhengli has pioneered experiments that enable bat coronaviruses to directly infect human cells without the traditional need for an intermediate host such as a civet cat, pangolin, mink and pig. Despite being a highly controversial research field, Shi has openly published her GoF research. It is noteworthy that a substantial portion of this research was originally done with scientists from the University of North Carolina at Chapel Hill. [61]

Despite the severe COVID-19 outbreak in the United States, several other American lab groups, such the Galveston National Laboratory (another BSL4 facility which is part of the University of Texas system) openly claimed that WIV had impeccable standards and that the COVID-19 virus could simply not have emerged from the facility.[62] The U.S. Department of Education

---

60. Three network graphs outlining key entities that are linked to WIV and the specific nature of those relationships can be found in Annex A. A full set of network diagrams outlining all of WIV's domestic as well as transnational institutional linkages based off of joint publications and grant awards can be found in Annex A as well. All data was collected using the automated search and knowledge representation capabilities of Data Abyss. https://www.dataabyss.ai/

61. For example, see Vineet Menachery, et. al., 'SARS-like cluster of circulating bat coronavirus pose threat for human emergence', Nature Medicine, Vol. 21, No. 12, December 2015.
WIV also conducts research on the Middle East Respiratory Syndrome (MERS), Zika, SARS and SARS-like viruses, Nipah, Ebola, HIV, and various insect-borne viruses such as Malaria.

investigated the links between the University of Texas and various Chinese labs (WIV in particular) as well as the Chinese state-owned telecommunications giant Huawei.[63] Apparently, the Director of the Galveston National Laboratory, Dr James Le Duc, visited WIV several times during the construction phase of WIV's BSL4 facility and provided advisory inputs [64].

Another key member of Shi's team is Dr Zhou Peng. He completed his Ph.D. training at the Australian Centre for Disease Preparedness (formerly known as the Australian Animal Health Laboratory) in Geelong, Australia. Zhou Peng's placement was jointly funded by the Chinese and Australian governments.[65] Zhou then completed a post-doctoral fellowship at the Duke-NUS Medical School in Singapore. [66]

GoF experiments are widely assessed to have little or no real scientific value. No current consequential coronavirus therapeutic, diagnostic, vaccine, or any other relevant breakthrough has been directly attributed to this work. In fact,

---

62. Hollie McKay, 'Prominent university bio lab urged to reveal extent of relationship with Wuhan lab at centre of coronavirus outbreak', Fox News, 1 May 2020.

63. For example, see Kate O'Keefe, 'U.S. Probes University of Texas Links to Chinese Lab Scrutinized Over Coronavirus', The Wall Street Journal, 1 May 2020.
Yuelong Shu, Nancy Cox, et. al., 'A ten-year China-US laboratory collaboration: improving response to influenza threats in China and the world, 2004-2014', BMC Public Health, No. 19, Vol. 520, 10 May 2019.

64. John Wayne Ferguson, 'Galveston bio lab explains connections to Wuhan', The Daily News, 22 April 2020.

65. Kelly Burke, 'Australian CSIRO in Geelong linked to coronavirus 'bat laboratory' theory', 7 News, 28 April 2020.

66. For example, see Peng Zhou, Shi, Zhengli, et. al., 'IFNAR2-dependent gene expression profile induced by IFN-alpha in Pteropus alecto bat cells and impact of IFNAR2 knockout on virus infection', PLOS ONE, Vol. 17 January 2018.

the University of North Carolina researchers suspended their collaboration with the WIV in October 2014 after the US government banned federal funding on all GoF studies on influenza, MERS, and SARS. However, Shi and her team continued their work at WIV after being officially licensed in 2015 by NIH to both continue bat coronavirus GoF research and receive American funds despite the ban and funding moratorium within the United States itself. [67] This is ironic indeed.

Besides its US partnerships, WIV has a strong French connection. The Institute was designed with substantial French technical assistance[68] followed by a scientific exchange program that never fully materialized. Only a token French researcher (there were supposed to be up to 50) was ever able to spend time at WIV. These developments generated concern within French intelligence and security circles[69] given the nature of the experiments being done at WIV and the fact that WIV had a 'Military Management Division'. The Military Management Division clearly indicated an official PLA presence in WIV. [70] Shi Zhengli also individually maintains French linkages with INSERM, a leading French biomedical research institute with strong infectious disease control research capabilities. Critically,

---

67. Christina Lin, 'Why US outsourced bat virus research to Wuhan', Asia Times, 22 April 2020.
68. Both Institut Pasteur and Institut Merieux were heavily involved in the physical design and development of key management and scientific protocols.
   Shi Zhengli obtained her doctorate at Montpellier 2 University in Montpellier, France.
69. Glen Owen, 'Wuhan virus lab was signed off by EU Brexit chief Michel Barnier in 2004 – despite French intelligence warnings that China's poor bio-security reputation could lead to a catastrophic leak', The Guardian, 23 May 2020.
70. Ibid.

INSERM houses a BSL4 lab in Lyon where GoF experiments have been conducted on H5N1 and H5N1 viruses.[71] Shi has maintained a particularly close relationship specifically with Dr. Branka Horvat who conducts high-risk research on Nipah and has made official visits to WIV to discuss this research under Shi's research group structure.[72] Shi was hosted by Horvat and the INSERM team at the BSL4 lab in Lyon on 23-24 September 2019 as part of an event organized by former French Prime Minister Jean-Pierre Raffarin and French biotechnology industry leader Alain Merieux. This event was also attended by Lu Shaye, Chinese Ambassador to France. [73]

71. 'The P4 Jean Merieux-Inserm Laboratory expands making it one of the largest facilities in the world', Merieux Foundation, 18 May 2015.
https://www.fondation-merieux.org/en/news/the-p4-jean-merieux-inserm-laboratory-expands-making-it-one-of-the-largest-facilities-in-the-world/
Olivier Ferraris, et. al., 'The NS Segment of H1N1pdm09 Enhances H5N1 Pathogenicity in a Mouse Model of Influenza Virus Infections', Viruses, Vol. 10, No. 504, September 2018.
72. 'Professor Branka HORVAT in French National Institute of Health and Medical Research visited WIV', Wuhan Institute of Virology, 1 August 2016.
http://english.whiov.cas.cn/Exchange2016/Seminars/201712/t20171212_187686.html
'The French Ambassador to China bestowed medals on Two Scientists in Wuhan Institute of Virology', WIV Newsletter, No. 11, July 2016.
Branka Horvat, et. al., 'Reprogrammed Pteropus Bat Stem Cells as A Model to Study Host-Pathogen Interaction during Henipavirus Infection', Microorganisms, Vol. 9, No. 12, December 2021.
73. 'Perspectives for Reinforcing Scientific Cooperations', Ecole Normale Superieure Lyon, 30 September 2019.
http://www.ens-lyon.fr/en/article/research/perspectives-reinforcing-scientific-cooperations

Bat Coronavirus GoF 'Breakthroughs' in 2010-2016: International Cooperation in a Potential Bioweapons Research

Joint Sino-US-Australian teams[74] published several GoF studies in leading scientific journals such as Nature and Archives of Virology in 2010, 2013, and 2015. These studies showed how a bat coronavirus can directly infect human cells without the need for an intermediate mammalian host.[75] Additional experiments enabled these researchers to make these lab-modified bat coronavirus more transmissible than bat coronaviruses found in nature.[76] These experiments sparked major debates within the scientific and security/defense communities.

However, the points made in opposition to these experiments were ignored by this transnational network of bat coronavirus GoF researchers. They continued their work openly at various institutions in China, Australia, and the United States, amongst

---

74. The Australian Centre for Disease Preparedness, Australia's BSL4 lab in Geelong (outside of Melbourne) have refrained from making comments so far, despite the fact that extensive research was conducted on bat coronaviruses in this facility with Dr. Shi even spending time there as a visiting scientist in 2006.

75. See Shi Zhengli, Ralph Baric, et. al., 'A SARS-like cluster of circulating bat coronaviruses
shows potential for human emergence', Nature Medicine, Vol. 21, No. 12, December 2015.
Joanna Mazet, Peter Daszak, Shi Zhengli, et. al., 'Isolation and characterization of a bat SARS-like
coronavirus that uses the ACE2 receptor', Nature, Vol. 503, No. 28, November 2013.
Fang Li, Linfa Wang, Shi Zhengli, et. al, 'Angiotensin-converting enzyme 2 (ACE2) proteins of different bat species confer variable susceptibility to SARS-CoV entry', Archive of Virology, Vol. 155, 22 June 2010.

others. The clearest evidence of this disregard is a subsequent 2016 study in which the same group of lead researchers clearly crossed into bioweapons research. In this study, Shi Zhengli and her team at WIV along with Peter Daszak from EcoHealth Alliance used reverse genetics method to constructed a full-length infectious cDNA clone of a SARS-like bat coronavirus strain (called SL-CoV WIV1 or rWIV1) and a related mutant clone called rWIV1-GFP-ΔX. The SL-CoV WIV1 strain contained the Open Reading Frame X (ORFX) gene, while rWIV1-GFP-ΔX strain deleted the ORFX gene. [77]

By comparing the functions of these two recombinant strains of viruses, they found that ORFX could inhibit interferon production and activate NF-κB. Their results demonstrated for the first time that the unique ORFX in the WIV1 strain is a functional gene involving modulation of the host immune response. In other words, this study demonstrated how to reverse engineer infectious clones of SL CoV and how a viral gene can

---

76. See Shi, Zhengli, Ralph Baric, et. al., 'A SARS-like cluster of circulating bat coronaviruses
    shows potential for human emergence', Nature Medicine, Vol. 21, No. 12, December 2015.
    Joanna Mazet, Peter Daszak, Shi Zhengli, et. al., 'Isolation and characterization of a bat SARS-like
    coronavirus that uses the ACE2 receptor', Nature, Vol. 503, No. 28, November 2013.
    Fang Li, Linfa Wang, Shi Zhengli, et. al, 'Angiotensin-converting enzyme 2 (ACE2) proteins of different bat species confer variable susceptibility to SARS-CoV entry', Archive of Virology, Vol. 155, 22 June 2010.
77. Shi Zhengli, Peter Dazsak, et. al., 'Bat Severe Acute Respiratory Syndrome-Like Coronavirus WIV1 Encodes an Extra Accessory Protein, ORFX, Involved in Modulation of the Host Immune Response', Journal of Virology, Vol. 90, No. 14, July 2016.

modulate its pathogenicity.[78] And the rWIV1-GFP-ΔX is a mutant clone that has higher pathogenicity than its parental strain of rWIV1, since it replicates efficiently and does not have this ORFX gene that exists between ORF6 and 7. It is interesting that no more journal publications about any further study of the ORFX gene could be found since then. In addition, the sequence of the small protein expressed by ORFX gene (Genbank: ATO98224.1) could not find any homology with any known protein in the Genbank search. Where did this gene come from? Why was the ORFX gene never found in any other bat coronavirus strains collected in WIV or globally?

In addition, the SARS-CoV-2 genome also does not have this ORFX gene. Does the absence of ORFX have anything to do with the pathogenicity of SARS-CoV-2 if this virus was a natural or engineered derivant of bat coronavirus? It should be noted that the infection by wild type SARS-CoV-2 virus leads to severe multi-organ failure and at the same time around 40% of all confirmed COVID-19 infections were asymptomatic. [79]

All of this research was done publicly with the knowledge and awareness of possibly thousands of peers. Moreover, most high-

---

78. Shi Zhengli, Peter Dazsak, et. al., 'Bat Severe Acute Respiratory Syndrome-Like Coronavirus WIV1 Encodes an Extra Accessory Protein, ORFX, Involved in Modulation of the Host Immune Response', Journal of Virology, Vol. 90, No. 14, July 2016.

79. Daniel Oran and Eric Topol, 'Prevalence of Asymptomatic SARS-CoV-2 Infection', Annals of Internal Medicine, 1 September 2020.
Qiuyue Ma, et. al., 'Global Percentage of Asymptomatic SARS-CoV-2 Infections Among the Tested Population and Individuals With Confirmed COVID-19 Diagnosis: A Systematic Review and Meta-analysis', JAMA Network Open, Vol. 4, No. 12, 14 December 2021.

risk GoF experiments were 'outsourced'[80] to China in response to domestic criticisms of tinkering with nature in other Western countries, especially the United States. Dr Simon Wain-Hobson, a leading virologist at Institut Pasteur in Paris, openly warned that GoF experiments are potentially dangerous especially if there is a leak from the lab. [81]

The links between the United States and the WIV might well have extended beyond scientific collaboration. US$3.7 million of US-taxpayer provided funds were transferred to WIV from NIH (in full) to specifically fund bat coronavirus GoF research projects despite identical work being shut down in the United States itself.[82] This link and flow of American public funds raises the question whether this grant was an erroneous one-off or if it was the tip of the iceberg indicating much broader links between Chinese and American labs. After initial denials, NIH Director Anthony Fauci has officially acknowledged that US$600,000 was subcontracted to WIV as part of a US$3.7 million grant awarded to Daszak's EcoHealth Alliance. These US taxpayer-provided funds specifically supported bat coronavirus GoF research projects at the same time that identical work was banned and shut down in the United States itself.' [83]

80. Christina Lin, 'Why US outsourced bat virus research to Wuhan', Asia Times, 22 April 2020.
81. Jef Akst, 'Lab-Made Coronavirus Triggers Debate', The Scientist, 16 November 2015.
Simon Wain-Hobson, 'An Avian H7N1 Gain-of-Function Experiment of Great Concern', mBio, Vol. 5, No. 5, September/October 2014.
82. Shawna Williams, 'NIH Cancels Funding for Bat Coronavirus Research Project', The Scientist, 28 April 2020.

GoF Research on Nipah Virus: High-Probability Bioweapons Research With (At Least) International Awareness

World-renowned physician, vaccine developer, and biomedical scientist Dr Steven Quay recently testified in a U.S. Congressional hearing that his team have identified evidence that WIV was conducting dangerous experiments on Nipah virus. Nipah is a BSL4-level pathogen and US Centers for Disease Control and Prevention (US CDC)-designated Bioterrorism Agent.

Dr. Quay made this detection in raw RNA-Seq sequencing reads which were deposited by WIV itself produced from five December 2019 patients infected with SARS-CoV-2. Research involving Nipah infectious clones has never been reported to have occurred at the WIV and these patient samples were also reported to contain reads from several other viruses: Influenza A, Spodoptera frugiperda rhabdovirus and Nipah. Other scientists erroneously interpreted the presence of these virus sequences as indicative of co-infections of the patients in question by

83. Harriet Alexander, 'Fauci and NIH defend giving $600K to Wuhan to study how viruses can transmit from bats to humans before COVID-19 outbreak - after being accused of funding 'gain of function' research in heated argument with Rand Paul', Mail Online, 26 May 2021.
https://www.dailymail.co.uk/news/article-9618623/Fauci-NIH-confirm-600-000-public-money-went-Wuhan-two-weeks-Rand-Paul-row.html
It should also be noted that this US$600,000, while specifically targeted towards bat coronavirus GoF research, represents a mere fraction of the US$337 million that has been given to China for biomedical research (including virology) by the Gates Foundation. For additional information, see:
Tracy Qu, 'The Bill & Melinda Gates Foundation is spending millions in China, a fraction of its total funding', South China Morning Post, 6 May 2021.

these pathogens or laboratory contamination. However, Quay's analysis clearly demonstrates that Nipah genes are actually encapsulated in synthetic vectors, which was specifically designed for the assembly of an infectious Nipah clone. Quay and his team also note that contamination of patient sequencing reads by an infectious Nipah clone of the highly pathogenic Bangladesh strain could indicate a significant breach of BSL4 protocols.

Quay documents the presence of Nipah sequences, Bangladesh strain, interpreted as likely for assembly of a Nipah infectious clone, found in raw sequencing reads by WIV from five patients infected with SARS-CoV-2 sampled by the Wuhan Jin Yin-Tan Hospital at the beginning of the COVID-19 outbreak.[84] The Bangladesh strain of Nipah virus was often associated with high levels of oral shedding and is one of the most transmissible and pathogenic strains of Nipah viruses. The five patients experienced COVID-19 illness onset between 12 December 2019 and 23 December 2019 and were admitted to intensive care between 20 December 2019 and 29 December 2019 with all BALF (bronchoalveolar lavage fluid) sampling conducted on 30 December 2019and 10 January 2020. BioProject PRJNA605983 containing the analyzed samples was actually registered by WIV with GenBank on 11 February 2020 and consists of nine RNA sequencing (RNA-Seq) BALF datasets. NGS (next-generation sequencing) was undertaken at the WIV using BGI MGISEQ-2000 and Illumina MiSeq 3000 sequencers [85].

---

84. Peng Zhou, Shi Zheng-Li, et. al., 'A pneumonia outbreak associated with a new coronavirus of probable bat origin', Nature, Vol. 579, 12 March 2020.
85. Peng Zhou, Shi Zheng-Li, et. al., 'A pneumonia outbreak associated with a new coronavirus of probable bat origin', Nature, Vol. 579, 12 March 2020.

Some mistakenly interpreted[86] the presence of these virus sequences as indicative of co-infection of early Wuhan COVID-19 infected patients with these microbes. However, Quay analyzed the presence of a sequence H7N9 Hemagglutinin A segment 4 gene and found in a synthetic vector in these COVID-19 patient samples. He concluded that contamination was the likely cause while his colleague Dr Zhang Daoyu[87] identified the presence of a Nipah infectious clone in the datasets.

Nipah was designated a a priority research area at WIV[88]. However, after a search using Google Scholar and Pubmed, only two publications by WIV-affiliated authors were found in the 2018-2020 year period: a general overview of phylogeny, transmission and protein structure[89] and an article relating to rapid detection assay research, but which only concerns N gene pseudotyped Nipah virus, rather than a fully assembled Nipah infectious clone.[90] Interestingly, WIV Chief Biosafety Officer

86. For example, see Sandeep Chakraborty, 'There was a simultaneous outbreak of the zoonotic Nipah henipavirus in Wuhan - 4 out of 5 patients have the virus in Jinyintan Hospital, along withSARS-Cov2, in their metagenome - which seems to have resolved by itself', OSF, 1 October 2020.
   Mohammed Abouelkhair, 'Non-SARS-CoV-2 genome sequences identified in clinical samples from COVID-19 infected patients: Evidence for co-infections', PeerJ. 2 November 2020.
87. Steven Quay, Daoyu Zhang, et. al., 'Vector sequences in early WIV SRA sequencing data of SARS-CoV-2 inform on a potential large-scale security breach at the beginning of the COVID-19 pandemic', Zenodo, 19 September 2021.
88. Shi Zheng-li, 'Inter-nation collaboration Sino-French NiV taskforce 2019', Nipah Virus International Conference, 9-10 December, Singapore.
   https://cepi.net/wp-content/uploads/2020/06/2019-Nipah-Conference-Proceedings.pdf
89. Bangyao Sun, et. al., 'Phylogeography, Transmission, and Viral Proteins of Nipah Virus', Virologica Sinica, Vol. 33, No. 5, 2018.

Yuan Zhiming is on public record openly stating that WIV is working on synthetic biology studies to manipulate the proteins of Nipah viruses as well as Ebola that involve animal models. [91]

Over the course of Dr. Quay's Nipah-focused investigation he and his team detected other contaminating sequences, including HIV, Simian Virus and Woodchuck Hepatitis Virus that are all synthetic vector-related and not related to primary patient infection. These findings converge with previous findings on significant contamination at Wuhan sequencing facilities was previously documented by Dr. Zhang Daoyu[92] Middle Eastern Respiratory Syndrome (MERS) and SARS-CoV-1 genomes recovered from agricultural sequencing datasets. Those sequences are consistent with an infectious Nipah clone and numerous other synthetic sequences[93] were found in samples from the earliest sequenced COVID-19 patients in Wuhan. Quay notes

---

90. Liping Ma, et. al., 'Rapid and specific detection of all known Nipah virus strains' sequences with reverse transcription-loop-mediated isothermal amplification'. Frontiers in Microbiology, Volume 10, Article 418, March 2019

91. 'U.S China Dialogue and Workshop on the Challenges of Emerging Infections, Laboratory Safety, Global Health Security and Responsible Conduct in the Use of Gene Editing in Viral Disease Research', Draft Version 4, Harbin Veterinary Research Institute – Chinese Academy of Agricultural Sciences, 8-10 January 2019. This document was obtained via a Freedom of Information request from the University of Texas System.

92. Steven Quay, Daoyu Zhang, et. al., 'Vector sequences in early WIV SRA sequencing data of SARS-CoV-2 inform on a potential large-scale security breach at the beginning of the COVID-19 pandemic', Zenodo, 19 September 2021.
Daoyu Zhang, et. al., 'Unexpected novel Merbecovirus discoveries in agricultural sequencing datasets from Wuhan, China', ArXiv 6 June 2021.

93. Steven Quay, et. al., 'Contamination or Vaccine Research? RNA Sequencing data of early COVID-19 patient samples show abnormal presence of vectorized H7N9 hemagglutinin segment', Zenodo, 3 July 2021.

that this could indicate serious contamination problems at WIV. Quay fundamentally assesses that the finding of Nipah gene sequences attached to synthetic vectors (presumably for assembly as a full length infectious Nipah clone of the highly pathogenic Bangladesh strain) in datasets of the earliest sequences COVID-19 patients in Wuhan is potentially a significant breach of BSL4 protocols. [94]

Summary

Chinese pathogen facilities are closely networked with many Western laboratories which provided significant assistance, including physical design and construction of facilities, joint design and execution of the most high-risk experiments, and even direct transfer of research funds to Chinese institutions such as WIV. Indeed, under the mentorship of the Western scientists, Chinese virology labs have impressively grown in capability and coverage of dangerous pathogens.GoF studies have become their unique expertise with the cloning of Nipah virus being clear evidence of their accelerating ambition.

---

94. Steven Quay, et. al., 'Contamination or Vaccine Research? RNA Sequencing data of early COVID-19 patient samples show abnormal presence of vectorized H7N9 hemagglutinin segment', Zenodo, 3 July 2021.

CHAPTER THREE

Critical Assistance from Virology Networks Abroad

CHAPTER 3 [95]

Critical Assistance from Virology Networks Abroad

This chapter examines the invaluable foreign assistance to the two Chinese BSL4 laboratories in Wuhan and Harbin and the Institute Pasteur of Shanghai, especially during their formative years. Chinese pathogen laboratories have now acquired considerable expertise and are no longer dependent on foreign mentors. However, transnational collaboration is still mutually useful in this field. External networks have helped to strengthen the top Chinese laboratories to the extent that they can operate autonomously. Given the rising capability of these labs, China is on the road to becoming a 'virology power' second to none.

---

95. Segments of this chapter have previously appeared in Ryan Clarke and Lam Peng Er, 'Coronavirus Research Networks in China: Origins, International Linkages and Consequences', Centre for Non-Traditional Security Studies, May 2021, Singapore. They have been published with the consent of the Centre for Non-Traditional Security Studies.
https://rsis-ntsasia.org/wp-content/uploads/2021/06/NTS-Asia-Monograph-Coronavirus-Research-in-China-by-Ryan-Clarke-and-Lam-Peng-Er-May2021-1.pdf

USAID and PREDICT Project

Since 2009, the United States Agency for International Development (USAID) has funded the PREDICT project (US$200 million total funding) as part of its Emerging Pandemic Threats (EPT) program. The Trump Administration ended this program in March 2020. PREDICT's mandate was to enhance global surveillance capability, which includes novel sample collection of viruses in nature and subsequent physical sample distribution and data sharing.[96] These activities were meant to more rapidly and accurately detect 'zoonotic spillover events' (i.e., animal viruses making the 'species jump' and infecting humans). Much work done by PREDICT was on bat coronaviruses in tropical Asia, especially in Yunnan province of China, and Assam and Nagaland in Northeast India. [97]

A major recipient of PREDICT funds (as well as NIH funds)[98] and other material support is the EcoHealth Alliance, a non-profit organization based in New York city. EcoHealth Alliance also focuses on tropical Asia, including Southeast Asia, and has been openly endorsed by USAID. The Head of EcoHealth Alliance, Dr. Peter Daszak, is one of the lead WHO investigators tasked to examine the origins of the COVID-19 pandemic.

---

96. For example, see USAID PREDICT Semi-Annual 2019 Report. https://ohi.sf.ucdavis.edu/sites/g/files/dgvnsk5251/files/files/page/SAR2019-draft-final-compressed.pdf
97. Ibid.
98. For example, see Peter Daszak, 'Understanding the Risk of Bat Coronavirus Emergence', NIH Grant Database. https://grantome.com/grant/NIH/R01-AI110964-06

Daszek featured prominently in many documentaries such as 'Coronavirus, Explained' where he openly discussed his work in bat caves in Yunnan.[99] Daszak has supported the WIV (including publicly calling Shi Zhengli a 'hero' [sic.]). Daszek has provided a blueprint strategy to prevent a repeat of the '2019-nCoV outbreak'. The reality check is that despite marketing itself as the expert team in the virology field, the EcoHealth Alliance clearly missed this outbreak.[100]

EcoHealth Alliance also has a strong relationship with the University of California at Davis, another major partner of USAID's PREDICT Program. UC Davis hosts the One Health Institute, which received a US$85 million grant from USAID in October 2019 for 'capacity building' in Southeast Asia.[101] The One Health Initiative's mandate and mission overlap with that of

---

99. For a recent mainstream American media example, see Julie Zaugg, 'The virus hunters who search bat caves to predict the next pandemic', CNN, 27 April 2020.

See also Simon Anthony, Peter Daszak, et. al., 'Global patterns in Coronavirus diversity', Virus Evolution, Vol. 3, No. 1, 2017.

Michael Letko, et. al., 'Bat-borne virus diversity, spillover, and emergence', Nature Reviews Microbiology, Vol. 18, 2020.

Shi Zhengli, Peter Daszak, et. al., 'Bats Are Natural Reservoirs of SARS-Like Coronaviruses', Science, 2005.

Peter Daszak, et. al., 'Global hotspots and correlates of emerging zoonotic diseases', Nature Communications, Vol. 8, No. 1124, 24 October 2017.

Shi Zhengli, Peng Zhou Peng, Peter Daszak, et. al., 'Fatal swine acute diarrhoea syndrome caused by an HKU2-related coronavirus of bat origin', Nature, Vol. 556, No. 7700. April 2018.

Shi Zhengli, Peter Daszak, et. al., 'Discovery of a rich gene pool of bat SARS-related coronaviruses provides new insights into the origin of SARS coronavirus', PLOS Pathogens, 30 November 2017.

100. For example, see Peter Daszak, et. al., 'A strategy to prevent future epidemics similar to the 2019-nCoV outbreak', Biosafety and Health, Vol. 2, No. 1, March 2020.

EcoHealth Alliance. The Executive Director of the One Health Initiative (and scientific collaborator with Daszak) is Dr. Jonna Mazet. The One Health Initiative is housed in UC Davis's School of Veterinary Medicine with associated laboratory and other physical clinical research infrastructure.

EcoHealth Alliance has a relatively flat management structure and is not officially tied to any academic institution. This allows the EcoHealth Alliance to serve as the 'tip of the spear' for bat coronavirus surveillance work in Yunnan and Northeast India. Perhaps this 'sub-contracted' fieldwork represents activities that One Health Initiative and PREDICT program personnel cannot carry out personally in those Asian localities. Daszak and his team have joint publications with Shi Zhengli and Zhou Peng at WIV. Similarly, Mazet has joint publications with Shi and Daszak.[102] Their close transnational collaboration in virology is evidenced by these publications.

To these Western scientists, the WIV team worked as their local team in collecting field samples, harboring various bat species, exploring GOF studies in labs and conducting field testing of genetically modified pathogens. This type of collaboration appears to provide a unique way to get things done while keeping the Western scientists' hands clean without doing the dirty jobs.

---

101. Kat Kerlin, '$85M to Develop a One Health Workforce for the Next Generation - USAID Award Supports New Project Led by UC Davis One Health Institute', University of California at Davis, 9 October 2019.

102. For example, see Peter Daszak, Joanna Mazet, Shi Zhengli, et. al., 'Joint China-US Call for Employing a Transdisciplinary Approach to Emerging Infectious Diseases', Ecohealth, Vol. 12, No. 4, 2015.97. Ibid.

But do they know or how do they manage the risks if there are military interests from the PLA behind these projects?

Global Virome Project: A Privatized Transnational Enterprise

Mazet, Daszak and Dr. Dennis Carrol serve on the Global Leadership Team of the Global Virome Project (GVP). The GVP is a consultancy for infectious disease control programs and 'managing partner investment and optimizing return on investment'. Dr. Carrol previously headed USAID's Emerging Pandemic Threats Program that supported PREDICT. [103]

Dr. Gao Fu (George Gao), Director of the Chinese Center for Disease Control and Prevention in Beijing (Chinese CDC), endorsed the GVP in 2018.[104] Gao was at the Institute of Microbiology at the Chinese Academy of Sciences then. Gao did his doctorate at Oxford (1991), conducted research at the University of Calgary, and then returned to Oxford for a post-doctoral fellowship. Gao then worked at Harvard Medical School in 1999 (funded by the UK's Wellcome Trust) and eventually

---

103. For more information, see http://www.globalviromeproject.org/who-we-are
104. See, for example, George Gao, Joanna Mazet, Peter Daszak, Peter, et. al., 'The Global Virome Project', Science, Vol. 359, No. 6378, 23 February 2018.
105. Chinese Academy of Sciences (CAS), 'Gao Fu'. http://people.ucas.ac.cn/~GeorgeGao
106. Another famous figure in the field of epidemiology in the PRC is Professor Zhong Nanshan, reputed to be the key scientist who successfully tackled the 2003 SARS pandemic in the Chinese Mainland. That he studied at St Bartholomew's Hospital in London and the University of Edinburgh Medical School reveals the critical scientific assistance from abroad for Chinese students in this field.

became a Lecturer at Oxford (2001-2004).[105] As the Director of the China CDC, Gao is a key figure in China's international linkages in virology research.[106] The Chinese CDC in Beijing manages pandemics in that country and has a branch with a laboratory in Wuhan that is located only several hundred meters from the Huanan Seafood Market, the still-official point of origin of the COVID-19 outbreak according to the CCP.

Another key member of the GVP team is Dr. Jennifer Gardy. She simultaneously serves on its Leadership Board while being the Deputy Director of the Malaria Team at the Bill and Melinda Gates Foundation. Earlier, Gardy was at the British Columbia Centre for Disease Control and the University of British Columbia's School of Population and Public Health, where she held the Canada Research Chair in Public Health Genomics. Her research focused on the use of genomics to understand pathogen transmission, and to incorporate techniques drawn from genomics, bioinformatics, modeling, information visualization, and the social sciences. [107]

French Assistance: From Central to Peripheral Role in WIV

France has strong historical links to the city of Wuhan. Since the

---

107. For more information, see Jennifer Gardy, 'Leadership – Global Virome Project', Global Virome Project.
http://www.globalviromeproject.org/who-we-are/leadership/jennifer-gardy.
See also Jennifer Gardy, 'What We Do – Malaria', Bill and Melinda Gates Foundation.
https://www.gatesfoundation.org/What-We-Do/Global-Health/Malaria/Strategy-Leadership/Jennifer-Gardy

advent of the Dengist reform era, French companies and educational institutions have helped to develop Wuhan as a biotechnology hub.[108] Then French Foreign Minister Michel Barnier signed the bilateral agreement to build the BSL4 lab at the WIV in 2004. [109]

Apparently, the French side expected to play a leading role even after the design, construction and development of the WIV lab. However, these aspirations were mistaken. In reality, the WIV's collaboration with the French was a temporary 'build-operate-transfer' model instead of a long-term 'mentor-mentee model'. The latter model was appropriate when Chinese virology lagged far behind its French counterparts and required considerable technical assistance. However, this is no longer the case when many Chinese researchers have gained world class expertise in virology. Simply put, the WIV today does not require French scientific leadership.

Institut Pasteur and Institut Merieux led in the physical design and development of key management and scientific protocols of WIV in its initial developmental stages. Upon the construction

---

108. See, for example, Wuhan Institute of Virology (WIV), 'Exchanges - Wuhan Institute of Virology'.
    http://english.whiov.cas.cn/Exchange2016/ and Wuhan Institute of Virology (WIV), 'Partnerships - Wuhan Institute of Virology'.
    http://english.whiov.cas.cn/International_Cooperation2016/Partnerships/. See also Wuhan Institute of Virology (WIV), 'Joint Research Units'.
    http://english.whiov.cas.cn/International_Cooperation2016/Joint_Institutes2016/
109. Glen Owen, 'Wuhan virus lab was signed off by EU Brexit chief Michel Barnier in 2004 – despite French intelligence warnings that China's poor bio-security reputation could lead to a catastrophic leak', The Guardian, 23 May 2020.

and completion of the WIV complex, a Franco-Sino scientific exchange program was to follow. But that did not happen. Only a token French researcher was a visiting researcher at WIV when the original agreement stipulated that up to 50 researchers from France were to work inside WIV.[110] Besides these disappointments, French intelligence and security circles [111] were also concerned about biosecurity at WIV and its Military Management Division (MMD). Presumably, the MMD represented the PLA in WIV. Regardless, Gabriel Gras, a former French government official who directly supervised the implementation of biosecurity standards and protocols over a multi-year period at WIV, stated in June 2021 that there is a '0 per cent' chance the COVID-19 virus leaked from the Institute. [112] No specific evidence was provided for this assertion.

In June 2016, then French Ambassador to China Maurice Gourdault-Montagne bestowed the medal of Knight of the National Order of Merit (French: Chevalier de L'Ordre National du Mérite) and the medal of Knight of the Order of Academic Palms (French: Chevalier dans l'Ordre des Palmes académiques)

110. Glen Owen, 'Wuhan virus lab was signed off by EU Brexit chief Michel Barnier in 2004 – despite French intelligence warnings that China's poor bio-security reputation could lead to a catastrophic leak', The Guardian, 23 May 2020.

111. Ibid.

112. John Power, 'Exclusive | '0 per cent' chance: former French official who oversaw safety standards at Wuhan lab dismissed leak theory', South China Morning Post, 11 June 2021.

113. Wuhan Institute of Virology (WIV), 'The French Ambassador to China bestowed medals on Professor Zhiming Yuan and Professor Zhengli Shi in Wuhan Institute of Virology', 1 August 2016.
http://english.whiov.cas.cn/Exchange2016/Foreign_Visits/201712/t20171215_187978.html

on Shi Zhengli as well as fellow WIV colleague Dr. Yuan Zhiming. The award coincided with the ceremony where control of WIV's BSL4 lab was formally handed over to the Chinese.[113] French ambassadors and other senior officials have frequently visited WIV since 2014 (Table 1). Besides the WIV, the French government and scientific establishment also have close ties to the Institute Pasteur of Shanghai. Both French-supported virology labs in Wuhan and Shanghai have a close horizontal partnership under CAS.

Table 1

WIV: Close Sino-Franco Collaboration

Date of Official Visit	French Personnel Involved	French Government
29 October 2014	Ambassador Maurice Gourdault-Montagne	Government
24 September 2015	Counselor for Science and Technology of the Embassy of France, Mr. Pierre Lemonde	Government
16 December 2016	Dr. Herve Bourhy of Institut Pasteur	Government – visit under the auspices of The EMERGENGES 2016 Program launched by the French Embassy in China which supports French-Chinese cooperation in emergent infectious diseases.
12 September 2017	Wuhan Consul General Olivier Guyonvarch	Government

29 January 2018	French Senator for Overseas Civic Affairs M. Christophe- Andre Frassa	Government
26 March 2018	Ambassador Jean- Maurice Ripert	Government
22 May 2018	General Coordinator of French-Sino Cooperation on Prevention and Control of Emerging Infectious Diseases Jean-Michel Hubert	Government
24 January 2019	Wuhan Consul General Olivier Guyonvarch, Counselor from the Embassy of France in China, and Pierre Lemonde, Science and Technology Attaché from Consulate General of France in Wuhan Mr. Yann Moreau	Government

Source: Foreign Visits, Wuhan Institute of Virology.
http://english.whiov.cas.cn/Exchange2016/Foreign_Visits/index_1.
html

Institute Pasteur of Shanghai (IPS), Chinese Academy of Sciences

Institut Pasteur (IP) established its first presence in China in 1899. Historically, IP has provided biomedical education in Mainland China and Hong Kong. In August 2004, CAS, the Shanghai Municipal Government and the Institut Pasteur in Paris signed a cooperation agreement to create the IPS, CAS.[114] This agreement followed the signing of a letter of intent in January 2004 in Paris, in the presence of then Chinese President Hu Jintao and then French Prime Minister Jean-Pierre Raffarin.

However, the IPS has a different governance structure from other Institut Pasteur labs in the world. Besides its organizational ties to CAS, IPS has a strong CCP presence at the management level with Si Shengli serving as the CCP Secretary while Chen Fengwei serves as the Secretary General of Discipline and Inspection.[115] The CCP and CAS now play leading roles in these previously French-influenced institutions, IPS and WIV. Nevertheless, IPS is a symbol of cordial Sino-French diplomatic ties with the French Ambassador to China, Laurent Bili, visiting IPS in December 2019. [116]

A key researcher of interest at IPS is Dr. Cui Jie who conducts high-risk pathogen research on bat coronaviruses and previously was on the staff of Shi Zhengli at WIV and Linfa Wang at Duke-

---

114. 'Inauguration of the Intitut Pasteur of Shanghai – Chinese Academy of Sciences', Press Release, Institut Pasteur-Chinese Academy of Sciences (IPS-CAS), Shanghai, 10 October 2004.
https://www.pasteur.fr/en/inauguration-institut-pasteur-shanghai-chinese-academy-sciences

115. Institut Pasteur-Chinese Academy of Sciences (IPS), 'Senior Management - Institut Pasteur of Shanghai'.
http://english.shanghaipasteur.cas.cn/Overview2016/ms2016/sm2016/
Four out of the five-person management team at IPS are Chinese nationals.

116. Institut Pasteur-Chinese Academy of Sciences (IPS), 'A delegation led by the Ambassador of France in China visited Institut Pasteur of Shanghai, CAS', 10 December 2020.
http://english.shanghaipasteur.cas.cn/IPIN2016/News2016/201912/t20191210_227526.html

NUS Medical School (Duke-NUS) in Singapore. He also completed postdoctoral fellowships at Penn State University and the University of Sydney.[117] While working under Shi at WIV, Cui became known for his hazardous on-site field work inside bat caves in Yunnan where he has stated that he was bitten by a bat and had to self-quarantine as a result.[118] It is unclear as to why Cui left Shi's team to join IPS given Cui's established track record of working alongside Shi to conduct high-risk bat coronavirus research. It is also noteworthy that Cui's official IPS staff profile omits his previous position at WIV. [119]

J-GRID and HVRI[120] – A Jointly Managed Lab on Avian Flu in Harbin

The Japan Initiative for Global Research Network on Infectious Diseases (J-GRID) brings together top Japanese virologists and

---

117. "Principal Investigators 2016: Jie CUI', Institut Pasteur of Shanghai – Chinese Academy of Sciences.
http://sourcedb.shanghaipasteur.cas.cn/yw/Talent2016/PI2016/202106/t20210624_6116681.html
118. Keoni Everington, 'Video shows Wuhan lab scientists admit to being bitten by bats', Taiwan News, 15 January 2021.
https://www.taiwannews.com.tw/en/news/4102619
119. For clear evidence of Cui's membership of Shi's research group, please see Jie Cui, Fang Li, and Zheng-Li Shi, 'Origin and evolution of pathogenic coronaviruses', Nature Reviews Microbiology, Vol. 17, December 2018.
120. Three network graphs outlining key entities that are linked to HVRI and the specific nature of those relationships can be found in Annex B. A full set of network diagrams outlining all of WIV's domestic as well as transnational institutional linkages based off of joint publications and grant awards can be found in Annex B as well. All data was collected using the automated search and knowledge representation capabilities of Data Abyss.
https://www.dataabyss.ai/

other related specialists and oversees joint programs in Thailand, Vietnam, Zambia, India, Indonesia, Philippines, Ghana, Myanmar, and China. The Japanese universities involved include Osaka University, Nagasaki University, University of Tokyo, Hokkaido University, Okayama University, Kobe University, Tohoku University, Tokyo Medical and Dental University, and Niigata University. [121]

J-GRID lead researchers at the University of Tokyo are responsible for the Chinese partnerships and have established a strong relationship with HVRI. The University of Tokyo team is the only international group that has strong scientific relationships characterized by jointly run labs at HVRI. In contrast to Institut Pasteur, the University of Tokyo team has a symmetrical peer-to-peer laboratory partnership structure with HVRI colleagues. The University of Tokyo team is led by Dr. Yasushi Kawaguchi from the Institute of Medical Sciences who intimated that he visited labs in Beijing on a bi-monthly basis.

Dr. Yoshihiro Kawaoka is a member of this leadership team and is the Chief of the Joint China-Japan Joint Research Group on Avian Influenza Virus housed in HVRI.[122] Kawaoka is a key scientist in China's transnational virology research network. He

---

121. 'Division of Infectious Diseases Research, Department of Research Promotion, Japan Agency for Medical Research and Development, 'Research Activities of Japan Initiative for Global Research Network on Infectious Diseases (J-GRID)', July 2018.
122. Division of Infectious Diseases Research, Department of Research Promotion, Japan Agency for Medical Research and Development, 'Research Activities of Japan Initiative for Global Research Network on Infectious Diseases (J-GRID)', July 2018.

also has an appointment at the University of Wisconsin at Madison and has long-time scientific partnerships with Dutch avian influenza GoF specialists Dr. Ron Fouchier at Erasmus University in Holland and Dr. Chen Hualan at HVRI.[123] Kawaoka has joint publications with Chen Hualan.

While Kawaoka's work with his colleagues at HVRI was focused on avian flu viruses, he has diversified to COVID-19 research too. In a July 2020 study, Kawaoka and his international team assessed the replicative ability and pathogenesis of SARS-CoV-2 isolates in Syrian hamsters. They found that SARS-CoV-2 isolates replicated efficiently in the lungs of hamsters and caused severe pathological lung lesions that shared characteristics with SARS-CoV-2–infected human lungs. They also found that SARS-CoV-2–infected hamsters mounted neutralizing antibody responses and were protected against future SARS-CoV-2 reinfections. In addition, passive transfer of convalescent serum to previously uninfected hamsters efficiently suppressed the replication of the virus in the lungs. Kawaoka and his colleagues claimed that their findings prove that this 'Syrian hamster model' helps to better understand SARS-CoV-2 pathogenesis and testing vaccines and antiviral drugs.[124]

---

123. For example, see Hualan Chen, Yoshihiro Kawaoka, et. al., 'A Single-Amino-Acid Substitution in the NS1 Protein Changes the Pathogenicity of H5N1 Avian Influenza Viruses in Mice', Journal of Virology, Vol. 82, No. 3, February 2008.
    Hualand Chen, Yoshihiro Kawaoka, et. al., 'A Duck Enteritis Virus-Vectored Bivalent Live Vaccine Provides Fast and Complete Protection against H5N1 Avian Influenza Virus Infection in Ducks', Journal of Virology, Vol. 85, No. 21, November 2011.
124. Yoshihiro Kawaoka, et. al., 'Syrian hamsters as a small animal model for SARS-CoV-2 infection and countermeasure development', PNAS, Vol. 117, No. 28, 14 July 2020.

India's National Centre for Biological Sciences and WIV

The Indian government investigated a bat coronavirus study in the Northeast Indian state of Nagaland carried out by researchers from India, Singapore, China and the United States. The investigation focused on scientists from India's National Centre for Biological Sciences (NCBS), WIV, Uniformed Services University of the Health Sciences (US), and Duke-NUS. The enquiry sought to determine if scientists obtained bat and human bio samples without proper permission and ethical protocol.[125] The investigation has now been concluded.

The Indian government was concerned that bat and human bio samples from India were shared with WIV. A five-member team from the Indian Council of Medical Research investigated this research in Nagaland and then submitted their findings to the Indian Ministry of Health.[126] One concern was triggered by an October 2019 study published in PLOS Neglected Tropical Diseases, a new journal funded by the Bill and Melinda Gates Foundation. This study focuses on human bat hunters who had continuous exposure to bat-borne pathogens, namely filoviruses.[127] The study concluded that Nagaland has several filoviruses in bats with the accompanying possibility for filovirus

---

125. Bindu Shajan Perappadan, 'Study on bats and bat hunters in Nagaland to be probed', The Hindu, 3 February 2020.
126. Ibid.
127. Pilot Dovih, Shi Zhengli, et. al., 'Filovirus-reactive antibodies in humans and bats in Northeast India imply zoonotic spillover', PLOS Neglected Tropical Diseases, Vol. 13, No. 10, 31 October 2019.

transmission from bats to humans.

The co-authors of this study include WIV scientists, including Shi Zhengli, and researchers from NCBS and Duke-NUS. NCBS acknowledged that WIV provided reagents[128] for this study, which could be classified as biological materials. The US Defense Threat Reduction Agency (DTRA) funded this research via Duke-NUS.[129] Duke-NUS then channeled funds to the NCBS in Bangalore as well as WIV for various forms of technical and scientific assistance.[130] The US-funded partnership between Duke-NUS, NCBS, and WIV took place openly as evidenced by their joint publications.

This multi-dimensional relationship developed in spite of geopolitical rivalries, trade disputes, and other factors that would have disrupted many other transnational networks. Although people have argued that this demonstrated that effective collaboration could be established in the public health and science domain beyond the political concerns, it is a serious question to ask whether there is any mechanism to address national security issues if the partnership involved partners with malign or military intentions. They could be 'strange bedfellows' in bat research indeed.

---

128. Reagents encompass a range of biological or chemical materials that are necessary to carry out key laboratory tests and analyses.
129. Ibid.
130. Pilot Dovih, Shi Zhengli, et. al., 'Filovirus-reactive antibodies in humans and bats in Northeast India imply zoonotic spillover', PLOS Neglected Tropical Diseases, Vol. 13, No. 10, 31 October 2019.

Links Between WIV and Canada's National Microbiology Lab

Canada's National Microbiology Lab (NML) in Winnipeg has links with WIV, though more in key logistical (namely viral sample sharing) and critical knowledge transfer domains. These are strategic modes of interactions that are not always immediately apparent. They do not immediately manifest themselves in the form of joint publications and joint grant award publicity. This case of cooperation between various researchers at NML and the WIV highlights the opaque nature of this transnational network of pathogen research.

In July 2019 leading Ebola researcher Dr. Qiu Xiangguo and her entire research team were escorted out of their lab and were taken into custody by the Royal Canadian Mounted Police. Apparently, Qiu was planning to ship dangerous pathogens including Ebola and Henipah virus (including Nipah virus) samples to WIV. Qiu was fired but the NML stated that her dismissal was unrelated to this clandestine shipment.[131] Qiu also made at least five trips to China between 2017-2018 to train staff at WIV. The Canadian government acknowledged that the costs were borne by third-parties and not Public Health Canada. It is also established that Qiu met with collaborators in Beijing during her trips. Some Canadian colleagues at the NML were worried that Qiu's trips might have national security issues. [132]

---

131. Tom Blackwell, 'Dismissal and investigation by RCMP of Winnipeg co-inventor of Ebola drug stuns colleagues', National Post, 16 July 2019.

Qiu is one of the inventors of ZMapp, the most effective therapeutic for Ebola virus so far. One of her key collaborators, Wang Hualei, is linked to the Academy of Military Medical Sciences, a Chinese military medical research institute in Beijing.[133] Qiu also obtained many scientific awards in Canada for her research and held an academic appointment at the University of Manitoba.

It is unbelievable that a top microbiologist in Canada would risk her whole career to ship very sensitive and dangerous pathogen samples to another country by breaching the basic security protocol and approval process, which should be common sense for a top scientist at her level. This also suggested a very strong interest or demand in these samples from the Chinese side.

Laying the Transnational Foundation for GoF Experiments: Dutch HPAI H5N1 Experiments

The transnational collaboration of GoF experiments can be traced to research on HPAI H5N1 viruses. Dr. Ron Fouchier at Erasmus Medical Center in Rotterdam, Holland was a pioneer on

---

132 . Tom Blackwell, Tom, 'In mystery investigation of two Canadian scientists, a request for Ebola, henipavirus from the Wuhan lab', National Post, 5 May 2020.
See also Karen Pauls, 'Canadian government scientist under investigation trained staff at Level 4 lab in China', CBC News, 3 October 2019.

133 . Karen Pauls, Karen, 'Canadian scientist sent deadly viruses to Wuhan lab months before RCMP asked to investigate', CBC News, 14 June 2020.
Hualei Wang, Qiu Xiangguo, et. al., 'Equine-Origin Immunoglobulin Fragments Protect Nonhuman Primates from Ebola Virus Disease', Journal of Virology, Vol. 93, No. 5, March 2019.

HPAI H5N1. Avian flu specialist Dr. Chen Hualan at HVRI has benefited significantly from this research. Returning the compliment, Fouchier has cited the work done by Chen and her colleagues at HVRI as a justification for his own controversial HPAI H5N1 GoF experiments in Holland.[134] Chen did not appear to collaborate directly with Fouchier but with Dr. Yoshihiro Kawaoka, a long-time collaborator of Dr. Fouchier. [135] While this connection between Fouchier and Chen may have one slight degree of separation, it is significant nonetheless because they are directly or indirectly part of the same transnational network.

Fouchier has conducted controversial experiments that successfully engineered HPAI H5N1 viruses to transmit between ferrets without direct contact. Ferrets are the mammals that most closely genetically resemble humans.[136] This work was highly controversial with many leading virologists and other scientists warning that Fouchier was directly engaging in GoF research under the guise of public health.

---

134 . Center for Infectious Disease Research and Policy (CIDRP), 'Dutch researcher resumes H5N1 transmission studies', University of Minnesota, 28 February 2013.

135 . For example, see Hualan Chen, Yoshihiro Kawaoka, et. al., 'A Single-Amino-Acid Substitution in the NS1 Protein Changes the Pathogenicity of H5N1 Avian Influenza Viruses in Mice', Journal of Virology, Vol. 82, No. 3, February 2008. Hualand Chen, Yoshihiro Kawaoka, et. al., 'A Duck Enteritis Virus-Vectored Bivalent Live Vaccine Provides Fast and Complete Protection against H5N1 Avian Influenza Virus Infection in Ducks', Journal of Virology, Vol. 85, No. 21, November 2011.

136 . For example, see Ron Fouchier, et. al., 'Airborne transmission of influenza A/H5N1 virus between ferrets', Science, Vol. 22, No. 336:6088, June 2012. Ron Fouchier, et. al., 'The potential for respiratory droplet-transmissible A/H5N1 influenza virus to evolve in a mammalian host', Science, Vol. 22, No. 336:6088, June 2012.

The Dutch government did take notice and forced Fouchier to obtain a European Union-compliant Export License prior to pursuing further HPAI H5N1 GoF research. This EU regulatory regime is to prevent the unauthorized proliferation of weapons of mass destruction. An Export License was not granted to Fouchier and he unsuccessfully challenged this decision in a Dutch court in September 2013. Initially, some analysts believed that this court ruling would end this type of GoF research.[137] However, in 2019 the US government (which had previously successfully pressured the Dutch government to shut down Fouchier's research) quietly lifted the moratorium on HPAI H5N1 GoF research. This about-turn by the US is indeed a puzzle. Fouchier resumed his experiments at Erasmus.[138] Arguably, Fouchier's pioneering GoF research sets the foundation for the bat coronavirus GoF research carried out at WIV and avian flu at HVRI.

Summary

While China benefited from indispensable international virology expertise, it did not yield control of its labs to any foreign government or international organization. These labs were closely supervised by the state (national and provincial), CCP, Chinese Academy of Sciences and Chinese Academy of

---

137 . Martin Enserink, 'Flu Researcher Ron Fouchier Loses Legal Fight Over H5N1 Studies', American Association for the Advancement of Science (ScienceMag), 25 September 2013.

138 . Jocelyn Kaiser, 'EXCLUSIVE: Controversial experiments that could make bird flu more risky poised to resume', American Association for the Advancement of Science (ScienceMag), 8 February 2019.

Agricultural Sciences. Our case studies of the two BSL4 labs in Wuhan and Harbin, and the IPS support this observation. Thanks to critical support from virology networks abroad, top Chinese labs can now 'stand on one's own two feet'. Indeed, China is emerging to be a 'Great Virology Power' ready for the next global pandemic.

CHAPTER FOUR

Chinese Academy of Medical Sciences, Constituent High-Risk Pathogen Research Units, and Transnational Linkages

CHAPTER 4

Chinese Academy of Medical Sciences, Constituent High-Risk Pathogen Research Units, and Transnational Linkages

Historical Origins and Current Organizational Structure

The U.S.-based Rockefeller Foundation formally established the Peking Union Medical College Hospital (PUMC) in 1917. Penang-born Dr. Wu Lien-Teh, the first Nanyang Chinese to obtain a medical degree from Cambridge University, was deeply involved in the PUMC's early preparatory establishment. Wu, who was known for his role in ending the great Manchurian Plague of 1910-11, added credibility to the establishment.[139] With Wu serving as a founding father, virology research was in the 'DNA' of the PUMC.

---

139. Kevin Tan, 'The Plague Fighter: Dr Wu Lien-Teh and His Work', National Library, Singapore, 1 July 2020.
https://biblioasia.nlb.gov.sg/vol-16/issue-2/jul-sep-2020/plague
Yu-lin Wu, Memories of Dr. Wu Lien-teh, Plague Fighter, World Scientific, 1995.

PUMC evolved over the Republican period, Japanese invasion, Chinese civil war, Great Leap Forward and Cultural Revolution. Notwithstanding the turbulent past century, PUMC maintained its top nationwide position and offered American-style medical education along the Johns Hopkins model with an eight-year Medical Degree program. Nevertheless, PUMC was not immune to the upheavals and disruptions in 20th century China. In 1951 the CCP took over PUMC and nationalized it on the suspicion that PUMC was operating as a front for American 'imperialism' in China. PUMC's name was changed to China Union Medical College. While the PUMC's overall medical curriculum was maintained, its medium of instruction was changed from English to Chinese.

The PLA assumed control of the PUMC in 1952 until 1956. During this time, the PLA reduced the duration of medical education to one year for those who aspired to become a medical officer in the Army [140]. After regaining its autonomy in 1956 and its PUMC name restored, it merged with the Chinese Academy of Medical Sciences (CAMS) in 1957 and has operated as a single institution since. During the Cultural Revolution (1966-1976), PUMC was shuttered and renamed the Beijing Anti-Imperialism Hospital. In 1979, the institution reopened under the name of Capital University of Medical Sciences before its original PUMC name was finally restored in 1985.[141] This restoration of the PUMC name was interpreted by some at the time as being a core

---

140. Mary Augusta Brazelton, 'Western Medical Education on Trial: The Endurance of Peking Union Medical College, 1949–1985'. Twentieth-Century China, Vol. 40, Issue 2, 2015.

component of Beijing's re-engagement with the West in the domain of biomedical sciences.[142] However, despite the name change, the Chinese government has maintained its direct control of PUMC, especially in high-risk pathogen research.

Presently, CAMS/PUMC operates a full-spectrum, nationwide infrastructure of laboratories, including BSL3/4, hospitals and educational facilities. CAMS/PUMC is under the National Health Commission, a cabinet-level executive department of the State Council responsible for formulating national health policies. Many top PUMC alumni and PUMC professors were trained in the West over the past century. Although these linkages were temporarily severed during the Mao era, they were re-established during Deng's reform and opening. Some prominent doctors and scientists of PUMC were Wu Jieping: University of Chicago[143], Huang Jiasi: University of Michigan [144], Zhan Qimin: University of California (San Francisco), University of Texas, SW Medical Center, University of Pittsburgh School of Medicine,[145] Tang Fei Fan: Yale and Harvard,[146] Xin Lu: Oxford, [147] Feng Chuanhan: orthopedics training in the UK[148] and Lin Qiaozhi: Chicago Medical School. [149]

---

141. Mary Augusta Brazelton, 'Western Medical Education on Trial: The Endurance of Peking Union Medical College, 1949–1985'. Twentieth-Century China, Vol. 40, Issue 2, 2015.
142. 'Peking Hospital Takes Back Pre-1949 Name', New York Times, 9 June 1985.
143. 'An Introduction of Wu Jieping Fellow', Wu Jieping Medical Foundation, https://www.wjpmf.org.cn/aboutwjp.html
144. 'U-M Chinese Alumni – Huang Jiasi', University of Michigan, https://sites.lsa.umich.edu/chinese-alumni/huang-jiasi-%E9%BB%84%E5%AE%B6%E9%A9%B7/
145. 'ZHAN Qimin', Shenzhen Bay Laboratory, http://www.szbl.ac.cn/en/scientificresearch/researchteam/371.html

Current CAMS president, Dr. Wang Chen, graduated from the Capital University of Medical Sciences, University of Texas.[150] The transnational links between CAMS/PUMC and the West past and present are evidenced by the many eminent PUMC alumni and professors trained abroad. CAMS/PUMC not only conducts research, provides clinical care and performs clinical trials, it also advises the Chinese government on public health policy and serves a frontline function in the event of public health emergencies. For example, PUMC sent multiple technical assistance teams to Wuhan over the course of the COVID-19 outbreak in the city. [151]

CAMS has 19 research institutes, six hospitals and eight schools under its umbrella. Its expert team comprises 24 members from the Chinese Academy of Sciences (CAS) and Chinese Academy of Engineering (CAE), 1,073 PhD supervisors and 1,437 supervisors for master's students. CAMS Academic Advisory Committee has six academic divisions and 219 members, all of whom are

---

146. 'Dr. Tang Fei-fan: The 'Louis Pasteur' of the East', Nspirement, https://www.nspirement.com/2016/12/02/dr-tang-fei-fan-the-louis-pasteur-of-the-east.html

147. 'Xin Lu'. Chinese Academy of Medical Sciences Oxford Institute, https://www.camsoxford.ox.ac.uk/team/xin-lu

148. 'Awardee of Medical Sciences and Materia Medica Prize: Feng Chuanhan', Holeung Ho Lee Foundation, http://www.hlhl.org.cn/english/showsub.asp?id=414

149. Guowei Wright, 'Lin Qiaozhi: The Steady Pulse of a Quiet Faith' in Carol Lee Hamrin, ed., with Stacey Bieler, Salt and Light: Lives of Faith that Shaped Modern China (Eugene, OR., Wipf and Stock Publishers, Pickwick Publications, 2008.

150. 'Profile Chen Wang: new President of CAMS and PUMC', The Lancet, Vol. 391, 16 June 2018.

151. Tang Bo, 'Coronavirus Pandemic: Last assisting medical team leaves Wuhan', CGTN, 16 April 2020.

advertised as top scientists. There are 23 national platforms for intramural scientific research, including six State Key Laboratories and five National Clinical Research Centers. Eighty-nine extramural research institutions or units have been collaborating with other domestic institutions since 2019. [152]

Within the field of virology at CAMS, the Institute of Medical Biology (IMB; Kunming), Institute of Medicinal Biotechnology (IMBT; Beijing), Institute of Laboratory Animal Sciences (ILAS; Beijing), Institute of Pathogen Biology (IPB; Beijing) and Christophe Merieux Lab primates, to identify direct infection pathways to humans. [153]

---

152. 'Chinese Academy of Medical Sciences and Peking Union Medical College are seeking global talents', NatureCareers, 2022.
https://www.nature.com/naturecareers/employer/79137
153. Interview with former senior biodefence officer, Washington DC, 23 December 2021.

Figure 2: Organizational Diagram of the Chinese Academy of Medical Sciences

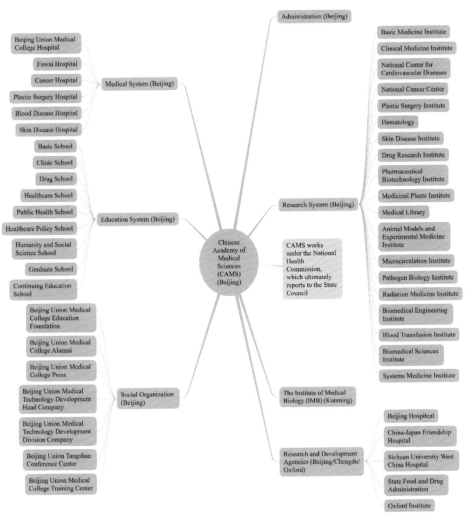

Source: '組織機構', Chinese Academy of Medical Sciences.
http://www.cams.ac.cn/yxgk/zzjg/index.htm

How Does CAMS/PUMC Operate? –
Structures and Principles[154]

CAMS/PUMC operates along an American-style biomedical research and hospital network system with interlinking research institutes, laboratories, clinical facilities, medical education and technology commercialization operations that are designed to be mutually reinforcing and beneficial across the entire network. For example, specific Principal Investigators (PIs) within a specialized lab/s will be tasked with analyzing samples and providing technical opinions on complex patient cases coming from clinical care. They may also be asked to develop new technologies to address these complex challenges, be it in the form of new drugs, diagnostic tests, vaccines, prophylactics, or bioinformatics software.

As part of these activities, CAMS/PUMC PIs will interact with and seek inputs or guidance from international collaborators who work in a similar domain area, especially in the United States and Europe. These activities are designed to enhance clinical activities and position CAMS as a world leader in both patient care, scientific knowledge generation and biomedical technology development. [155]

---

154. A full set of network diagrams outlining all of CAMS/PUMC's institutional linkages based off of joint publications and grant awards can be found in Annex C. All data was collected using the automated search and knowledge representation capabilities of Data Abyss.
https://www.dataabyss.ai/

In addition, non-clinician scientists are enabled to be deeply embedded in the flow of clinical activities and to configure their own respective scientific research agendas around current and emerging clinical priorities within the CAMS/PUMC system. Under a CAMS-style system, virtually all research is applied and directly linked to clinical priorities and other national priorities set by the Chinese government. 'Blue sky', or more open-ended research without clearly pre-determined required outcomes, is largely absent within the CAMS system.

While the basic structure of CAMS/PUMC resembles an American-style system, material differences have emerged over time. First, like other leading biomedical research institutes in China, all members of the CAMS/PUMC leadership team and leading clinicians and scientists are strongly encouraged, if not outright required, to be CCP members and carry out party work in addition to their clinical/scientific work.[156] While Chinese government control over CAMS/PUMC is usual under China's system of governance, this marks a substantial divergence from counterparts in other countries.

---

155. In the domain of biotechnology development, CAMS has extensive industry linkages, institutional holdings in various companies and a track record of commercializing research. In-depth research and analysis of these activities will be provided in future work.

156. Ryan Clarke and Lam Peng Er, 'Coronavirus Research Networks in China: Origins, International Linkages and Consequences', Centre for Non-Traditional Security Studies, May 2021, Singapore. https://rsis-ntsasia.org/wp-content/uploads/2021/06/NTS-Asia-Monograph-Coronavirus-Research-in-China-by-Ryan-Clarke-and-Lam-Peng-Er-May2021-1.pdf

Second, under China's Civil-Military Fusion Law, there is a possibility that CAMS/PUMC (or any other biomedical research institute in China) can be repurposed and directly controlled by the Chinese government under specific contingencies, including lab accidents.[157] The Civil-Military Fusion Law is an overarching legal framework within which CAMS/PUMC must operate.

Third, international scientific collaborations appear to be more tenuous and vulnerable to immediate disruption due to external non-scientific factors, especially in more strategically sensitive fields. This is evidenced by the email conversations between Dr. James LeDuc and his counterparts at UTMB and the National Academy of Sciences (NAS) regarding their access to the BSL4 lab in Kunming being denied 'due to the current US-China situation' and a new CCP Party secretary 'recently arriving' in June/July 2019. These developments appear to have even surprised LeDuc as these respective teams had been jointly engaging in scientific publications and conferences without any apparent issues. [158]

There was no specificity or rationale provided nor were there any timelines or conditions for BSL4 lab access being granted. This was also in spite of LeDuc and his colleagues jointly

---

157. Ibid. For additional analysis of the Civil-Military Fusion Law, please see 'Alibaba and Ant Group: Involvement in China's Military-Civilian Fusion Initiative', RWR Advisory Group, 2 October 2020.
For a more in-depth discussion, please see Ryan Clarke, 'Emerging Global Pandemic Risks Come from Engineered Viruses in Chinese Labs, Not the Jungle or Bat Caves', Epoch Times, 4 September 2021.

organizing a lab safety and global health security conference with the Institute of Medical Sciences, CAMS in Kunming, Yunnan province.[159] This also suggests that Dr. LeDuc and his counterparts at UTMB might not have full knowledge on all projects in the BSL4 lab in Kunming, nor did they have oversight of the lab safety operation of this BSL4 lab. What is noteworthy is that the Kunming BSL4 lab is designed for experiments on dangerous pathogens with large primates (monkeys, most suitable for human-like experiments). [160]

The sudden denial of access due to a change in the political environment in this incident also raises serious concerns. There is no established mechanism to address security issues if the intellectual knowledge and technologies involved in these public health or medical science international collaborations are freely transferred without any monitoring or oversight. Can we ensure the safety operation protocols are strictly followed by every partner of international collaborations? Can bioterrorism be

---

158. These email conversations were legally obtained via a Freedom of Information Request made by US Right to Know Executive Director Gary Ruskin and shared with Ryan Clarke. Additional documentation is available upon request.
   For example, please see Pei-Yong Shi, 'Spike mutation D614G alters SARS-CoV-2 fitness', Nature, Vol. 592, 2021.
   Qi Chen, Chao Shan, Shi Peiyong, et. al., 'Treatment of Human Glioblastoma with a Live Attenuated
   Zika Virus Vaccine Candidate', mBio, Vol. 9. Iss. 5, September/October 2018.
   'CAS-NAS Workshop on Emerging Infections and Global Health Security Held', Beijing Institutes of Life Sciences, Chinese Academy of Sciences, 1 October 2015.
   http://english.biols.cas.cn/news/news/201701/t20170109_173250.html
159. These email conversations were voluntarily shared with Ryan Clarke by Gary Ruskin.
160. Demaneuf, Giles, 'BSL-4 laboratories in China: Kunming, Wuhan, Harbin', Medium, 27 April 2022.

incubated in the name of developing surveillance or prevention tools and open international collaboration? Is this simply a blind spot, or intentionally ignored? Do we not need a security protocol when dealing with international science or health collaborations in which a totalitarian dictatorship is involved?

Last but not least, China's National Security Law poses major challenges to international data sharing, especially in the field of virology. It is unclear whether researchers at CAMS/PUMC (or any other biomedical research institute in China) are able to freely share data and other related information regarding pathogens that have been recently discovered or are being analyzed within CAMS/PUMC on a priority basis due to perceived acute public health risks. Notably, Chinese companies are often expressly forbidden from 'exporting' basic financial statements outside of China to foreign auditors, regulators, potential investors, or even existing shareholders. This even includes Chinese companies that are publicly listed on American or British stock exchanges. [161] While this example derives from a different domain, it nonetheless can be used to possibly infer how the Chinese government, which exerts direct control over CAMS/PUMC, would likely view international data sharing in the domains of virology research.

---

161. This assessment is based on Ryan Clarke's direct experience covering the Chinese market during his time in the investment banking sector.
    For additional analysis, please see 'The Risk Exposure of U.S. Investors Holding Chinese Sovereign Bonds', RWR Advisory Group, 28 October 2020.
    'President's Working Group on Financial Markets: Report on Protecting United States Investors from Significant Risks from Chinese Companies', US Department of Treasury, 24 July 2020.

CAMS IMB: SARS-CoV-2
Vaccine Developer in Kunming

IMB was established in 1958 and occupies a prominent position within the CAMS network. The institute houses a WHO Collaborating Center of Enteroviruses and is the largest research and production base for live attenuated oral poliomyelitis vaccine (OPV) in China. The IMB is constructing a national key project, titled 'Kunming National High-level Biosafety Research Center for Non-Human Primates'.[162] This institute has also received funding from the Gates Foundation for research on polio vaccines. [163]

Approved by the National Development and Reform Commission (NDRC), this IMB initiative will become a critical fundamental research platform for discovering, monitoring, controlling and preventing infectious diseases in China. The IMB will serve as a national center of excellence for high-level biosafety research lab (BSL3/4) governance and operations thereby enabling key studies in etiology,[164] epidemiology and

---

162. For example, see 'About Us, Institute of Medical Biology – Chinese Academy of Medical Sciences', https://www.imbcams.ac.cn/en/aboutus
'Homepage, Institute of Medical Biology – Chinese Academy of Medical Sciences', https://www.imbcams.ac.cn/en

163. 'Committed Grants: Institute of Medical Biology, Chinese Academy of Medical Sciences', Bill & Melinda Gates Foundation, November 2015 and April 2012. https://www.gatesfoundation.org/about/committed-grants/2015/11/opp1130833 and
https://www.gatesfoundation.org/about/committed-grants/2012/04/opp1049425

164. Etiology is the study of animal behavior.

pathogenesis of infectious diseases.[165] **Table 2** shows a data table on IMB facility size and number of research staff. Please see **Figure 3** for a full organizational diagram.

Table 2: Key IMB Research Staff and Their Transnational Linkages

Research Groups Listed	Head	Estimated Number of Staff	Is Group/ Lab Head Western-Educated	If Yes, Which Institutions?
Central Lab	Yu Jiankun	16	Yes	University of Manitoba (Postdoc)
Vaccine Lab	Hu Yunzhang	13	No	N/A
Centre of Drug Safety Evaluation	Ma Kaili	8	No	N/A
Small Animal Trial Centre	Tang Donghong	14	No	N/A
Team of Primate Animal Experimental Models	He Zhanlong	10	No	N/A
Biological Product Room 5	Liao Guoyang	10	No	N/A
Molecular Epidemiology Lab	Sun Qiangming	10	Yes	University of Maryland, College Park (Postdoc)

---

165. For example, please see 'About Us, Institute of Medical Biology – Chinese Academy of Medical Sciences', https://www.imbcams.ac.cn/en/aboutus

Molecular Immunity Lab	Ma Yanbing	14	Yes	University of Manitoba (Postdoc)
Virus Immunity Lab	Li Qihan	23	Yes	Massachusetts Institute of Technology (Postdoc)
Medical Genetics Lab	Yang Shaoqing	20	Yes	University of Birmingham and George Washington University
Biological Product Room 3	Cun Wei	11	Yes	University of Kentucky
Vaccine Diagnostic Technology Team	Xie Zhongping	7	No	N/A

Source: '科學研究', **Institute of Medical Biology, Chinese Academy of Medical Sciences.**
https://www.imbcams.ac.cn/kxyj/kydw

Figure 3: Organizational Diagram of the Institute of Medical Biology

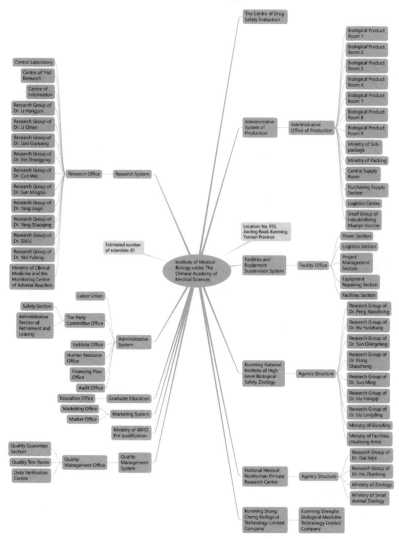

Source: '關于我們', Institute of Medical Biology, Chinese Academy of Medical Sciences. https://www.imbcams.ac.cn/

In June 2021 it was officially announced that the Chinese government had reportedly begun constructing a new SARS-CoV-2 vaccine factory that could produce between 500 million and one billion doses per year. The new vaccine development, called the IMBCAMS SARS-CoV-2 Vaccine, was credited to IMB. This vaccine was developed using human and non-human primate samples as opposed to the mRNA vaccines developed by Western companies that utilize synthetic genetic material.[166] For a SARS-CoV-2 vaccine to clear Chinese patient safety and efficacy standards, IMB would have to conduct a large-scale exercise that involves (at least) accessing SARS-CoV-2 viral samples from across China, or establishing clinical trial collaboration with foreign countries, designing and executing clinical trials and structuring modalities for technology transfer for industrial-scale production.

---

166. 'China builds new plant for IMBCAMS COVID-19 vaccine -state media', Reuters, 9 June 2021.
https://www.reuters.com/world/asia-pacific/china-builds-new-plant-imbcams-covid-19-vaccine-state-media-2021-06-09/
'COVID-19 vaccine reaches phase-2 trials in China', Xinhua, 22 June 2020.
http://english.nmpa.gov.cn/2020-06/22/c_502093.htm
'New Vaccine Industrial Base Project in Kunming High-tech Industrial Development Zone', Yunnan Investment Promotion, 21 January 2022.
https://invest.yn.gov.cn/ENArticleInfo.aspx?id=19069
For additional information on the methods used to develop the IBMCAMS vaccine, please see
Heng Li, et. al., 'Self-Assembling Nanoparticle Vaccines Displaying the Receptor Binding Domain of SARS-CoV-2 Elicit Robust Protective Immune Responses in Rhesus Monkeys', Bioconjugate Chemistry, Vol. 32, 2021.
Qianhui Wu, et. al, 'Evaluation of the safety profile of COVID-19 vaccines: a rapid review', BMC Medicine, Vol. 19, Issue 173, 2021.

Galveston National Laboratory/UTMB: From American BSL4 Capacity Builder and Gain of Function (GoF)[167] Research Partner to Abrupt Access Denial in Kunming[168]

Recently legally obtained email communications between Dr. James LeDuc at UTMB in Galveston and CAMS reveal that IMB houses a BSL4 lab. This lab appeared to be engaging in joint high-risk virology research with UTMB that is made only available to a select few Chinese scientists.[169] Previously, many analysts assumed that China only had two BSL4 labs, one at WIV and one at HVRI.

The point person between the Galveston lab and CAMS was Dr. Shi Pei-Yong. Shi has conducted research involving the manipulation of spike proteins of the SARS-CoV-2 virus to make

---

167. GoF experiments are a controversial domain within biomedical science, defense and security, and other related fields. They are separate and distinct from other scientific methods and approaches. GoF experiments are designed to enable pathogens to develop new properties (e.g., increased transmissibility, increased lethality and drug resistance) for them to generate better information on how viruses could leap from one species to another. This can enable rapid early detection, containment and local/regional/international pandemic prevention. However, this also makes viruses more dangerous than their natural form.

168. A full set of network diagrams outlining all of UTMB's institutional linkages with all Chinese virology research institutes based off of joint publications and grant awards can be found in Annex K. All data was collected using the automated search and knowledge representation capabilities of Data Abyss. https://www.dataabyss.ai/

169. These email conversations were voluntarily shared with Ryan Clarke by Gary Ruskin.
Please also see Yuan Zhiming, 'Current status and future challenges of high-level biosafety laboratories in China', Journal of Biosafety and Biosecurity, Vol. 1, Issue 2, September 2019.

the pathogen more infectious than the variants that were circulating naturally.[170] This may have represented a common interest with his counterparts in Kunming. Shi has also worked extensively with the PLA's Academy of Military Medical Sciences (AMMS) and CAMS/PUMC on other infectious disease projects that involve the manipulation of viruses, such as chimeric Zika vaccine development and Zika GoF studies using mouse models.

One of Shi's key collaborators, Qi Chen, is the director of the Virology Lab at the Institute of Microbiology and Epidemiology (AMMS).[171] Despite these well-established linkages, the UTMB team was shut out of the BSL4 lab in Kunming that they helped develop. Dr. Chao Shan also held simultaneous dual appointments at WIV[172] and on LeDuc's team at UTMB in Galveston. Chao has several joint publications with Shi and

170. For example, please see Pei-Yong Shi, 'Spike mutation D614G alters SARS-CoV-2 fitness', Nature, Vol. 592, 26 October 2020.
171. Qi Chen, Chao Shan, Shi Peiyong, et. al., 'Treatment of Human Glioblastoma with a Live Attenuated
   Zika Virus Vaccine Candidate', mBio, Vol. 9. Iss. 5, September/October 2018.
   Xiao Feng I, et al., 'Development of a chimeric Zika vaccine using a licensed live-attenuated flavivirus vaccine as backbone', Nature Communications, Vol. 9, No. 673, 2018.
   Chao Shan, et. al., 'An Infectious cDNA Clone of Zika Virus to Study Viral Virulence, Mosquito Transmission, and Antiviral Inhibitors', Cell Host Microbe, Vol. 19, No. 6, 8 June 2016.
172. For additional information on high-risk pathogen research at the Wuhan Institute of Virology and its transnational linkages, please see Ryan Clarke and Lam Peng Er, 'Coronavirus Research Networks in China: Origins, International Linkages and Consequences', Center for Non-Traditional Security Studies, May 2021, Singapore.
   https://rsis-ntsasia.org/wp-content/uploads/2021/06/NTS-Asia-Monograph-Coronavirus-Research-in-China-by-Ryan-Clarke-and-Lam-Peng-Er-May2021-1.pdf

others demonstrating GoF research. In one 2020 PNAS study, Chao, Shi and colleagues took a pre-epidemic Asian Zika virus strain (FSS13025 isolated in Cambodia in 2010) and inserted the 'V473M' substitution that significantly increased neurovirulence[173] in neonatal mice and produced higher viral loads in the placenta and fetal heads in pregnant mice. This E-V473M mutant strain was further studied in competition experiments in cynomolgus macaques. The results showed that this mutation increased Zika's fitness for viral generation in macaques, a clear demonstration of GoF that was based on the reverse genetics techniques that had been used in other high-risk studies. [174]

UTMB also played a key technical role in the Chinese Academy of Sciences - National Academy of Sciences Workshop on the Challenges of Emerging Infections, Laboratory Safety and Global Health Security in October 2015.[175] LeDuc and the UTMB team also provided lab biosafety training to IMB staff working in BSL3 labs (which are also GoF-capable) and advised on biocontainment engineering.[176] LeDuc viewed these activities as a major contribution to the Chinese BSL4 scientific ecosystem and

---

173. Neurovirulence refers to infection of the brain.
174. Chao Shan, et. al., 'A Zika virus envelope mutation preceding the 2015 epidemic enhances virulence and fitness for transmission', PNAS, Vol. 117, No. 33., 18 August 2020.

    For additional GoF work conducted by Galveston/UTMB's Pei-Yong Shi and colleagues at AMMS involving Zika viruses in mice, please see Ling Yuan, et. al., 'A single mutation in the prM protein of Zika virus contributes to fetal microcephaly', Science, Vol. 17, No. 358, 17 November 2017.
175. 'CAS-NAS Workshop on Emerging Infections and Global Health Security Held', Beijing Institutes of Life Sciences.
    http://english.biols.cas.cn/news/news/201701/t20170109_173250.html

utilized the example to support grant applications for additional funding for international BSL4 training and capacity building programs. In one such example, in October 2016 LeDuc obtained a grant from the US Army Medical Research and Materiel Command in Fort Detrick, Maryland to establish the National Biocontainment Training Centre. The primary purpose of this center is to provide international BSL4-related training, funding and capacity building.[177] It is unclear whether any US funding obtained by LeDuc has flowed to joint research with IMB. However, LeDuc did provide direct BSL4 management training to IMB staff in 2017. [178]

There has also been additional joint training between IMB and UTMB. In September 2014, Dr. Curtis Klages (a veterinarian UTMB) and Miguel Grimaldo (also from UTMB) were invited to review the animal facilities at IMB in Kunming and advise on BSL4 technical specifications and performance requirements. They were also asked to provide training on laboratory

---

176. James LeDuc and Thomas Ksiazek, National Biocontainment Training Center, Annual Report, Grant Number: W81XWH-09-2-0053, US Army Medical Research and Materiel Command, Fort Detrick, Maryland 21702-5012, June 2014. https://careersdocbox.com/87871061-Nursing/Prepared-for-u-s-army-medical-research-and-materiel-command-fort-detrick-maryland.html

177. James LeDuc, National Biocontainment Training Center, Award Number: W81XWH-11-2-0148, US Army Medical Research and Materiel Command, Fort Detrick, Maryland 21702-5012, October 2016.

178. 'Galveston National Lab Director LeDuc Provided Early Contact Between the NIAID and the Wuhan Lab; Fauci Invited by LeDuc to 'Informal Discussions' with a Dozen Senior Chinese Scientists', Mining Awareness, 24 October 2021. https://miningawareness.wordpress.com/2021/10/24/galveston-national-lab-director-leduc-provided-early-contact-between-the-niaid-and-the-wuhan-lab-fauci-invited-by-leduc-to-informal-discussions-with-a-dozen-senior-chinese-scientist/.

management, facility operations, and facility personnel training.[179] Collaborations continued throughout 2014 with a focus on the specialized maintenance needs of high containment laboratories. IMB staff members from Kunming also traveled to UTMB in January 2015 for specialized engineering training. [180]

In 2013, Dr. Liu Longding and Dai Qing traveled to UTMB to participate in an intensive two-week biocontainment engineering fellowship. Liu and Dai worked with UTMB biocontainment engineers to focus on critical components of facility operation and management. This was in preparation for the opening of the IMB BSL4 laboratory that was still under construction in Kunming at the time.[181] The training program was customized to the needs of Liu and Dai and included:

- Laboratory Facilities and Primary Containment Requirements
- Primary Containment Equipment
- Filtration Systems
- Liquid and Solid Waste Decontamination

179. James LeDuc, National Biocontainment Training Center, Award Number: W81XWH-11-2-0148, US Army Medical Research and Materiel Command, Fort Detrick, Maryland 21702-5012, October 2016. https://apps.dtic.mil/sti/pdfs/AD1022067.pdf

180. James LeDuc, National Biocontainment Training Center, Award Number: W81XWH-11-2-0148, US Army Medical Research and Materiel Command, Fort Detrick, Maryland 21702-5012, October 2016. https://apps.dtic.mil/sti/pdfs/AD1022067.pdf

181. James LeDuc, National Biocontainment Training Center, Award Number: W81XWH-11-2-0148, US Army Medical Research and Materiel Command, Fort Detrick, Maryland 21702-5012, October 2016. https://apps.dtic.mil/sti/pdfs/AD1022067.pdf

- Mechanical Systems - Ventilation and Controls
- Laboratory Facility Adjustment and Testing
- Decontamination Methodologies and Procedures
- L4 Specialized Equipment & Other Laboratory Equipment
- BSL4 Suits - Setup, Maintenance and Usage
- Annual Maintenance Shutdowns and Record Keeping
- Special Topics on Biocontainment Operation [182]

UTMB's collaboration with the IMB continued throughout 2013 when Dr. Shi Jiandong and Dr. Guo Lei participated in BSL2 and BSL3 training at the National Biocontainment Training Centre at UTMB. This training was also provided in preparation for the opening of the new biocontainment laboratory that was nearing completion in Kunming. [183]

Serial Passaging GoF Experiments on SARS-CoV-2 in Mice: A National Exercise with AMMS, CAMS/PUMC and the Beijing Institute of Lifeomics

In September 2020, He Yuxian from CAMS/PUMC and a joint team of researchers from AMMS, Beijing Institute of Lifeomics, and Institute of Military Cognition and Brain Sciences published

---

182. James LeDuc, National Biocontainment Training Center, Award Number: W81XWH-11-2-0148, US Army Medical Research and Materiel Command, Fort Detrick, Maryland 21702-5012, October 2016.
https://apps.dtic.mil/sti/pdfs/AD1022067.pdf
183. JJames LeDuc, National Biocontainment Training Center, Award Number: W81XWH-11-2-0148, US Army Medical Research and Materiel Command, Fort Detrick, Maryland 21702-5012, October 2016.
https://apps.dtic.mil/sti/pdfs/AD1022067.pdf

a study that describes their use of SARS-CoV-2 serial passaging. The rationale for this study is to improve the efficacy of vaccines.[184] Serial passaging involves continuously selecting for the most infectious viral strains, isolating them, and then combing and reinserting them back into mice to produce new viral strains that are more infectious, lethal and/or drug/vaccine-resistant than SARS-CoV-2 viruses found in nature. In this experiment, even though the research team justified it as an animal model to study vaccine efficacy and validated a recombinant vaccine in this system, the mouse-adapted new SARS-CoV-2 strain pose a serious risk of rapid spread among mouse population if there is any release or leakage to the animal world. This would create a huge animal reservoir that can further incubate other dangerous SARS-CoV-2 variants. The majority of He Yuxian's co-authors on this study come from overtly PLA-run institutions.

Notably, none of the most effective SARS-CoV-2 vaccines produced globally have been developed through serial passaging, or any other GoF techniques. Given the current rates of protection against the development of severe disease provided by current vaccines, there is no clear civilian scientific justification to develop additional vaccines that protect against artificially enhanced SARS-CoV-2 viruses. In addition, one of the reasons that many vaccine developers avoid doing serial passages of this novel virus, SARS-CoV-2, is because we still know too little about this virus. The world is still facing the challenges of its

---

184. Gu Hongjing, et. al. 'Adaptation of SARS-CoV-2 in BALB/c mice for testing vaccine efficacy', Science, Vol. 369, No. 6511, 25 September 2020.

naturally generated variants, shall we create more risks with serial passages of this virus on animals that were not a natural reservoir for it? The CAMS/PUMC study suggests that GoF research methods that were being used at WIV[185] on bat coronaviruses continue to be used at CAMS, AMMS, Institute of Military Cognition and Brain Sciences and the Beijing Institute of Lifeomics.

CAMS/PUMC Researchers Create a Non-Human Primate Host for Previously Low-Risk Middle Eastern Respiratory Syndrome (MERS) with Dutch Assistance

The MERS virus that emerged from Saudi Arabia's Eastern Province in 2012 generated modest outbreak clusters across the Middle East and limited clusters in Southeast and South Asia, as well as South Korea in 2015. Although there were human-to-human transmissions in nosocomial outbreaks in hospitals, the MERS virus was not well adapted for continuous human-to-human transmission. It is listed on the WHO Priority Pathogen list; however, its pandemic potential remains limited. MERS-

---

185. For example, please see Shi, Zheng-Li, Baric, Ralph et. al., 'A SARS-like cluster of circulating bat coronaviruses shows potential for human emergence', Nature Medicine, Vol. 21, No. 12, December 2015.

Mazet, Jonna, Daszak, Peter, Zheng-Li, Shi et. al., 'Isolation and characterization of a bat SARS-like coronavirus that uses the ACE2 receptor', Nature, Vol. 503, No. 28, November 2013.

Li, Fang, Wang, Linfa, Shi, Zheng-Li, et. al, 'Angiotensin-converting enzyme 2 (ACE2) proteins of different bat species confer variable susceptibility to SARS-CoV entry', Archive of Virology, Vol. 155, 22 June 2010.

CoV has been identified in dromedaries in several countries in the Middle East, Africa and South Asia. The origins of the virus are not fully understood but, according to the analysis of different virus genomes, it is believed that it may have originated in bats and was transmitted to camels sometime in the distant past.48

A group of CAMS/PUMC researchers infected non-human primates with the MERS coronavirus in a study in 2014. In the study titled, 'An animal model of MERS produced by infection of rhesus macaques with MERS coronavirus', Yao Yanfeng, Bao Linlin, Deng Wei and Qin Chuan from CAMS/PUMC set out to determine whether monkey models were effective to study the pathogenesis of MERS infections. In this CAMS/PUMC study, the research team sourced its MERS samples from Dr. Ron Fouchier in Erasmus and utilized them to directly infect the lungs of Rhesus Macaques and observe their physiological responses. The researchers reported that infected monkeys showed clinical signs of disease, virus replication, histological lesions and neutralizing antibody production. They also reported that they could confirm that the monkey model supports viral growth, and manifests respiratory and generalized illness along with tissue pathology. These CAMS/PUMC researchers claim to have conducted similar experiments on mouse, ferret and guinea pig models but decided not to publish the data. [186]

Although the animal model studies will benefit the studies on

---

186. Yao Yanfeng, et. al., 'An Animal Model of MERS Produced by Infection of Rhesus Macaques With MERS Coronavirus', Journal of Infectious Diseases, Vol. 209, No. 2, 15 January 2014.

vaccine, antiviral as well as viral pathogenesis, the adaptation of MERS-CoV in primates has intrinsic risks of obtaining viral variants that have enhanced transmissibility in primates. Then, whether these variants also have higher transmissibility in humans, causing more efficient human-to-human transmission, becomes a great concern and bioethics issue. Dr. Bao Linlin is of particular interest in this MERS study as well as her multiple studies on H7N9 and other GoF research on avian influenza viruses. Bao operates under ILAS at CAMS and conducts GoF research that is virtually identical to the research conducted by Ron Fouchier [187]. Both Bao and Fouchier have engineered avian influenza (H7N9 and H5N1) viruses that could transmit between ferrets via droplets.[188] However, while Fouchier's research was criticized and has periodically ceased under EU regulations related to weapons of mass destruction, Bao's research has continued with no apparent restrictions.

Chinese Academy of Medical Sciences Oxford Institute (COI) – A Model of Governance

COI is a joint biomedical research and educational institute

---

187. For example, please see Ron Fouchier, et. al., 'Airborne transmission of influenza A/H5N1 virus between ferrets', Science, 22, 336:6088 (June 2012).
   Ron Fouchier, et. al., 'The Potential for Respiratory Droplet–Transmissible A/H5N1 Influenza Virus to Evolve in a Mammalian Host', Science, 22;336:6088 (June 2012).
   Martin Enserink, 'Flu Researcher Ron Fouchier Loses Legal Fight Over H5N1 Studies', American Association for the Advancement of Science (ScienceMag), 25 September 2013.
   https://www.science.org/content/article/flu-researcher-ron-fouchier-loses-legal-fight-over-h5n1-studies,

between CAMS/PUMC and the Nuffield Department of Medicine at Oxford University. In addition to Oxford, Nuffield runs the Mahidol Oxford Tropical Medicine Research Unit (MORU) in Bangkok with clinical facilities and field sites across Thailand, Myanmar, Laos, Cambodia, Vietnam, Indonesia, Bangladesh and India. [189]

---

188. For example, please see Linlin Bao, et. al., 'Novel Avian-Origin Human Influenza A(H7N9) Can Be Transmitted Between Ferrets via Respiratory Droplets', Journal of Infectious Diseases, Vol. 209, Issue 4, 15 February 2014.

Linlin Bao, et. al., 'Transmission of H7N9 influenza virus in mice by different infective routes', Virology Journal, Vol. 11, Article No. 185, 2014.

Ron Fouchier, et. al., 'Airborne Transmission of Influenza A/H5N1 Virus Between Ferrets'.

Ron Fouchier et. al., 'Gain-of-Function Experiments on H7N9', Science, 3 August 2013.

https://www.science.org/doi/full/10.1126/science.1243325

Ron Fouchier, et. al., 'The Potential for Respiratory Droplet–Transmissible A/H5N1 Influenza Virus to Evolve in a Mammalian Host'.

Martin Enserink, 'Flu Researcher Ron Fouchier Loses Legal Fight Over H5N1 Studies: Dutch court confirms that export license is needed to publish certain influenza paper', Science, 25 September 2013.

https://www.science.org/content/article/flu-researcher-ron-fouchier-loses-legal-fight-over-h5n1-studies

Robert Roos, 'Fouchier study reveals changes enabling airborne spread of H5N1', Center for Infectious Disease Research and Policy, University of Minnesota, 21 June 2012.

https://www.cidrap.umn.edu/news-perspective/2012/06/fouchier-study-reveals-changes-enabling-airborne-spread-h5n1

Jocelyn Kaiser, 'EXCLUSIVE: Controversial experiments that could make bird flu more risky poised to resume:

Two 'gain of function' projects halted more than 4 years ago have passed new U.S. review process', Science, 8 February 2019.

Martin Enserink, 'Scientists Brace for Media Storm Around Controversial Flu Studies', Science, 23 November 2011.

https://www.science.org/content/article/scientists-brace-media-storm-around-controversial-flu-studies

189. Ryan Clarke is a former MORU staff member and has worked across the entire regional operation.

While COI and MORU are two officially separate organizations, they are organized under Nuffield. Traditionally, there has been regular interaction between scientists, especially related to research on tropical diseases. Interactions between MORU staff and their China-based COI counterparts had stopped during the COVID-19 period.[190] The Oxford staff serve as the official leadership with Professor Tao Dong as the director, Professor Chris Conlon as clinical director, Darren Nash as finance director, Dr. Ricardo Fernandes as the group leader of Cancer Immunology, and Associate Professor Roman Fischer as the head of Discovery Proteomics. CAMS staff are not in official leadership positions and appear to be seconded to COI from other CAMS institutes. [191]

Contrary to many other Western countries, the United Kingdom appears to have avoided inadvertent funding to, jointly publishing with, or transferring sensitive dual-use technology or know-how related to high-risk pathogen research to Chinese institutes. This contrasts sharply with practices of other countries such as the United States, Australia, Canada, France, Holland and even Japan. [192] COI has remained focused on more standardized, analytical and classification tasks related to cancer screening and treatment as well as determining the efficacy of various treatment

---

190. Interview with multiple senior MORU staff on 1, 4 and 7 February 2022.

191. 'Principal Investigators in Oxford', Chinese Academy of Medical Sciences Oxford Institute,
https://www.camsoxford.ox.ac.uk/PIs/principal-investigators-oxford
'Principal Investigators China', Chinese Academy of Medical Sciences Oxford Institute,
https://www.camsoxford.ox.ac.uk/PIs/principal-investigators-china

regimes for infectious diseases, including SARS-CoV-2. The focus of COI has remained focused on providing clinical and scientific descriptions in order to generate fundamental knowledge. [193]

This consistent focus can be largely attributed to a combination of a strong commitment by the British government, Oxford University and Wellcome Trust (the primary funder of Nuffield's international public health activities) to serve low-income groups who are vulnerable to tropical diseases. International Nuffield operations, such as MORU, are not necessarily focused on leading in next generation technology development but rather validating innovative deployment models in low-resource settings.[194] This same overall philosophy has traditionally been present within COI as well.[195] However, with recent governance challenges related to the inability to communicate with COI personnel, it is unclear as to how Nuffield will continue to exercise the same

---

192. Ryan Clarke and Lam Peng Er, 'Coronavirus Research Networks in China: Origins, International Linkages and Consequences', Center for Non-Traditional Security Studies, May 2021, Singapore.
https://rsis-ntsasia.org/wp-content/uploads/2021/06/NTS-Asia-Monograph-Coronavirus-Research-in-China-by-Ryan-Clarke-and-Lam-Peng-Er-May2021-1.pdf

193. For example, please see Tao Dong, et. al, 'Clinical and epidemiological features of COVID-19 family clusters in Beijing, China', Journal of Infection, Vol. 81, Issue 2, 1 August 2020.
Tao Dong, et. al., 'Interferon-Induced Transmembrane Protein 3 Genetic Variant rs12252-C Associated With Disease Severity in Coronavirus Disease 2019', The Journal of Infectious Diseases, Vol. 222, Issue 1, 1 July 2020.
Chi Zhang, 'A Novel Scoring System for Prediction of Disease Severity in COVID-19', Frontiers in Cellular and Infection Microbiology, Vol. 10, Issue 318, June 2020.

194. Assessments based on Ryan Clarke's work with MORU across Southeast Asia.

195. Assessments based on Ryan Clarke's work with MORU across Southeast Asia.

degree of oversight as during the period prior to the SARS-CoV-2 outbreak.

As the Chinese diplomats are gradually adopting increasingly aggressive strategies when dealing with international relations issues under Xi Jinping's leadership, it is clear that many Chinese have also adopted the mentality that Chinese people should set the rules for the world, not the West. This is what they called 'East Rising while West Declining'. Have some Chinese scientists also adopted a similar mentality after they have mastered the knowledge and technologies of high-risk pathogen research? Do they think that they should be the ones who define the rules of bioethics and bioweapon conventions? Or at a minimum, have some of these Chinese researchers with PLA backgrounds embraced this mentality?

Historical Overview and Current Organizational Structure of the Institute of Pathogen Biology (CAMS)

The Institute of Pathogen Biology (IPB) is one of the institutes under the flagship of the CAMS/PUMC. IPB was founded in May 2006 in Beijing and through CAMS falls under the National Health Commission, a cabinet-level executive department of the State Council responsible for formulating national health policies. Dr. Jin Qi is the Director of IPB. He completed a postdoctoral fellowship at the United States Centers for Disease Control and Prevention.[196] IPB has 22 additional Senior Scientists listed as full-time faculty on its official website.[197] IPB has 22 additional Senior Scientists listed as full-time faculty on its official website. [198]

Table 3: Transnational Linkages of Senior Scientists in IPB[199]

Featured Researchers	Transnational Linkages	CCP Membership?
CUI Sheng [200]	Graduated with a PhD from the Italian International School for Advanced Study (SISSA) in 2004	Unknown
DENG Tao [201]	Graduated with DPhil degree in Molecular Virology, conferred in 2006 by Sir William Dunn School of Pathology, Oxford University	Unknown
HE Yuxian [202]	Studied in University of Ulm, Germany. Previously worked as a visiting scholar at the Allen Diamond AIDS Research Center of Rockefeller University, a postdoctoral researcher at the New York University Institute of Public Health, and an assistant researcher at the LFK Institute of the New York Blood Center	Unknown
JIN Qi [203]	Graduated from Beijing Medical College and was a postdoctoral researcher at the U.S. Center for Disease Control and Prevention	Unknown
ZHANG Leiliang [204]	Held a postdoc at Harvard Medical School and the University of Florida.	Unknown

196. 'Faculty', Institute of Pathogen Biology, Chinese Academy of Medical Sciences. http://www.mgc.ac.cn/IPB_en/faculty.html
197. Ibid.
198. 'Faculty', Institute of Pathogen Biology, Chinese Academy of Medical Sciences. http://www.mgc.ac.cn/IPB_en/faculty.html
199. Only a few of the 20 listed scientists' open-source profiles are available online.
200. CUI Sheng's profile on ORCID. https://orcid.org/0000-0001-6329-3582
201. 'DENG Tao', Institute of Microbiology, Chinese Academy of Sciences. http://english.im.cas.cn/people_/facultyandstaff/KLPMI/202012/t20201204_256026.html

The official mission of IPB is to (i) conduct fundamental research to provide a domestic platform for the improvement of infectious disease research; (ii) conduct directed applied research to augment nationwide efforts regarding the prevention and treatment of infectious diseases; (iii) conduct research and development to build up domestic infectious disease-related and biotechnology industries; (iv) and provide policy-relevant inputs to inform decision-making on the prevention and control of infectious diseases at the national level. [205]

IPB facilities cover 10,000 square meters of space for lab experiments and offices with over 3,000 pieces of equipment valued at an estimated CNY150 million. IPB hardware and software are focused primarily on immunology, cell biology, morphology, structural biology, and bioinformatics.[206] IPB is formally a member of both the National Major Basic Research Program (973 Program) and the now-defunct (at least officially) National High-Tech Development Program (863 Program).[207] The 863 program was a major initiative that was modeled on the American Strategic Defense Initiative. It was officially active

202. 'HE Yuxian's publication profile on the website of X-Mol Academic Platform.
     https://www.x-mol.com/university/faculty/188213
203. JIN Qi's profile on X-MOL.
     https://www.x-mol.com/university/faculty/210903
204. 'ZHANG Leiliang's profile on the website of Shandong First Medical University.
     https://stic.sdfmu.edu.cn/info/1012/1196.htm#
205. 'Director of IPB', IPB, CAMS & PUMC.
     http://www.mgc.ac.cn/IPB_en/index.html
     'Institute of Pathogenic Biology, Chinese Academy of Medical Sciences 2022 Recruitment Notice', Institute of Pathogen Biology, Chinese Academy of Medical Sciences, 20 May 2022.
     http://www.gaoxiaojob.com/zhaopin/zhuanti/zgyxkxybyswxyjs2019/index.html

from 1983 to 2016. [208]

The 863 Program had initially focused on developing seven strategic priority areas, namely laser technology, space platforms, biotechnology, information technology (including artificial intelligence), automation and manufacturing technology, energy, and advanced materials.[209] One of the key achievements of Project 863 was the invention of the quad core Loongson-3 processor that is now part of the Tianhe-1A supercomputer, one of the world's most powerful that also has military applications.[210] In 2011, Huang Kexue was imprisoned in the United States after being convicted of stealing biotechnology intellectual property from Dow AgroSciences and Cargill between 2003 and 2008 and passing it to Project 863. [211]

206. '金奇（研究員。男，朝鮮族,).
金奇（研究員。男，朝鮮族）_百度百科 (baidu.com)
207. '金奇（研究員。男，朝鮮族）.
金奇（研究員。男，朝鮮族）_百度百科 (baidu.com)
208. 'Qiang Zhi and Margaret Pearson, 'China's Hybrid Adaptive Bureaucracy: The Case of the 863 Program for Science and Technology', Governance: An International Journal of Policy, Administration, and Institutions, Vol. 30, No. 3, July 2017.
Julian Gewirtz, 'The Futurists of Beijing: Alvin Toffler, Zhao Ziyang, and China's 'New Technological Revolution,' 1979–1991', The Journal of Asian Studies, Vol. 78, No. 1, February 2019.
209. 'Tai Ming Cheung, Fortifying China: The Struggle to Build a Dual-Use Economy, Cornell University Press, 2019

Figure 4: Organizational Graph of the Institute of Pathogen Biology

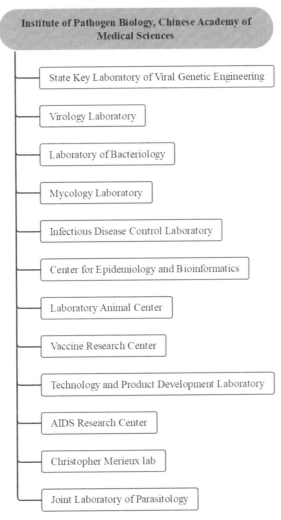

Source: The website of 'Institute of Pathogen Biology at Chinese Academy of Medical Sciences'.
http://www.mgc.ac.cn/IPB_en/index.html

Engineering Synthetic, Replicative SARS-CoV-2 Viruses at the Christophe Merieux Laboratory (CML) of IPB

While most of the daily flow of clinical, laboratory, research and educational activities within IPB can be classified as standard, there is high-risk research being conducted, some of which with international cooperation. In October 2021, researchers from the IPB-controlled CML in Beijing developed their own synthetic SARS-CoV-2 virus in the lab, which they refer to as the 'SARS-CoV-2-GFP replicon', with the logic that experimentation on this synthetic virus would more fully inform treatment options.[212] As the SARS-CoV-2 replicon generated by this

210. "Designing Quad-Core Loongson-3 Processor', Institute of Computing Technology, Chinese Academy of Sciences, 10 September 2009.
http://english.ict.cas.cn/rh/rps/200909/t20090910_36875.html
Michael Raska, 'Scientific Innovation and China's Military Modernization', The Diplomat, 3 September 2013.
https://thediplomat.com/2013/09/scientific-innovation-and-chinas-military-modernization/
Nabeel Mancheri and Viswesh Rammohan, 'China's 'leapfrogging' in high performance computing', The Strategist, 15 November 2013.
https://www.aspistrategist.org.au/chinas-leapfrogging-in-high-performance-computing/
Alex Joske, Picking Flowers, Making Honey: The Chinese Military's Collaboration with Foreign Universities, Policy Brief Report No. 10, Australian Strategic Policy Institute, 30 October 2018.
https://ad-aspi.s3.ap-southeast-2.amazonaws.com/2018-10/Picking%20flowers%2C%20making%20honey_0.pdf?VersionId=H5sGNaWXqMgTG_2F2yZTQwDw6OyNfH.u
211. "Chinese scientist Huang Kexue jailed for trade theft', BBC, 22 December 2011.
https://www.bbc.com/news/business-16297237
212. Bei Wang, Chongyang Zhang, Xiaobo Lei, Lili Ren, Zhendong Zhao and He Huang, 'Construction of Non-infectious SARS-CoV-2 Replicons and Their Application in Drug Evaluation', Virologica Sinica, Vol. 36, No. 5, October 2021.
https://www.ncbi.nlm.nih.gov/pmc/articles/PMC8034055/

synthetic virus does not have functional structure genes and NSP-1 gene, this replicon is not infectious, even though it can replicate and produce reporter proteins efficiently in their experiments.[213] While this work aimed to avoid high-risk experiments of producing infectious SARS-CoV-2 clones in the BSL-3 labs, it is just one step away from generating full length infectious clones via adding back missing genes using the same reverse engineering methods.

This work on SARS-CoV-2 shares fundamental similarities with some of the work that was done by Ralph Baric in 2002 when he was developing synthetic SARS-CoV-1 viruses in his lab at UNC - Chapel Hill. Baric filed US Patent Number US 7,279,327 B2 on 19 April 2002. The first case of the SARS-CoV-1 outbreak in China was in Guangdong province in November 2002. [214]

The April 2002 US patent describes the bioengineering work as producing an infectious, replication-defective coronavirus that was specifically targeted for human lung epithelium – a literal description of SARS-CoV-1. This patent lays out the fact that these researchers knew that the ACE receptor, ACE2 binding

---

213. Bei Wang, Chongyang Zhang, Xiaobo Lei, Lili Ren, Zhendong Zhao and He Huang, 'Construction of Non-infectious SARS-CoV-2 Replicons and Their Application in Drug Evaluation', Virologica Sinica, Vol. 36, No. 5, October 2021. https://www.ncbi.nlm.nih.gov/pmc/articles/PMC8034055/
214. Ryan Clarke, 'Emerging Global Pandemic Risks Come from Engineered Viruses in Chinese Labs, Not the Jungle or Bat Caves'.
Please also see Kristopher Curtis, Boyd Yount and Ralph Baric, United States Patent, Patent No: US 7,279,327 B2, Date of Application: 19 April 2022, Date of Patent Grant: 9 October 2007.
https://patentimages.storage.googleapis.com/a8/c0/6a/0584dd67435ef2/US7279327.pdf

domain, the S1 spike protein and other elements could be synthetically modified in laboratory settings. This could be done using existing gene sequencing technologies (even back in 2002) to utilize computer code to turn this genetic sequence into a pathogen or an intermediate host of a pathogen. [215]

This 2021 study conducted by IPB, PUMC, and CML used a different version of the strategies: generating assembly-defective replicon, but not replication-defective replicon as used by Dr. Baric's group. But in principle, once a scientist has mastered the reverse engineering methods to produce SARS-CoV-2 cDNA clones, it is straightforward to obtain full infectious viral clones if no bioethics committees are blocking the effort.

Key Transnational Linkages of IPB[216] and CML[217]

CML was co-founded by the Merieux Family Foundation and

---

215. Ryan Clarke, 'Emerging Global Pandemic Risks Come from Engineered Viruses in Chinese Labs, Not the Jungle or Bat Caves'.
    Please also see Kristopher Curtis, Boyd Yount and Ralph Baric, United States Patent, Patent No: US 7,279,327 B2, Date of Application: 19 April 2022, Date of Patent Grant: 9 October 2007.
    https://patentimages.storage.googleapis.com/a8/c0/6a/0584dd67435ef2/US7279327.pdf.
216. A full set of network diagrams outlining all of IPB's institutional linkages based off of joint publications and grant awards can be found in Annex D. All data was collected using the automated search and knowledge representation capabilities of Data Abyss.
217. A full set of network diagrams outlining all of CML's institutional linkages based off of joint publications and grant awards can be found in Annex E. All data was collected using the automated search and knowledge representation capabilities of Data Abyss.
    https://www.dataabyss.ai/

CAMS. The lab is formally part of the IPB at CAMS and seeks to identify 'emerging and infectious pathogens and conducts research on the etiology and epidemiology of acute viral respiratory infections'. In addition, the lab states that its primary 'goal is to identify the viral and bacterial agents responsible for severe pneumonia in children under the age of five'.[218] Given this self-declared pediatric mission, it is unclear why this lab would be engineering synthetic SARS-CoV-2 viruses.

CML is also part of the GABRIEL Network of over 70 international scientists conducting joint research, education and training programs. The GABRIEL network has three official objectives:

- to publish and share the expertise, tools and knowledge required for advanced applied research in emerging countries, particularly in the field of pathogenic agent identification and monitoring;
- to conduct international, collaborative epidemiological studies in conjunction with people working in local healthcare and biomedical research and/or private partners; and
- to help improve public health policies by introducing surveillance studies, and generating reliable and accurate epidemiological data. [219]

218. 'Christophe Merieux Laboratory', Merieux Foundation.
    https://www.fondation-merieux.org/en/what-we-do/enhancing-research-capabilities/research-laboratories/christophe-merieux-laboratories/
219. 'GABRIEL Network, Merieux Foundation,
    https://www.fondation-merieux.org/en/what-we-do/enhancing-research-capabilities/gabriel-network/

It is unclear as to how this October 2021 study corresponds to or forwards any of these declared objectives.

CML also articulates more specific scientific and technological objectives related to the entire spectrum of virology and the epidemiology of respiratory infections:

- Development of technology platform of unknown virus identification and discovery of unknown respiratory viruses in respiratory samples;
- Development of multiplex assays for respiratory pathogens;
- Molecular evolution of new emerging respiratory viruses;
- Identification of biomarkers for diagnosis, treatment assessment and prediction of respiratory infections. [220]

CML shares BSL-3 laboratories with ILAS and CAMS. CML officially acknowledges collaborations with the following premier Chinese institutions, some of which also have an established track record of high-risk pathogen research, namely ILAS:

- Center for Disease Control and Prevention (CDC) of Beijing
- Peking Union Medical College Hospital (PUMCH)
- Beijing Children Hospital (BCH)

---

220. 'Christophe Merieux Laboratory – Beijing, China', Gabriel Network. https://www.gabriel-network.org/laboratoires/christophe-merieux-laboratory/research-activities/?lang=en#menu

- ChaoYang Hospital (CYH)
- Shanghai CDC
- Jiangsu Provincial CDC
- Shandong Provincial Academy of Medical Sciences
- Institute of Laboratory Animal Sciences (ILAS)[221] , CAMS [222]

CAMS is a Primary Driver of China's Emerging Position as a World Leader in High-Risk Virological Research

CAMS/PUMC represents a major component of China's ambition to become the world's leading virological center of expertise. However, its GoF research has not been subjected to any meaningful scrutiny from the international scientific community regarding potential public health risks versus benefits. CAMS/PUMC has successfully absorbed American expertise to develop and operationalize its own BSL4 lab in Kunming. This lab is now able to independently conduct high-risk virological research.

CAMS/PUMC is now a world leader in the development of synthetic viruses in the lab, including SARS-CoV-2 viruses, and

---

221. For examples of high-risk pathogen research conducted at ILAS, please see Linlin Bao, et. al., 'Novel Avian-Origin Human Influenza A(H7N9) Can Be Transmitted Between Ferrets via Respiratory Droplets', Journal of Infectious Diseases, Vol. 209, Issue 4, 15 February 2014.
Linlin Bao, et. al., 'Transmission of H7N9 influenza virus in mice by different infective routes', Virology Journal, Vol. 11, Article No. 185, 2014.
222. 'Christophe Merieux Laboratory – Beijing, China', Gabriel Network. https://www.gabriel-network.org/laboratoires/christophe-merieux-laboratory/research-activities/?lang=en#menu

engineering dangerous pathogens found in nature. This marks a major development in that CAMS/PUMC has the capability to engineer a range of viruses for various applications, even if it is not possible to acquire a sufficient number of natural samples. Access to samples is no longer a scientific bottleneck or a source of Western leverage against Chinese institutes such as CAMS/PUMC.

CAMS/PUMC researchers are capable of conducting high risk research on-shore and only with fellow Chinese domestic counterparts. They are no longer dependent on international expertise or knowhow to conduct this research. This is a recent development and is strategically significant. Simply put, China is emerging as a comprehensive leader with an autonomous capability in cutting edge virology research.

CHAPTER FIVE

Guangzhou Institute of Respiratory Health, CCP Integration, and International Connectivity

- Historical Overview and Current Organizational Structure

- Huyan Institute's Relationship with the CCP: Strong Municipal Ties in Guangzhou, Establishment of Internal Party Branch and Lack of Formal Linkages to Beijing

- Transnational Linkages of GIRH/Huyan Institute

CHAPTER 5

Guangzhou Institute of Respiratory Health, CCP Integration, and International Connectivity

In 1971, the First Affiliated Hospital of Guangzhou Medical College established a 'chronic bronchitis prevention team' at the calling of then-Premier Zhou Enlai. In 1979, Guangzhou Medical College (now named Guangzhou Medical University) founded the Guangzhou Institute of Respiratory Diseases (GIRD) as one of the first respiratory disease research institutes in China.[223] In August 2017, GIRD was renamed the Guangzhou Institute of Respiratory Health (GIRH, also known as the Huyan Institute). The Huyan Institute has played an active role in combating SARS in 2003 as well as multiple H5N1, H1N1, H7N9, H5N6, and MERS outbreaks in China, including the clinical treatment of patients. [224] In subsequent years, it received multiple national honors for having an 'advanced grass-roots party organization' (in 2003) and aiding 'civilization construction' (in 2005). [225]

---

223. Guangzhou Institute of Respiratory Health.
   http://www.gird.cn/show_list.php?id=11
224. Ibid.

Apparently, GIRH continues to retain its local Guangzhou-based governance and does not formally fall under the control of CAS, CAMS, or the State Council. This GIRH governance structure is unique in China for an institute of this domestic significance and not witnessed in any other peer virology research institute in the country. The institute's director is Zhong Nanshan, arguably China's most well-known and respected virologist. Zhong graduated from Beijing Medical College in 1960, and received further training from 1979-81 in the Department of Respiratory Medicine of the University of Edinburgh, where he received a MD.[226] In 2020, Zhong was awarded the Medal of the Republic, the highest state honor, for his 'outstanding contribution to fighting the COVID-19 epidemic'. [227]

Zhong, of Fujianese ancestry, was born in Nanjing in 1936. Both his parents received medical training, with Zhong's father returning from the State University of New York to China in 1946. During the Mao era, Zhong's father established a virology laboratory at Sun Yat-sen University in Guangzhou where viral specimens were isolated and reproduced.[228] Zhong Nanshan's

---

225. 'The history of the Huyan Institute,' Guangzhou Institute of Respiratory Disease Institute Overview, 24 Aug. 2011, archived at https://web.archive.org/web/20120825030305/http://www.gird.cn/girdweb/Article-565.aspx

226. 'Journal Editor-in-Chief,' website of the Journal of Thoracic Disease, https://jtd.amegroups.com/about/editorInChief; 'Brief introduction of Academician Zhong Nanshan,' Guangzhou Institute of Respiratory Disease Academician Column, 2 Aug. 2011, archived at https://web.archive.org/web/20120825010142/http://www.gird.cn/girdweb/Article-460.aspx

227. 'Zhong Nanshan: outspoken doctor awarded China's top honour', Xinhua, 8 Sept. 2020. http://www.xinhuanet.com/english/2020-09/08/c_139352929.htm; 'Respiratory disease expert wins alumni award', University of Edinburgh, 16 April 2020, https://www.ed.ac.uk/news/2020/respiratory-disease-expert-wins-alumni-award

current laboratory is about an hour's walk from the Guangzhou hospital where his father had worked. Zhong Nanshan's family suffered greatly in the Cultural Revolution, during which Zhong's father was labeled a 'reactionary academic'. The laboratory of Zhong's father was apparently dismantled in the 1960s, and his research assistants were sent to the countryside for ideological reeducation. Red Guards attacked Zhong Nanshan's mother, who reportedly committed suicide in 1968. Zhong married Li Shaofen, a basketball player whose team had been supported by Premier Zhou Enlai. With his wife's help, Zhong Nanshan was able to return to Guangzhou in 1971 with a medical position. [229]

Since that time, Zhong has largely remained in Guangdong. From 1992 to 2002, he served as party secretary and/or rector of

228. 'ZHONG Nanshan', Chinese Academy of Engineering, 7 March 2017.
https://web.archive.org/web/20170306224833/http://www.cae.cn/cae/jsp/
introduction.jsp?oid=2011123111535267114551
'Xinlin Stories of SHEN Jieping: Going through the adversities and growing up out of struggles', YCWB, 17 July 2021.
http://news.ycwb.com/2021-07/17/content_40145876.htm
'Three Generations of Medical Professionals: Listening to the story of their family's heritage told by ZHONG Nanshan's son', Xinhua, 19 August 2020.
'Doctor ZHONG Nanshan', Peking University, 12 September 2019.
https://news.pku.edu.cn/bdrw/f09c73a1063a43b0a02132aff3d51f6a.htm
229. 'Doctor ZHONG Nanshan', Peking University, 12 September 2019.
https://news.pku.edu.cn/bdrw/f09c73a1063a43b0a02132aff3d51f6a.htm
'Xinlin Stories of SHEN Jieping: Going through the adversities and growing up out of struggles', YCWB, 17 July 2021.
http://news.ycwb.com/2021-07/17/content_40145876.htm
'ZHONG Nanshan's wife wears the number Five in China's Female National Basketball Team', Sina, 16 June 2003.
http://news.sina.com.cn/c/2003-06-16/02521173575.shtml
'The Fifty Superstars of China's Basketball Hall of Fame: ZHONG Nanshan's wife in the first cohort of female basketball in China', 163.com, 27 September 2015.
https://www.163.com/sports/article/AVH5TGT800052UUC.html

Guangzhou Medical College (the institution which GIRD/GIRH belongs to and later renamed as GMU); from July 1992 to July 1994, Zhong served as both party secretary and rector, a relatively unusual distinction for GMC/GMU. In 1992, Zhong was named a 'model worker,' and in 1996, Zhong became an academician of the Chinese Academy of Engineering. In 2008, he also joined the 11th National People's Congress in Beijing. [230]

As an especially high honor, Guangzhou Medical University and the State Key Laboratory of Respiratory Diseases in 2011 supported the creation of the 'Zhong Nanshan Medical Foundation of Guangdong Province', with Zhong Nanshan serving as the foundation's 'honorary chairman' and with participation from industry, venture capital, and party groups. The foundation lists goals and activities including poverty alleviation, covid-19 pandemic resource distribution, science popularization, scientific research funding, and funding for graduate students. [231] A researcher at GIRH serves as the foundation's chairman and a former asset management financier serves as the foundation's party secretary. [232]

---

230. 'Brief introduction of Academician Zhong Nanshan,' Guangzhou Institute of Respiratory Disease Academician Column, 2 Aug. 2011, archived at https://web. archive.org/web/20120825010142/http://www.gird.cn/girdweb/Article-460. aspx; 'Past leaders', Guangzhou Medical University School Profile, archived at https://web.archive.org/web/20220330042623/https://www.gzhmu.edu. cn/10009021

231. 'About' and 'Organization' pages, Zhong Nanshan Medical Foundation of Guangdong Province, http://www.znsmf.org/jijinhuijianjie/ and http://www. znsmf.org/zjjg/

232. 'Management' page, Zhong Nanshan Medical Foundation of Guangdong Province, http://www.znsmf.org/zjwrh/

Zhong has sometimes invited controversy related to activities outside of GIRH. In April 2022, the Financial Times reported that Zhong Nanshan may have improperly profited from pharmaceutical businesses, whose products he promoted, paralleling earlier allegations of questionable business dealings. Zhong has gained substantial prominence in recent months for promoting a 'traditional Chinese medicine' under the trade name 'lianhua qingwen' as a treatment for Covid-19. China's government has helped distribute these capsules extensively both domestically and internationally. [233]

It also appears that Zhong Nanshan has publicly argued with Beijing neuroscientist Rao Yi, both about official preferences for certain medicines and about plagiarism allegations facing other academicians.[234] On 22 December 2002, the first SARS patient was transferred from Heyuan City People's Hospital to GIRH. The patient subsequently developed respiratory failure and infected some of the institute's staff.[235] Confronted by this

---

233. Primrose Riordan, Gloria Li, Chan Ho-him and Hudson Lockett, 'China Covid-19 tsar pushed treatments without revealing business ties', Financial Times, 25 April 2022.
    'Kuwaitis praise traditional Chinese medicine for treating COVID-19,' Xinhua, 4 March 2021; Cao Zinan, 'Respiratory expert Zhong Nanshan's latest views on COVID-19', China Daily, 15 April 2020.; She Jingwei, 'Expert: Chinese medicine Lianhua Qingwen capsule proven effective for COVID-19', CGTN, 5 May 2020.

234. '官方最新回應：鐘南山院士是曹雪濤等論文調查複核專家組組長', Sohu, 3 February 2021.
    https://www.sohu.com/a/448494013_100226214
    Jane Cai, 'Shanghai needs food, not TCM Covid-19 medicine Lianhua Qingwen: medical experts', South China Morning Post, 20 April 2022.

235. Guangzhou Institute of Respiratory Health.
    http://www.gird.cn/show_list.php?id=11

medical crisis, Zhong rallied his medical 'troops' to view the hospital as a 'battlefield' with every doctor a 'fighter'. [236]

A similar analogy refers to the institute as the 'Whampoa Military Academy' of respiratory medicine for its role in training large numbers of leading respiratory doctors and scientists in China. [237] The historic Whampoa was a prominent, nationalist officer training center in Guangzhou during the Republican period, forming a power base for Kuomintang leader Chiang Kai-shek. GIRH also contains several centers with 'national' titles, including, a National Clinical Research Center for Respiratory Diseases and a National Clinical Drug Trial Institute (with a respiratory specialty), five national key clinical specialties (respiratory medicine, critical care medicine, allergic disease, oncology, and thoracic surgery), and one national key (secondary-level) discipline designation (for respiratory medicine).[238] GIRH has over 350 hospital beds within the First Affiliated Hospital of Guangzhou Medical University. The

---

236. 'SARS Technology is declaring war against you', Chinese Academy of Sciences, 2 May 2003.
    https://www.cas.cn/zt/kjzt/fdgx/ggqy/200305/t20030502_1709485.shtml
237. 'Building leadership and establishing brand reputation, without forgetting the mission of serving people: Commemorating the first Party branch's pioneering deeds made by the Guangzhou Institute of Respiratory Health in the First Affiliated Hospital of GUANGZHOU Medical University', Guangzhou Institute of Respiratory Health, 5 June 2019.
    http://www.gird.cn/show.php?id=62.
238. Guangzhou Institute of Respiratory Health.
    http://www.gird.cn/show_list.php?id=11; 'National Key Disciplines', China Academic Degrees and Graduate Education Development Center, PRC Ministry of Education, http://www.cdgdc.edu.cn/xwyyjsjyxx/zlpj/zdxkps/zdxk/; 'Introduction', State Key Laboratory of Respiratory Diseases, http://www.sklrd.cn/show_list.php?id=10

institute also houses a State Key Laboratory that has an area of 12,800 square meters. Since 2003, GIRH staff numbers have increased exponentially from 83 to 552 after the SARS epidemic. [239] The structure is presented in **Figure 5** below.

Figure 5: GIRH Organization

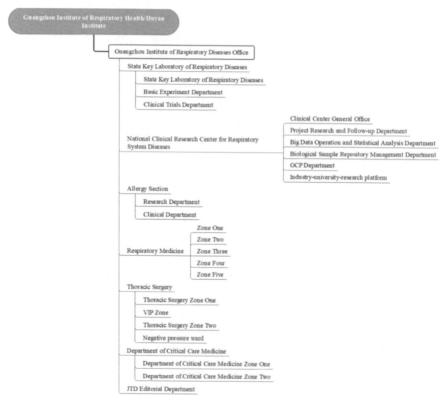

Source: Guangzhou Institute of Respiratory Health.
http://www.gird.cn/show_list.php?id=11

---

239. Guangzhou Institute of Respiratory Health.
http://www.gird.cn/show_list.php?id=11

CHAPTER FIVE | 137

GIRH-CCP Ties

As a Chinese government-funded research organization, GIRH maintains strong ties with the Chinese Communist Party (CCP). GIRH's website notes that during the 2003 SARS outbreak, Cheng Donghai served as the CCP branch secretary at GIRD.[240] In August 2013, Cheng Donghai reportedly was transferred and Huang Qinghui became the new CCP branch secretary, although Huang also appears to have been listed as a party secretary for GIRD in 2012. [241] Huang has been active in public roles on behalf of GIRH, including with businesses and with research institutions in other provinces. Huang's specialty is in insomnia, sleep apnea, and other sleep-related issues, and he has led the sleep section of the Guangzhou Medical Association. [242]

In the late 2000s, Liu Youning, a respiratory disease doctor who worked on SARS at the PLA General Hospital and PLA Institute of Respiratory Diseases, served as deputy director of the academic

---

240. It is difficult to determine Cheng Donghai's background, but while at GIRH, Cheng authored or co-authored several publications about health policy or about Zhong Nanshan. For instance, Cheng, Ruan Jizheng, and Zhong Nanshan in 2006 published an article criticizing the increasingly market-dominated trend of Chinese healthcare, citing among others Marx, Lionel Jospin, and Rousseau ('Thoughts on the health system after SARS' [SARS 事件後對衛生體制的反思], Medicine and Philosophy 醫學與哲學 10, no. 218 (Oct. 2006). For an example of his writing praising Zhong, see Cheng, 'On Nanshan Styles', Modern Hospital 7, no. 12 (Dec. 2007), which among other topics notes Zhong's anger at foreigners' 'demonization' of China.

241. Guangzhou Institute of Respiratory Health.
    http://www.gird.cn/show_list.php?id=11; Huang Xiaoliang, 'Revisit the oath of joining the party,' Guangzhou Institute of Respiratory Disease institute news, 20 June 2012, archived at https://web.archive.org/web/20120827072216/http://www.gird.cn/girdweb/Article-816.aspx

committee of Zhong Yongnian's laboratory, in addition to scholars from a variety of institutes belonging to CAS and Guangdong and northeast Chinese universities.[243] GIRH reported having 123 party members in 2011, and now claims to have had 175 CCP members by 2013. In October 2013, the CCP party committee of Guangzhou Medical University decided to let GIRH have its own 'general party branch,' a status which is usually for grassroots party groups with 50 to 100 party members. GIRH's general party branch, like typical CCP party branches, is tasked with propaganda activities, discipline inspection, training cadres, and other basic grassroots party functions, but it is not clear why the GMU party committee apparently waited to grant GIRH's party organization the higher 'general' designation. [244]

242. On Huang, see 'Always follow the party for the masses' welfare,' Zhong Nanshan Medical Foundation of Guangdong Province, 4 Aug. 2021, http://www.znsmf.org/news/720.html; 'Indoor air quality survey and respiratory disease,' Sina, 20 Aug. 2014, http://jiaju.sina.com.cn/news/20140820/375596_2.shtml; 'Investigation visit to Zhengzhou campus,' Henan University News, 12 April 2021, https://news.henu.edu.cn/info/1083/113389.htm; '2021 Academic Annual Meeting of the Sleep Medicine Branch,' Guangzhou Online Science and Technology Workers' Home, 28 Aug. 2021, https://xhfw.gzast.org.cn/portal/gzwskjgzzzj/xhfw-detail-society.action?id=78400; 'Mid-term report meeting of Lianhua Qingwen,' State Key Laboratory of Respiratory Disease News, 2 Mar. 2018, http://www.sklrd.cn/show.php?id=702

243. On the academic committee, see 'Academic Committee,' State Key Laboratory of Respiratory Diseases, posted January 23, 2011, https://web.archive.org/web/20120311175913/http://www.gird.cn/sklrd/Article-144.aspx; On Liu, see 'Our Family's 'White Haired General,'' The Paper, 3 November 2021, https://www.thepaper.cn/newsDetail_forward_15212620; 'Liu Youning personal website,' Medcon Conference platform, https://www.sciconf.cn/cn/person-detail/50?user_id=wUtevF5lLL4MV9lBh8geRQ_d_d

244. Guangzhou Institute of Respiratory Health. http://www.gird.cn/show_list.php?id=11. On number of party members in 2011, see 'Party branch work,' Guangzhou Institute of Respiratory Disease, archived at https://web.archive.org/web/20120825030253/http://www.gird.cn/girdweb/List-50.aspx

Given its leading role in taming the first SARS pandemic, GIRH has received support from all levels of local and national governments. For example, in May 2003, Zhong Nanshan discussed the institute's work with then Premier Wen Jiabao, who warmly praised Zhong's work on SARS.[245] In 2009, Wang Yang, now a member of the Politburo Standing Committee of the CCP and Chairman of the National Committee of the CPPCC, made an official visit to mark the 30th anniversary of GIRH. Wang urged GIRH staff to continue 'expanding cages, building nests and attracting phoenixes, and never stop the pace of reform and innovation'. [246]

The currently listed leaders of GIRH are Zhong Nanshan, He Jianxing, Li Shiyue, Zheng Jinping, and Huang Qinghui.[247] Zheng Jinping, a respiratory and geriatrics doctor and a Jiusan Society member[248], also serves on the Guangzhou City Committee of the Chinese People's Political Consultative Conference. Zheng also previously served in the 11th Guangdong People's Congress where he represented Guangzhou.[249] Zheng has been noted for helping to develop China's first guidelines for pulmonary function tests. [250]

---

245. 'Zhong Nanshan: Wisdom, passion, and responsibility' in Zhongguo Gaoxin Keji (Chinese Emerging High Technology), 12 January 2021.
     http://www.zggxkjw.com/content-18-9320-1.html
246. Guangzhou Institute of Respiratory Health.
     http://www.gird.cn/show_list.php?id=11
247. Ibid.
248. The Chinese government recognizes eight minor 'democratic' parties which accept the leading role of the Communist Party. These parties hold minor, but occasionally influential, representation in China's national legislative chambers. The Jiusan Society, one of the eight minor parties, is traditionally oriented around intellectuals and people in universities, and it has often been led by physicians.

Aside from Zhong, all of these leaders received their higher education in Guangzhou. Different biographies for Li list him as a visiting scholar at Heidelberg University (Germany) and at the U.S. Food and Drug Administration (USFDA), while He visited Barnes-Jewish Hospital in St. Louis.[251] Perhaps unusually, while He (a lung cancer and surgery specialist) ranks beneath Zhong at GIRH, He has served as chief physician and president of the First Affiliated Hospital which contains GIRH. [252]

Chen Rongchan was formerly a top leader at GIRH, just a level below Zhong Nanshan. Chen had trained under Zhong as well as

249. 'Zheng Jinping', Guangzhou Medical University.
https://www.gzhmu.edu.cn/10021716
'Zheng Jinping, the Member of the City's Committee of the Chinese People's Political Consultative Conference (CPPCC): Suggesting building an extra Infectious Disease Unit for Guangzhou National Respiratory Health Medical Center', Guangzhou Institute of Respiratory Health, 5 June 2019.
http://www.gird.cn/show.php?id=458
'The Representative of the 11th People's Congress of Guangdong Province', The Standing Committee of Guangdong Provincial People's Congress, 11 February 2009.
http://www.gdrd.cn/rdgzxgnr_4349/rddbmd/syjrddb/202006/t20200601_172252.html
250. 'Professor Zheng Jinping of Guangzhou Medical University presided over drafting of the country's first guidelines for pulmonary function testing', Work News, Guangzhou Medical University, archived at https://webcache.googleusercontent.com/search?q=cache:unQHjbDx598J:https://tzb.gzhmu.edu.cn/info/1039/1114.htm+&cd=1&hl=en&ct=clnk&gl=sg
251. 'The Supervisor for Graduate Studies of Master Program', State Key Laboratory of Respiratory Disease.
http://www.sklrd.cn/show.php?id=1027
'Shiyue LI 李時悅 ', Chinese University of Hong Kong, 4 July 2019.
https://www.surgery.cuhk.edu.hk/atccs2019/Shiyue%20LI.pdf
252. 'President He Jianxing', Current Leadership, First Affiliated Hospital of Guangzhou Medical University, archived at https://web.archive.org/web/20180209005808/http://www.gyfyy.com/cn/list-170-745.html

briefly at McGill University in Canada. In 2018, he left GIRH to join and direct the Shenzhen Institute of Respiratory Diseases, a newer institution which in 2019 only had a handful of staff.[253] Chen's institute later recruited Zhong to serve as its 'honorary' leader with the hope of improving and 'internationalizing' the Shenzhen institute.[254] Chen is also said to enjoy political activities and once served in the People's Congress and Consultative Conference in Guangzhou. [255]

In addition to GIRH's leaders, Yang Zifeng, Ma Qinhai, Wang Jian, Luo Yuanming, Ran Pixin, Zhao Jincun, and Guan Weijie have all featured on GIRH's website, along with Lu Wenjiu and Xie Jiaxing for the latter's earlier accomplishments.[256] The work and activities of these figures are outlined in **Table 4** below.

253. 'A Cohort of Researchers', State Key Laboratory of Respiratory Disease.
    http://www.sklrd.cn/show.php?id=357
    'Chen Rongchang', Guangzhou Medical University, 5 January 2022.
    https://ygc.gzhmu.edu.cn/info/1121/1632.htm
254. 'ZHONG Nanshan is hired by People's Hospital of Shenzhen, as an Honorary Director for the Guangzhou Institute of Respiratory Health', People.Cn. 29 July 2021.
    http://sz.people.com.cn/n2/2021/0729/c202846-34842681.html
255. 'Chen Rongchang', X-MOL.
    https://www.x-mol.com/university/faculty/96389
256. 'Vehemently Celebrating Professor LI Shiyue of our Department is Nominated as the Directing Member in the 9th Committee of Chinese Thoracic Society', Guangzhou Institute of Respiratory Health, 9 July 2020.
    http://www.gird.cn/show.php?id=459

Table 4: Featured Researchers in GIRH and the State Key Laboratory of Respiratory Disease[257]

Researcher Name	Significance	International Experiences	CCP Membership
Yang Zifeng	Established a nationally adopted virus detection platform	Unknown	Unknown
Ma Qinhai	Participated in clinical researching of anti-viral medicine of Covid-19	Unknown	Unknown
Wang Jian	Leader of Pulmonary Vascular Disease Group, National Center for Respiratory Medicine	Senior Editor of UK-based journal Experimental Physiology, Editorial Board Member of the US-based journal Pulmonary Circulation, American Thoracic Society Member (ATS), Member of the ATS Pulmonary Circulation Academic Committee, Member of the American Heart Association, Member of the American Physiological Society	Unknown

257. Featured researchers listed on the website of State Key Laboratory of Respiratory Disease, http://www.sklrd.cn/en/show_list.php?id=22. See also 'Professor Luo Yuanming of SKLRD honored as Fellow of the Royal College of Physicians,' State Key Laboratory of Respiratory Disease News Information, 9 Feb. 2021, http://www.sklrd.cn/en/show.php?id=858

Luo Yuanming	NA	Member of the Expert Group on Respiratory Function Testing of the European Respiratory Association, Visiting Professor at King's College London, Head of Research and Innovation China Base for Clinical Medical Students at Imperial College London, Participant in the New Zealand Health Research Agency's Sino-New Zealand Cooperation Seminar, Chief China Representative of the European Respiratory Association, Fellow of the UK's Royal College of Physicians	Unknown
Ran Pixin	Secretary of the Party Committee of Guangzhou Medical University, Director of the State Key Laboratory of Respiratory Diseases	Unknown	Yes
Zhao Jincun	Deputy Director of the State Key Laboratory of Respiratory Diseases	Unknown	Yes

Guan Weijie	Principal of the Bronchiectasis Research Group of the State Key Laboratory of Respiratory Diseases	Short-term exposure to O3, NO2 and SO2 and its linkages to emergency department visits and hospital admissions due to asthma	Unknown
Lu Wenjiu	PI, State Key Laboratory of Respiratory Diseases, Guangzhou Medical University	Principal of research projects supported by the United States National Institutes of Health (NIH) Fund	Unknown
Xie Jiaxing	NA	Member of European Respiratory Society, Awarded the European Respiratory Society Scholarship to study at the National Heart and Lung Research Institute in the United Kingdom	Unknown

GIRH: Transnational Linkages[258]

Since 2007, GIRH has hosted around 100 or more foreign scientists from countries including the United States, United Kingdom, Canada, France, Belgium, Japan, and the United Arab Emirates. These foreign scientists visit GIRH under the domestic

---

258. For GIRH's institutional linkages based on joint publications and grant awards, see Annex F. All data was collected using the automated search and knowledge representation capabilities of Data Abyss.
https://www.dataabyss.ai/

talent development principle of 'please come in and then go out' (請進來, 走出去). 40 GIRH staff have also been sent to study outside of China. [259] GIRH has established partnerships with the Firestone Respiratory Health Research Institute (Canada), McMaster University, University of Toronto, Imperial College London, King's College, Johns Hopkins University, University of Hong Kong, Chinese University of Hong Kong, University of Macau, and Macau University of Science and Technology. Since 2013, GIRH has hosted and co-organized 22 international academic conferences and 24 national academic conferences. [260]

In February 2020, it was announced that GIRH would evenly share a US$115 million grant with Harvard University, provided by the large real estate developer China Evergrande Group. The grant aimed to drive new diagnostic technologies, vaccines, and other therapeutics in response to Covid-19.In response to the grant, Zhong Nanshan declared that 'We are extremely encouraged by the generous gesture from Evergrande to coordinate and support the collaboration and by the overwhelmingly positive response from our Harvard colleagues.'[261] However, two years later it emerged that Evergrande had reneged on all but US$12 million of the grant to its US-based recipients.[262] It is not clear how much of the grant has so far been distributed or canceled for GIRH.

---

259. 'International Cooperation and Communication', Guangzhou Institute of Respiratory Health.
http://www.sklrd.cn/show_list.php?id=47
260. 'International Cooperation and Communication', Guangzhou Institute of Respiratory Health.
http://www.sklrd.cn/show_list.php?id=47

GIRH leaders He Jianxing and Li Shiyue have spent many years working in the United States, helping to raise the institute's profile in international biomedical research. He and Li are affiliated with the American College of Chest Physicians, World Association of Bronchology and Interventional Pulmonology, Forum of International Respiratory Societies, Global Lung Function Initiative, and the journal Respiration, among other groups.[263] GIRH has an international English-language journal, the Journal of Thoracic Diseases (JTD), which lists receiving support from Italian and Brazilian medical societies. [264] Zhong Nanshan and He Jianxing are the journal's two top editors, while the broader editorial board has numerous ethnic Chinese doctors in mainland China, Taiwan, Britain, and the United

261. 'Ekaterian Pesheva, 'Scientists from Harvard, China to unite against coronavirus,' Harvard Gazette, 24 Feb. 2020, https://news.harvard.edu/gazette/story/2020/02/harvard-and-china-collaborate-on-coronavirus-therapies/; Jennifer Couzin-Frankel, 'With $115 million, more than 80 Boston researchers will collaborate to tackle COVID-19,' ScienceInsider, Science, 5 Mar. 2020, https://www.science.org/content/article/115-million-more-80-boston-researchers-will-collaborate-tackle-covid-19

    'Bill & Melinda Gates Foundation Dedicates Additional Funding to the Novel Coronavirus Response', Bill & Melinda Gates Foundation, 5 February 2020. https://www.gatesfoundation.org/ideas/media-center/press-releases/2020/02/bill-and-melinda-gates-foundation-dedicates-additional-funding-to-the-novel-coronavirus-response

262. Rebecca Ostriker and Deirdre Fernandes, 'Evergrande reneges on multimillion-dollar pledge to Harvard-led COVID project,' Boston Globe, 16 Jan. 2022, https://www.bostonglobe.com/2022/01/16/metro/evergrande-reneges-multimillion-dollar-pledge-harvard-led-covid-project-another-stumble-its-ties-school/

263. 'Shiyue LI 李時悦 ', Chinese University of Hong Kong, 4 July 2019. https://www.surgery.cuhk.edu.hk/atccs2019/Shiyue%20LI.pdf 'Zheng Jinping', Guangzhou Medical University. https://www.gzhmu.edu.cn/10021716

264. 'About the Journal', Journal of Thoracic Disease, AME Publishing Company, Hong Kong. https://jtd.amegroups.com/about

States, as well as non-ethnic Chinese doctors at prominent medical institutions in London, Berlin, Houston, New York, and elsewhere.[265] Unusually for a scholarly journal, JTD published in 2018 an extensive encomium (including five color photographs) to He Jianxing, who was one of the journal's founders.[266] Even more unusually, JTD's website features multimedia 'testimonials for JTD from eminent experts worldwide" highlighting its achievement in 'gaining more and more attention worldwide!'[267]

265. 'Editorial Team', Journal of Thoracic Disease, AME Publishing Company, Hong Kong.
     https://jtd.amegroups.com/about/editorialTeam
266. 'Prof. Jianxing He: ones with more motive power and willpower, a better traveler he is', Journal of Thoracic Disease, Vol. 10, No. 6, June 2018.
267. 'Testimonials', Journal of Thoracic Disease, AME Publishing Company, Hong Kong. https://jtd.amegroups.com/pages/view/testimonials

CHAPTER SIX

Academy of Military Medical Sciences (AMMS), Dual-Use Pathogen Research, and Transnational Linkages

CHAPTER 6

Academy of Military Medical Sciences (AMMS),
Dual-Use Pathogen Research, and Transnational Linkages

Historical Overview and Current Organizational Structure

AMMS is the highest medical research institution of the PLA. It was founded in Shanghai in August 1951 and moved to Beijing in 1958.[268] On 11 June 1951, the Central Military Commission (CMC) issued a 'telegram to establish the Academy of Military Medical Sciences' within the East China Military Region (MR), the Third and First Field Army, as well as the Central, South, Southwest, and Northeast MRs. On 1 August 1951 Gong Naiquan, then-Minister of Health of the East China MR, was appointed as the first Director in Shanghai. In its initial stages, AMMS established six departments covering physiology,

---

268. '中國人民解放軍軍事醫學科學院'.
　　中國人民解放軍軍事醫學科學院 _ 百度百科 (baidu.com)

biochemistry, medicine, chemistry, bacteria, and parasites. [269]

In December 1955 General Huang Kecheng, Minister of the PLA General Logistics Department expressed his views on the strategic significance of 'national defense construction' to Premier Zhou Enlai. General Huang focused specifically on China's needs to develop defensive capabilities regarding atomic weapons, biological weapons, and chemical weapons. In 1958, AMMS was moved from the Huangpu River north to the foot of Yanshan Mountain. In addition to the physical move, AMMS was administratively upgraded from a division-level unit to a military-level unit. The original departments (14 by 1958) were integrated and reorganized into 7 research institutes.[270] In November 1961, the executive meeting of the CMC decided that the AMMS should exercise corps-level authority and in 1970 this authority was made permanent by the CMC. [271]

In August 2003, the PLA Center for Disease Control and Prevention (PLA CDC) was formally established within AMMS.[272] The PLA CDC represents a separate capability from the officially civilian Chinese CDC. It is unclear if the PLA CDC and Chinese CDC represent intentionally redundant capabilities in the event of a public health emergency or if there are specific

269. '中國人民解放軍軍事醫學科學院'.
      中國人民解放軍軍事醫學科學院 _ 百度百科 (baidu.com)
270. '中國人民解放軍軍事醫學科學院'.
      中國人民解放軍軍事醫學科學院 _ 百度百科 (baidu.com)
271. '中國人民解放軍軍事醫學科學院'.
      中國人民解放軍軍事醫學科學院 _ 百度百科 (baidu.com)
272. '中國人民解放軍軍事醫學科學院'.
      中國人民解放軍軍事醫學科學院 _ 百度百科 (baidu.com)

complementarities. Chinese CDC reports to the National Health Commission (State Council) while PLA CDC ultimately reports to the Central Military Commission (CMC).

During the 2003 SARS outbreak in China, AMMS formed an industry partnership with BGI Genomics to fully sequence the entire genome of the virus. CAS) was also a key research partner in this exercise as was PUMC, which is part of the Chinese Academy of Medical Sciences (CAMS). This full genome sequencing of the then-novel SARS virus was instrumental in China's response efforts. [273]

In 2004, the PLA CDC was formally incorporated into China's broader public health system and in 2005. AMMS researcher Li Song is credited with leading the domestic development and production of 'Junkeaowei', a Chinese-produced version of the anti-influenza medicine Tamiflu. Junkeaowei was developed under the 'first imitate, then create' principle (' 先仿，再創 ' or alternatively ' 先入模，再出模：先仿，再創 '), that was driven by a perceived reluctance by Western pharmaceutical companies to offer China local production facilities and lower prices for anti-influenza treatments. [274]

In 2005, Roche finally licensed the Tamiflu technology that

273. 非典科技向你宣戰（圖）, Chinese Academy of Sciences, 2 May 2003.
     https://www.cas.cn/zt/kjzt/fdgx/ggqy/200305/t20030502_1709485.shtml
274. ' 深圳市東陽光實業發展有限公司 - 2015 年度報告 ', Shenzhen Dongguan Industrial Development Co., Ltd.
     http://file.finance.sina.com.cn/211.154.219.97:9494/MRGG/BOND/2018/2018-12/2018-12-12/9576048.PDF

underlies Junkeaowei, which includes the character for the armed forces (' 軍 ') in its name, for AMMS and its industrial partner, the Shenzhen Dongguan Industrial Development Co (SDIDC)., to manufacture. A 2015 document from SDIDC lists some of the funding it received from AMMS and Unit 62030 of the PLA for work on this drug, including CNY85 million in 2009 and CNY16 million in 2006.[275] Li is credited with spearheading a special production line with AMMS itself claiming that this proves that China has independent infectious disease protection, prevention, and control capabilities. Some commentators also claimed that this development saved China from national embarrassment over shortage of a needed drug. [276]

In August 2005, AMMS established and operationalized the 'three major forces' structure. This comprises of the (i) strategic planning force for military combat medical preparations to address strategic scientific and technological problems; (ii) specialized tactical force for counter-terrorism operations and public health emergency crisis response; and (iii) specialist technical unit for the PLA's disease prevention and control activities.

Based on publicly available information, AMMS consists of 11 research institutions and affiliated institutions, specifically 307

275. '深圳市東陽光實業發展有限公司 - 2015 年度报告', Shenzhen Dongguan Industrial Development Co., Ltd.
http://file.finance.sina.com.cn/211.154.219.97:9494/MRGG/BOND/2018/2018-12/2018-12-12/9576048.PDF

276. '中國人民解放軍軍事醫學科學院'.
中國人民解放軍軍事醫學科學院 _ 百度百科 (baidu.com)

hospitals, the PLA Medical Library, experimental instrument factory, experimental animal center, and various graduate student teams. Jilin and Heilongjiang Provinces are two key locations for research on military medicine, basic medicine, biotechnology, health equipment design, and drug development. These provincial bases are responsible for biodefense-related military missions and counter-terrorism operations, and strategic preparations for China's broader infectious disease prevention and control efforts. [277]

AMMS hosts 4 researchers from CAS and 7 from the Chinese Academy of Engineering. AMMS houses 3 National Key Laboratories, 1 National Engineering Laboratory, 4 National Engineering Research Centers. AMMS has 10 additional

277. '中國人民解放軍軍事醫學科學院'.
中國人民解放軍軍事醫學科學院 _ 百度百科 (baidu.com)
278. '中國人民解放軍軍事醫學科學院'.
中國人民解放軍軍事醫學科學院 _ 百度百科 (baidu.com)
279. Minnie Chan, 'How China's military took a frontline role in the coronavirus crisis', South China Morning Post, 17 March 2020.
Roxanne Liu and Se Young Lee, 'Chinese military researchers move a new COVID vaccine candidate into human trial', Reuters, 25 June 2020.
Josephine Ma, 'Domestic clinical trials planned for China's mRNA Covid-19 vaccine', South China Morning Post, 22 July 2021.
Anthony Esposito, 'Mexico to start late-stage clinical trial for China's mRNA COVID-19 vaccine', Reuters, 11 May 2021.
Zhuang Pinghui, 'Coronavirus: Indonesia, Mexico approve late-stage trials of Chinese mRNA vaccine hopeful', South China Morning Post, 1 September 2021.
Judy Babu, 'Nepal allows late-stage trials for Chinese mRNA vaccine candidate – Xinhua', Reuters, 28 August 2021.
'SARS-CoV-2 mRNA vaccine', DrugBank Online.
https://go.drugbank.com/drugs/DB15855
Gui-Ling Chen, et. al., 'Safety and immunogenicity of the SARS-CoV-2 ARCoV mRNA vaccine in Chinese adults: a randomized, double-blind, placebo-controlled, phase 1 trial', The Lancet Microbe, Vol. 3, Iss. 3, 1 March 2022.

laboratories, 1 Tianjin Engineering Center, and 1 Tianjin Key Laboratory. AMMS awards doctoral degrees in 6 disciplines and master's degrees in 36 fields [278]

Interestingly, in 2021 AMMS partnered with Yunnan Walvax Biotechnology and Suzhou Abogen Biosciences to develop an mRNA vaccine, commonly known as the ARCoV vaccine. Clinical trials have involved participants from Yunnan and Guangxi Provinces as well as Mexico, Indonesia, and Nepal. The ARCoV vaccine is currently in Phase 3 clinical trials.[279] It is noteworthy that mRNA vaccines were initially viewed with suspicion in China and were actively discouraged by the CCP.

Figure 6: Organizational Graph of the Academy of Military Medical Sciences

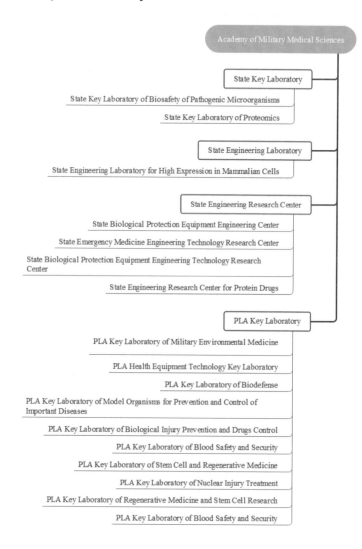

Source: '中國人民解放軍軍事醫學科學院'
中國人民解放軍軍事醫學科學院 _ 百度百科 **(baidu.com)**

Major General Chen Wei: Leading AMMS Virologist, Vaccine Developer, and Trusted CCP Adviser

A key PLA figure in AMMS is Major General Chen Wei（陳薇）, a virologist, epidemiologist, and recognized biodefense and biological anti-terrorism specialist. She was born in the small city of Lanxi in inland Zhejiang. Chen studied at Zhejiang and Tsinghua before completing a microbiology PhD at AMMS in 1998. She then was designated a part of the 'Class A talent pool' and continued to work as a researcher at AMMS.[280] Chen simultaneously joined the PLA and AMMS in 1991 at the age of 25 with some reports claiming that she had been 'specially' recruited into the PLA. Other reports claim that she visited an AMMS laboratory shortly before graduating from Tsinghua and became inspired by AMMS's mission and Korean War-era history.[281]

Chen studied at Tsinghua University from 1988-91, a time when

---

280 '戰鬥在抗疫一綫女院士陳薇：以最充分方案做最長期奮戰', Women.org. cn, 3 February 2020
https://www.women.org.cn/art/2020/2/3/art_24_163679.html
Minnie Chan and William Zheng, 'Meet the major general on China's coronavirus scientific front line', South China Morning Post, 3 March 2020.
'陳薇：軍中女英雄，國家棟梁才', 商業文化, Vol. 19, 2021.
https://gb.global.cnki.net/KCMS/detail/detail.aspx?dbcode=CJFD&dbname=CJFDLAST2021&filename=SYWH202119008&uniplatform=OVERSEAS_CHS&v=YHN-_0PpaIaIF-MWvC1uVBjbEEjLGX7sH3VvE8t80PP1b9beJ5u4KCIJfkd3jnS4
'陳微：從清華女神到護國戰神', 商業文化, Vol. 9, 2020.
https://gb.global.cnki.net/KCMS/detail/detail.aspx?dbcode=CJFD&dbname=CJFDLASN2020&filename=DXNB202009020&uniplatform=OVERSEAS_CHS&v=OkyRO4zZul7Mpx48ojvfTyBzNFQrQh5J8EjcxiUaR3BNoNhFVmSyTVUCjBjhCdQ0

many Beijing students were involved in the Tiananmen Square protests. Although many of the elite student leaders later fled overseas after the government crackdown, students who remained in China went through great political pressure to toe the party line or prove their political loyalties. At that period of time, the PLA did not have a good reputation among many young college students in Beijing, as more or less they knew some parts of the truth regarding the Tiananmen Square massacre. The other side of the coin on this issue was that CCP/PLA laid a particularly strong emphasis on loyalty to the CCP when they recruited college students. It is interesting to note that Zhao Hong, one of Chen's friends from the Tsinghua Chemical Engineering Department, joined Tsinghua's Communist Youth League in April 1991, roughly the same time that Chen was reported to have committed to AMMS, or serve the PLA [282].

After finishing her PhD, Chen had a remarkably fast rise in her career. AMMS made her a doctoral supervisor in microbiology in

281. '戰鬥在抗疫一線女院士陳薇: 以最充分方案做最長期奮戰', Women.org. cn, 3 February 2020
https://www.women.org.cn/art/2020/2/3/art_24_163679.html
Minnie Chan and William Zheng, 'Meet the major general on China's coronavirus scientific front line', South China Morning Post, 3 March 2020.
'陳薇: 軍中女英雄, 國家棟梁才', 商業文化, Vol. 19, 2021.
https://gb.global.cnki.net/KCMS/detail/detail.aspx?dbcode=CJFD&dbname=CJFDLAST2021&filename=SYWH202119008&uniplatform=OVERSEAS_CHS&v=YHN-_0PpaIaIF-MWvC1uVBjbEEjLGX7sH3VvE8t80PP1b9beJ5u4KCIJfkd3jnS4
'陳微: 從清華女神到護國戰神', 商業文化, Vol. 9, 2020.
https://gb.global.cnki.net/KCMS/detail/detail.aspx?dbcode=CJFD&dbname=CJFDLASN2020&filename=DXNB202009020&uniplatform=OVERSEAS_CHS&v=OkyRO4zZul7Mpx48ojvfTyBzNFQrQh5J8EjcxiUaR3BNoNhFVmSyTVUCjBjhCdQ0

2003, the Deputy Director of the Institute of Microbial Epidemiology in 2006, and the Director of the Institute of Bioengineering in 2012. Chen spent a few months in the United States in 2000, but it is not known where she was.[283] That same year the president of AMMS personally awarded Chen (only two years out of her PhD) an 'unprecedented' CNY5 million laboratory start-up grant. In 2001, right after 9/11, the PLA gave her an additional CNY 5 million grant to lead a project to genetically engineer drugs. By 2002, she was said to have a team of 50 people working with or under her on a PLA 'special drugs' project ('中國人民解放軍軍隊特需藥品中試基地'). Already, by 2003, she was personally greeted by then-CCP General Secretary Hu Jintao (see Image 1 below). [284]

282. '趙洪', Tsinghua University, 16 May 2021.
https://www.arts.tsinghua.edu.cn/info/1109/1549.htm
283. '潛心苦鑽研 十年磨一劍 —— 記我的同窗好友陳薇博士', 中國青年科技, Vol. 12, 2003.
https://gb.global.cnki.net/KCMS/detail/detail.aspx?dbcode=CJFD&dbname=CJFDN7904&filename=QNKJ200312004&uniplatform=OVERSEAS_CHS&v=Za9fP-KpdN_ybcCaqXh6e7e7w9FxyhRg_cG5E8iBcRlWzONBfB4_0y6axxYAPzhR
'陳薇：军中女英雄，國家棟梁才', 商業文化, Vol. 19, 2021.
https://gb.global.cnki.net/KCMS/detail/detail.aspx?dbcode=CJFD&dbname=CJFDLAST2021&filename=SYWH202119008&uniplatform=OVERSEAS_CHS&v=YHN-_0PpaIaIF-MWvC1uVBjbEEjLGX7sH3VvE8t80PP1b9beJ5u4KCIJfkd3jnS4
284 '潛心苦鑽研 十年磨一劍 —— 記我的同窗好友陳薇博士', 中國青年科技, Vol. 12, 2003.
https://gb.global.cnki.net/KCMS/detail/detail.aspx?dbcode=CJFD&dbname=CJFDN7904&filename=QNKJ200312004&uniplatform=OVERSEAS_CHS&v=Za9fP-KpdN_ybcCaqXh6e7e7w9FxyhRg_cG5E8iBcRlWzONBfB4_0y6axxYAPzhR
'陳薇：軍中女英雄，國家棟梁才', 商業文化, Vol. 19, 2021.
https://gb.global.cnki.net/KCMS/detail/detail.aspx?dbcode=CJFD&dbname=CJFDLAST2021&filename=SYWH202119008&uniplatform=OVERSEAS_CHS&v=YHN-_0PpaIaIF-MWvC1uVBjbEEjLGX7sH3VvE8t80PP1b9beJ5u4KCIJfkd3jnS4

Image 1: Hu Jintao Meets with Chen Wei in 2003

Source: '潛心苦鑽研 十年磨一劍：記我的同窗好友陳薇博士'，中國青年科技 [China Youth Science and Technology], Vol. 12, 2003, p. 13.

Chen was likewise chosen for a variety of prestigious science-related national and international roles. In 2008, she was named to an expert committee advising on relief efforts for the Sichuan earthquake as well as a committee overseeing security (including biological and chemical attacks) for the 2008 Beijing Olympics. In 2014, she was sent to Sierra Leone with PLA support to lead China's Ebola medical mission there. In 2019, she was made an academician of the Chinese Academy of Engineering. [285] In 2021, she became one of three Vice Chairmen of the China Association for Science and Technology. [286]

Chen has worked on teams developing vaccines for Anthrax and Ebola, including the first recombinant vaccine in China's national strategic reserves. [287] She became known as a leader in Biohazard Control (生 物 危 害 防 控).[288] In 2003, Chen devoted her laboratory to studying interferons [289] that could inhibit the SARS virus that was then spreading in China and is credited for developing an antiviral nasal spray that won her recognition as a 'Top Ten Outstanding Youth.'[290] Her anti-SARS medicine was reportedly tested on 14,000 medical staff at 30 hospitals to

285. ' 陳薇：軍中女英雄，國家棟梁才 ', 商業文化 , Vol. 19, 2021.
    https://gb.global.cnki.net/KCMS/detail/detail.aspx?dbcode=CJFD&dbname
    =CJFDLAST2021&filename=SYWH202119008&uniplatform=OVERSEAS_
    CHS&v=YHN-_0PpaIaIF-MWvC1uVBjbEEjLGX7sH3VvE8t80PP1b9beJ5u4KCI
    Jfkd3jnS4
    Frank Zhao, 'ACWF Executive Committee Member Chen Wei Promoted to
    Major General', All-China Women's Federation, 21 July 2015.
    https://web.archive.org/web/20200416163956/http://www.womenofchina.cn/
    html/news/china/15071648-1.htm
    Minnie Chan and William Zheng, 'Meet the major general on China's
    coronavirus scientific front line', South China Morning Post, 3 March 2020.
286. ' 中國科協第十屆全國委員會副主席人選公布 喬杰、向巧、陳薇三位女性
    當選 ', Women.org.cn, 31 May 2021.
    https://www.women.org.cn/art/2021/5/31/art_23_166394.html
287. ' 戰鬥在抗疫一綫女院士陳薇：以最充分方案做最長期奮戰 ', Women.org.
    cn, 3 February 2020
    https://www.women.org.cn/art/2020/2/3/art_24_163679.html
    Wan Lin, 'Anthrax human immunoglobulin enters trials, important to China's
    defense against biological and chemical attacks' Global Times, 6 June 2020.
    Frank Zhao, 'ACWF Executive Committee Member Chen Wei Promoted to
    Major General', All-China Women's Federation, 21 July 2015.
    https://web.archive.org/web/20200416163956/http://www.womenofchina.cn/
    html/news/china/15071648-1.htm
288. ' 戰鬥在抗疫一綫女院士陳薇：以最充分方案做最長期奮戰 ', Women.org.
    cn, 3 February 2020
    https://www.women.org.cn/art/2020/2/3/art_24_163679.html
289. Interferons are a natural substance that augment the human immune system to
    fight infections and other diseases. Interferons are naturally generated in the body
    by white blood cells and other cells but they can also be developed in laboratory
    settings.
290. Lin Lin, 'The Eighth Chinese Young Women in Science Awards', All-China
    Women's Federation, 12 January 2012.
    https://web.archive.org/web/20200416155646/http://www.womenofchina.cn/
    html/people/Crowd/137083-7.htm

evaluate its efficacy.[291] Chen had begun working on interferons while a student at Tsinghua in 1988. [292]

Chen was named a Major General of the PLA in 2015 and her appointment letter was personally signed by CCP Secretary General Xi Jinping. Xi had met with Chen publicly a year earlier and Xi may have also met her in 2008 when Xi and Chen were both involved with Olympics planning.[293] Chen also served as one of 268 PLA delegates to the 12th National People's Congress (NPC), but it appears she was not re-elected for the 13th NPC. Chen also served as a medical sector delegate to the 13th national-level CPPCC (one of 2,158 delegates in total), and according to China Discipline Inspection and Supervision Magazine, in March 2021 Chen had the honor of giving a speech before a full CPPCC session. [294]

Chen has also served in a variety of smaller party groups. She has served as a Director of the Association of Women in Science and

291. '科學家少將'陳薇', CKNI.
     https://gb.global.cnki.net/KCMS/detail/detail.aspx?dbcode=CYFD&dbnam
     e=CYFD2018&filename=N2018050116001696&uniplatform=OVERSEAS_
     CHS&v=V5i7DO3LGB-oo9mDEsrJp_wtn8T2Es_CZ7DY4NJKvYbcMFdoZYDU
     JzVIP27riIINRYmREKBe-_M%3d
292. '潛心苦鑽研 十年磨一劍 —— 記我的同窗好友陳薇博士', 中國青年科技,
     Vol. 12, 2003.
     https://gb.global.cnki.net/KCMS/detail/detail.aspx?dbcode=CJFD
     &dbname=CJFDN7904&filename=QNKJ200312004&uniplatform
     =OVERSEAS_CHS&v=Za9fP-KpdN_ybcCaqXh6e7e7w9FxyhRg_
     cG5E8iBcRlWzONBfB4_0y6axxYAPzhR
293. Frank Zhao, 'ACWF Executive Committee Member Chen Wei Promoted to
     Major General', All-China Women's Federation, 21 July 2015.
     https://web.archive.org/web/20200416163956/http://www.womenofchina.cn/
     html/news/china/15071648-1.htm

Technology, a 22,000-member group which 'links the party and government with female science and technology workers.'[295] She was a member of the Executive Committee of the All-China Women's Federation (ACWF) around 2015.[296] She has been frequently featured by the ACWF since early in the COVID-19 pandemic.[297] The 2016 yearbook of her hometown also claims that she was a member of the Standing Committee of the All-China Youth Federation, a major party group that has included Hu Jintao and Jiang Zemin, but Chen's possible ACYF affiliation does not appear in other biographies or descriptions of her. [298]

Chen is best known recently for leading the development of Convidecia, a vaccine against SARS-CoV-2 which first reported

294. '第十三屆全國人民代表大會代表名單（2980 名 吉林省 64 名）', Sohu, 25 February 2015.
   http://news.sohu.com/20130227/n367313787.shtml
   '十三屆全國政協女委員 440 名！女委員比例再提升！', Women.org.cn, 25 January 2018.
   https://www.women.org.cn/art/2018/1/25/art_19_154197.html
   '兩會這一刻', 中國紀檢監察, Vol. 6, 2021.
   https://gb.global.cnki.net/KCMS/detail/detail.aspx?dbcode=CJFD&dbname=CJFDLAST2021&filename=JANC202106011&uniplatform=OVERSEAS_CHS&v=imqwiUDjtamw0hcW19_2vETH6LZEqhCQnDVSvj83SYzEx0-7LOQqE9ahHrmRdyS_
295. '推動女科技工作者全面參與社會發展', Women.org.cn, 31 May 2021.
   https://www.women.org.cn/art/2021/5/31/art_22_166392.html
296. Frank Zhao, 'ACWF Executive Committee Member Chen Wei Promoted to Major General', All-China Women's Federation, 21 July 2015.
   https://web.archive.org/web/20200416163956/http://www.womenofchina.cn/html/news/china/15071648-1.htm
297. Search page for '陳薇' on the Chinese language website of the All-China Women's Federation (中華全國婦女聯合會), https://www.women.org.cn/jsearch/search.do?pagemode=result&appid=1&webid=1&style=1&pos=title%2Ccontent&pg=10&ck=o&tmp_od=0&q=%E9%99%88%E8%96%87&query=%E9%99%88%E8%96%87&radiobutton=1&Submit=%E6%90%9C%E7%B4%A2

a Phase 1 clinical trial in March 2020. The first officially publicized immunization with the vaccine was on 16 March and the Phase 2 trial began in Wuhan weeks later on 12 April.[299] However, a photo from 29 February shows Chen and several others receiving injections of the vaccine in front of a CCP flag, well before Phase 1 trial results were reported. People's Daily declared the image '#FAKENEWS', but an AMMS colleague verified the photo as part of an ethically-ambiguous attempt to protect scientists working in Wuhan at the time. [300]

In honor of Chen's vaccine work, Xi Jinping named her a 'People's Hero' later that year, on the same day that Zhong Nanshan was given the 'Medal of the Republic.'[301] The national Women and Children's Museum in Beijing subsequently created exhibits to honor both Chen and Zhong.[302] She later was

298. '科學家少將' 陳薇 ', CKNI.
    https://gb.global.cnki.net/KCMS/detail/detail.aspx?dbcode=CYFD&dbnam
    e=CYFD2018&filename=N2018050116001696&uniplatform=OVERSEAS_
    CHS&v=V5i7DO3LGB-oo9mDEsrJp_wtn8T2Es_CZ7DY4NJKvYbcMFdoZYDU
    JzVIP27riIINRYmREKBe-_M%3d
    '潜心苦鑽研 十年磨一劍 —— 記我的同窗好友陳薇博士', 中國青年科技,
    Vol. 12, 2003.
299. '陳薇: '除了勝利, 別無選擇 !', Women.org,cn, 16 November 2020.
    https://www.women.org.cn/art/2020/11/16/art_24_165256.html
    '與新冠病毒賽跑的女英雄 ——' 人民英雄' 陳薇談新冠疫苗研制心路歷程 ',
    Women.org.cn, 14 August 2020.
    https://www.women.org.cn/art/2020/8/14/art_24_164868.html
300. Jon Cohen, 'China's vaccine gambit', Science, Vol. 370, Iss. 6522, 11 December
    2020.
    https://www.science.org/doi/10.1126/science.370.6522.1263
301. 'Xi Focus: Xi signs order to award 4 persons for outstanding contribution in
    COVID-19 fight', Xinhua, 11 August 2020..
302. '中國婦女兒童博物館大型融媒體項目' 家風故事匯' 上綫', Women.org.
    cn, 28 December 2020.
    https://www.women.org.cn/art/2020/12/28/art_19_165462.html

prominent in presenting an inhaled spray form of the SARS-CoV-2 vaccine, paralleling her earlier SARS-CoV-1 work.[303] A few weeks before the March 2020 application of the vaccine, Chen gave an interview to CAS publication urging that epidemic prevention should 'never wait until the disease has happened' and that China should have:

'A powerful 'lead scientists' system so that they can spend their life studying and researching certain types of viruses and germs… [so] whenever an epidemic occurs, we will have the best and most authoritative team available and it will not be like what's happened now when the coronavirus came, and nobody is doing much.' [304]

Chen conducted her initial SARS-CoV-2 vaccine work from Wuhan. On 26 January 2020, Chen reportedly led a group of military doctors to Wuhan to see patients and carry out COVID-19 tests, building a site with capacity to test 1,000 people per day.[305] Within five days, she was also apparently involved

303. '打疫苗，還是'吸'疫苗？陳薇院士團隊又傳來好消息……', New.qq.com, 10 August 2021.
https://new.qq.com/rain/a/20210810a081vz00

304. Minnie Chan and William Zheng, 'Meet the major general on China's coronavirus scientific front line', South China Morning Post, 3 March 2020.
https://www.scmp.com/news/china/military/article/3064677/meet-major-general-chinas-coronavirus-scientific-front-line, 30 May 2022.

305. '陳薇：'除了勝利，別無選擇!', Women.org,cn, 16 November 2020.
https://www.women.org.cn/art/2020/11/16/art_24_165256.html
'與新冠病毒賽跑的女英雄 ——'人民英雄'陳薇談新冠疫苗研制心路歷程', Women.org.cn, 14 August 2020.
https://www.women.org.cn/art/2020/8/14/art_24_164868.html

with collecting plasma from recovered Wuhan patients (which she used to develop a plasma-based possible treatment for COVID-19) and visited the Director of Wuhan's Jinyintan Hospital.[306] The South China Morning Post reported in March 2020 that Chen began working from inside WIV, which other outlets do not seem to have reported.[307] It was also reported that, while Chen had praised the outcomes of an antiviral nasal spray she developed in 2003 for treating COVID-19, others within the PLA thought the spray had high costs and too many medical side effects. [308]

On the PLA-focused CCTV-7 channel, Chen spoke of her team's personal sacrifice for their mission in Wuhan, apparently emphasizing her comments by modifying the literary expression 'raise an army in a thousand days, use it in an hour' ('養兵千日, 用兵一時') to 'raise an army in a thousand days, use the army for a thousand days' ('養兵千日、千日用'). In other words, Chen stated that China must be comprehensively prepared and must be able to sustain emergency efforts for a long duration. [309]

Chen has a long and unusual record of associating with highly

---

306. ' 戰鬥在抗疫一綫女院士陳薇: 以最充分方案做最長期奮戰 ', Women.org. cn, 3 February 2020
      https://www.women.org.cn/art/2020/2/3/art_24_163679.html
307. Minnie Chan and William Zheng, 'Meet the major general on China's coronavirus scientific front line', South China Morning Post, 3 March 2020.
308. Minnie Chan and William Zheng, 'Meet the major general on China's coronavirus scientific front line', South China Morning Post, 3 March 2020.

309. ' 與新冠病毒賽跑的女英雄 ——' 人民英雄 ' 陳薇談新冠疫苗研制心路歷程 ', Women.org.cn, 14 August 2020.
      https://www.women.org.cn/art/2020/8/14/art_24_164868.html

nationalistic statements. Chen is, literally, a 'wolf warrior' scientist. In the film Wolf Warrior 2, which features a 'Dr. Chen' fighting a rare and deadly virus in Africa, was based on Chen Wei and her work in Sierra Leone (however, Chen appears murdered by an American mercenary in the film). Chinese media have nicknamed Chen 'God of War' ('戰神'), 'Ebola Terminator', and one who spends 'ten years sharpening her sword' ('十年磨一劍') with 'the courageous nature of a firm/steel warrior' ('鋼鐵戰士的血性本色'; a phrase also used to describe other CCP doctors). A friend claimed she is not influenced by money, 'worldly objects', or others' opinions, but is relentlessly and emotionally dedicated to her work. [310]

Chen has described herself as part of the military's scientific 'battleship' and has been quoted as saying that 'the vaccine must

310. '陳微：從清華女神到護國戰神', 商業文化, Vol. 9, 2020.
https://gb.global.cnki.net/KCMS/detail/detail.aspx?dbcode=CJFD&dbname=CJFDLASN2020&filename=DXNB202009020&uniplatform=OVERSEAS_CHS&v=OkyRO4zZul7Mpx48ojvfTyBzNFQrQh5J8EjcxiUaR3BNoNhFVmSyTVUCjBjhCdQ0
'潛心苦鑽研 十年磨一劍 —— 記我的同窗好友陳薇博士', 中國青年科技, Vol. 12, 2003.
https://gb.global.cnki.net/KCMS/detail/detail.aspx?dbcode=CJFD&dbname=CJFDN7904&filename=QNKJ200312004&uniplatform=OVERSEAS_CHS&v=Za9fP-KpdN_ybcCaqXh6e7e7w9FxyhRg_cG5E8iBcRlWzONBfB4_0y6axxYAPzhR
'陳薇：軍中女英雄，國家棟梁才', 商業文化, Vol. 19, 2021.
https://gb.global.cnki.net/KCMS/detail/detail.aspx?dbcode=CJFD&dbname=CJFDLAST2021&filename=SYWH202119008&uniplatform=OVERSEAS_CHS&v=YHN-_0PpaIaIF-MWvC1uVBjbEEjLGX7sH3VvE8t80PP1b9beJ5u4KCIJfkd3jnS4
'蘭溪籍科學家陳薇榮獲 '浙江驕傲' 年度致敬人物', Jinhua.gov.cn, 25 January 2021.
http://swb.jinhua.gov.cn/art/2021/1/25/art_1229168153_58839064.html

be developed independently by China!' and 'the patent is ours, the innovation is ours, so we don't need to look to anyone else on any occasion!'[311] On the risks she took in facing COVID-19, Chen said that she always feels she is a military professional and 'wearing the uniform means that this is what I should do.' [312]

Of course, the praises that she received from Chinese media (Chinese government mouthpieces in nature) has a strong element of exaggeration to serve the purpose of propaganda and establishing a role model for the society. Although the CCP did send medical professionals and resources to help African countries suffering Ebola outbreak in 2014, the contributions from them were primarily focused on setting hard quarantine protocols and helping build local capacities in surveillance and testing - it was far from 'terminating' Ebola.

Meanwhile, promoting military doctors like Chen will help establish the mental stereotype of fighting viruses as fighting a battle with enemies, which implies that all related sacrifices are warranted. This propaganda strategy serves as a unique brainwashing tool to make Chinese people obey any extreme zero-COVID policies. From this perspective, Chen is also a product of CCP's national propaganda campaign. Chen was

311. '不負時代 不辱使命', 中國新聞發布（實務版）, Vol. 3, 2022. https://gb.global.cnki.net/KCMS/detail/detail.aspx?dbcode=CJFD&dbname=CJFDAUTO&filename=XWSW202203008&uniplatform=OVERSEAS_CHS&v=EHfAJUoXF8U1iQASa4y9dcpgfgUlPTNMl6QZ5UW53tmXIjA_Yg4A3yPkhFSqgTRb
312. '不負時代 不辱使命', 中國新聞發布（實務版）, Vol. 3, 2022. https://gb.global.cnki.net/KCMS/detail/detail.aspx?dbcode=CJFD&dbname=CJFDAUTO&filename=XWSW202203008&uniplatform=OVERSEAS_CHS&v=EHfAJUoXF8U1iQASa4y9dcpgfgUlPTNMl6QZ5UW53tmXIjA_Yg4A3yPkhFSqgTRb

given the highest award for her actions in Wuhan, although the genuine death toll in WIV during the initial outbreak and origin of the outbreak remains unknowne. Was she responsible for taking down the WIV server that contained a database of previous WIV projects and results? Did her work actually create more difficulty for later independent international investigation of the origins of the outbreak?

Chen Wei and Qiu Xiangguo: Transnational Linkages Between AMMS and Canada's NML BSL4 Lab[313]

In September 2021, Canada's Globe and Mail reported that Chen Wei had collaborated on virus research with Qiu Xiangguo, a scientist who led the vaccine and antiviral sections of Canada's NML in Winnipeg, the only BSL4 lab in the country. Qiu and her husband Cheng Keding were fired from NML in January 2021. Qiu and some of her students also had security clearances revoked and police removed them from the lab in July 2019. [314]

---

313. A full set of network diagrams outlining all of AMMS's institutional linkages based off of joint publications and grant awards can be found in Annex G, surfaced high-risk AMMS linkages in Annex H, and keywords cloud of strategic AMMS partner organizations based on joint publications and joint grant awards in Annex I. All data was collected using the automated search and knowledge representation capabilities of Data Abyss.
    https://www.dataabyss.ai/

314. Robert Fife and Steven Chase, 'Chinese PLA general collaborated with fired scientist at Canada's top infectious disease lab', The Globe and Mail, 16 September 2021.
    Justin Ling, 'A brilliant scientist was mysteriously fired from a Winnipeg virus lab. No one knows why', Maclean's, 15 February 2022.
    Karen Pauls, ''Wake-up call for Canada': Security experts say case of 2 fired scientists could point to espionage', CBC News, 10 June 2021.

Months earlier, Qiu had sent Ebola[315] and Henipah virus [316] samples to WIV, with the apparent knowledge of NML's leaders. The Canadian government ordered NML scientists not to discuss Qiu and Chang with the media and initially sued the House of Commons speaker to prevent the release of information about Qiu and Chang's dismissal. [317] Qiu was born in Tianjin, studied in Tianjin and Hebei, joined NML in 2003, and primarily worked on Ebola. Qiu successfully identified monoclonal antibodies slowing the virus's development. Qiu was chosen as a Canadian

---

315. For one example of Qiu's Ebola research, please see Xiangguo Qiu, et. al., 'Equine-Origin Immunoglobulin Fragments Protect Nonhuman Primates from Ebola Virus Disease', Journal of Virology, Vol. 93, No. 5, March 2019.

316. Henipah virus is closely related to the Nipah virus, which is a haemorrhagic disease with an 80% lethality rate. At present, Nipah virus has only been clinically detected in Malaysia, Singapore, India, and Bangladesh. It is therefore unclear why Henipah virus samples were being illicitly sent to Chen Wei by Qiu Xiangguo. For additional information on Henipah/Nipah virus, please see:
Stephen Luby, et. al., 'Assessing the feasibility of Nipah vaccine efficacy trials based on previous outbreaks in Bangladesh', Vaccine, Vol. 39, Iss. 39, 15 September 2021.
Stephen Luby, et. al., 'Nipah Virus Transmission from Bats to Humans Associated with Drinking Traditional Liquor Made from Date Palm Sap, Bangladesh, 2011–2014', EID Journal, Vol. 22, No. 4, April 2016.
'Nipah Virus International Conference Proceedings', Coalition for Epidemic Preparedness Innovations, National Institute of Allergy and Infectious Diseases, and Duke-NUS Graduate School of Medicine, Singapore, 9-10 December 2019. https://cepi.net/wp-content/uploads/2020/06/2019-Nipah-Conference-Proceedings.pdf
Linfa Wang, et. al., 'Evidence of Henipavirus Infection in West African Fruit Bats', PLOS ONE, 23 July 2008.

317. Robert Fife and Steven Chase, Chinese PLA general collaborated with fired scientist at Canada's top infectious disease lab', The Globe and Mail, 16 September 2021.
Justin Ling, 'A brilliant scientist was mysteriously fired from a Winnipeg virus lab. No one knows why', Maclean's, 15 February 2022.
Karen Pauls, "Wake-up call for Canada': Security experts say case of 2 fired scientists could point to espionage', CBC News, 10 June 2021.

medical delegate to the Beijing Olympics, where Chen was also involved, and both scientists worked with Ebola and with many overlapping virologists in China. [318]

Qiu and Chen's scientific career paths also overlap at the Tianjin-based pharmaceutical firm CanSino Biotechnology, which was founded by a scientist from Tianjin who studied and worked in Canada (CanSino's only products all trace to AMMS).[319] Qiu's research was said to include collaborations with students from the AMMS Institute of Military Veterinary Sciences, the CAS Institute of Microbiology, and WIV (under CAS) as well as with the US Army Medical Research Institute of Infectious Diseases (USAMRIID). Qiu made several trips to China in 2017-18, including to train scientists in Wuhan. [320]

The first paper that Chen and Qiu collaborated on, published in 2016, explored modifying an adenovirus[321] base to foster immune responses to Ebola. Chen and Wei 'conceived and designed the study' alongside Hou Lihua. Hou is listed on the

---

318. Robert Fife and Steven Chase, Chinese PLA general collaborated with fired scientist at Canada's top infectious disease lab', The Globe and Mail, 16 September 2021.

Justin Ling, 'A brilliant scientist was mysteriously fired from a Winnipeg virus lab. No one knows why', Maclean's, 15 February 2022.

Karen Pauls, "Wake-up call for Canada': Security experts say case of 2 fired scientists could point to espionage', CBC News, 10 June 2021.

319. Jon Cohen, 'China's vaccine gambit', Science, Vol. 370, Iss. 6522, 11 December 2020.

https://www.science.org/doi/10.1126/science.370.6522.1263

320. Dany Shoham, 'Report: China and Viruses: The Case of Dr. Xiangguo Qiu', Begin-Sadat Center for Strategic Studies, 2020.

321. Adenoviruses are common viruses that are known to cause typical mild colds or flu-like symptoms.

paper as working at the Beijing Institute of Biotechnology but he was later identified by journalists as the AMMS colleague of Chen's via verification with the 29 February vaccine injection photo. The paper notes sponsorship from a variety of Chinese and Canadian institutes, as well as the firm CanSino. [322]

It should be noted that the vaccine that Chen worked on, Convidecia with CanSino, was the only domestically-developed Chinese vaccine to rely on an adenovirus. This is similar to the AstraZeneca and Sputnik vaccines, but unlike the Sinovac vaccine that is based on an inactivated coronavirus. However, the Chinese government did not drive a nationwide vaccination campaign with CanSino's Convedecia vaccine products. Instead, Sinovac and Sinopharm's inactivated vaccines were promoted as the main anti-COVID vaccines. This suggested that the results from clinical trials for Convidecia were poorer than the inactivated vaccines.

Is AMMS a Dual-Use Operation? High-Risk Virology Studies Identified on SARS-CoV-2 and African Swine Flu Virus

In 2021, researchers from WIV and the Chinese Communist Party Central Military Commission Joint Logistic Support Force

---

322. Xiangguo Qiu, Wei Chen, et. al., 'An Adenovirus Vaccine Expressing Ebola Virus Variant Makona Glycoprotein Is Efficacious in Guinea Pigs and Nonhuman Primates', The Journal of Infectious Diseases, Vol. 214 (Suppl 3), 2016.
Please also see Xiangguo Qiu and Wei Chen, 'Potent neutralizing monoclonal antibodies against Ebola virus isolated from vaccinated donors', MABS, Vol. 12, No. 1, 2020.

(CCP CMC JLSF, which AMMS is subordinated to) published a study describing a high-risk serial passaging experiment with a SARS-CoV-2 virus. One of the key scientists involved in this study was WIV's Shi Zhengli.[323] To further investigate the genetic susceptibility of SARS-CoV-2 during serial passage (a clear GoF technique) on different cells, this team identified nine cell lines (human, non-human primate, and swine) susceptible to the SARS-CoV-2 virus. These nine cell lines were then serially passaged with increasingly virulent variants of the SARS-Cov-2 virus and monitored to identify the most transmissible combinations.[324] There is no identifiable biomedical application for this type of research.

---

323. Zheng-Li Shi, Ben Hu, et. al., 'Genetic Mutation of SARS-CoV-2 during Consecutive Passages in Permissive Cells', Virologica Sinica, Vol. 26, 2021.
    For a more in-depth discussion on Shi Zheng-Li's high-risk pathogen research, see Ryan Clarke and Lam Peng Er, 'Coronavirus Research Networks in China: Origins, International Linkages and Consequences', Center for Non-Traditional Security Studies, May 2021, Singapore.
    https://rsis-ntsasia.org/wp-content/uploads/2021/06/NTS-Asia-Monograph-Coronavirus-Research-in-China-by-Ryan-Clarke-and-Lam-Peng-Er-May2021-1.pdf
    The following studies conducted at WIV demonstrate, in aggregate, how to engineer a bat coronavirus to directly infect humans without the need for an intermediate mammalian host for the first time in history:
    Shi, Zheng-Li, Baric, Ralph et. al., 'A SARS-like cluster of circulating bat coronaviruses shows potential for human emergence', Nature Medicine, Vol. 21, No. 12, December 2015.
    Mazet, Jonna, Daszak, Peter, Zheng-Li, Shi et. al., 'Isolation and characterization of a bat SARS-like
    coronavirus that uses the ACE2 receptor', Nature, Vol. 503, No. 28, November 2013.
    Li, Fang, Wang, Linfa, Shi, Zheng-Li, et. al, 'Angiotensin-converting enzyme 2 (ACE2) proteins of different bat species confer variable susceptibility to SARS-CoV entry', Archive of Virology, Vol. 155, 22 June 2010.

During the course of this serial passaging experiment, the viral loads of SARS-CoV-2 increased exponentially along with increased transmission fitness driven by evolutionary adaptations gained from serial passaging. These scientists note that human tissue (including lung, liver, colon, larynx, and skin), monkey (kidney), and swine (testicle) were most susceptible to SARS-CoV-2.[325] The key 'discovery' made by these scientists in this 2021 study is that the SARS-CoV-2 virus replicated most efficiently in human cell lines (classified as Huh-7, Calu-3, Caco-2 in this paper) and non-human primate cells (classified as Vero E6 in this paper) but less so in swine cells. The specific verification that the Vero E6 cell line is suitable for viral amplification is presented as a primary 'scientific breakthrough'. [326]

---

324. Zheng-Li Shi, Ben Hu, et. al., 'Genetic Mutation of SARS-CoV-2 during Consecutive Passages in Permissive Cells', Virologica Sinica, Vol. 26, 2021.
Additional scientific evidence demonstrating the clear GoF implications of this study for both animals and humans of this study can be found in:
Zheng-Li Shi, Yufei Zheng, et. al., 'SARS-CoV-2 rapidly adapts in aged BALB/c mice and induces typical pneumonia', Journal of Virology, Volume 95, Iss. 11, June 2021.
Li-Teh Liu, et. al., 'Isolation and Identification of a Rare Spike Gene Double-Deletion SARS-CoV-2 Variant From the Patient With High Cycle Threshold Value', Frontiers in Medicine, 6 January 2022.
325. Zheng-Li Shi, Ben Hu, et. al., 'Genetic Mutation of SARS-CoV-2 during Consecutive Passages in Permissive Cells', Virologica Sinica, Vol. 26, 2021.
Additional scientific evidence demonstrating the clear GoF implications of this study for both animals and humans of this study can be found in:
Zheng-Li Shi, Yufei Zheng, et. al., 'SARS-CoV-2 rapidly adapts in aged BALB/c mice and induces typical pneumonia', Journal of Virology, Volume 95, Iss. 11, June 2021.
Li-Teh Liu, et. al., 'Isolation and Identification of a Rare Spike Gene Double-Deletion SARS-CoV-2 Variant From the Patient With High Cycle Threshold Value', Frontiers in Medicine, 6 January 2022.

These researchers also noted their surprise that none of the tested bat cell lines supported SARS-CoV-2 replication. This finding appears to directly conflict with their own assertion in the introduction of their own paper that SARS-CoV-2 is natural in origin and entered the human population via bats.[327] This lack of viral replication in bat cell lines was also observed by scientists from the University of Hong Kong in a 2020 study that was published by the US CDC. [328]

This lack of SARS-CoV-2 replication in bat cell lines could also contradict the official position of Beijing that SARS-CoV-2 and the subsequent COVID-19 pandemic is the result of a zoonotic spillover event. How can the SARS-CoV-2 virus be reliably

---

326. Zheng-Li Shi, Ben Hu, et. al., 'Genetic Mutation of SARS-CoV-2 during Consecutive Passages in Permissive Cells', Virologica Sinica, Vol. 26, 2021.
Additional scientific evidence demonstrating the clear GoF implications of this study for both animals and humans of this study can be found in:
Zheng-Li Shi, Yufei Zheng, et. al., 'SARS-CoV-2 rapidly adapts in aged BALB/c mice and induces typical pneumonia', Journal of Virology, Volume 95, Iss. 11, June 2021.
Li-Teh Liu, et. al., 'Isolation and Identification of a Rare Spike Gene Double-Deletion SARS-CoV-2 Variant From the Patient With High Cycle Threshold Value', Frontiers in Medicine, 6 January 2022.
327. Zheng-Li Shi, Ben Hu, et. al., 'Genetic Mutation of SARS-CoV-2 during Consecutive Passages in Permissive Cells', Virologica Sinica, Vol. 26, 2021.
Additional scientific evidence demonstrating the clear GoF implications of this study for both animals and humans of this study can be found in:
Zheng-Li Shi, Yufei Zheng, et. al., 'SARS-CoV-2 rapidly adapts in aged BALB/c mice and induces typical pneumonia', Journal of Virology, Volume 95, Iss. 11, June 2021.
Li-Teh Liu, et. al., 'Isolation and Identification of a Rare Spike Gene Double-Deletion SARS-CoV-2 Variant From the Patient With High Cycle Threshold Value', Frontiers in Medicine, 6 January 2022.
328. Susanna Lau, et. al., 'Differential Tropism of SARS-CoV and SARS-CoV-2 in Bat Cells', Emerging Infectious Diseases, Vol. 26, No. 12, December 2020.

determined to originate from bats when the virus does not actually replicate in bat cells? Interestingly, this lack of transmissibility of the SARS-CoV-2 virus in bat cells is consistent with other leading researchers who have claimed that this virus is uniquely adapted to directly infect and transmit amongst human cells, not other animal species. [329]

Qi Chen is the Director of Virology at the Institute of Virology and Microbiology (IVM) under AMMS[330] . Qi has a well-established track record of conducting high-risk pathogen research with Chinese counterparts from WIV and CAMS as

---

329. Nikolai Petrovsky, et. al., 'In silico comparison of SARS-CoV-2 spike protein-ACE2 binding affinities across species and implications for virus origin', Scientific Reports, Vol. 11, 24 June 2021.

Steven Quay, 'A Bayesian analysis concludes beyond a reasonable doubt that SARS-CoV-2 is not a natural zoonosis but instead is laboratory derived', Zenodo, 29 January 2021.

Steven Quay and Angus Dalgleish, The Origin of the Virus: The hidden truths behind the microbe that killed millions of people, Clinical Press Ltd., September 2021.

Steven Quay and Richard Muller, 'The Science Suggests a Wuhan Lab Leak: The Covid-19 pathogen has a genetic footprint that has never been observed in a natural coronavirus', Wall Street Journal, 6 June 2021.
https://www.wsj.com/amp/articles/the-science-suggests-a-wuhan-lab-leak-11622995184

Birger Sørensen, Andres Susrud, and Angus Dalgleish, 'Biovacc-19: A Candidate Vaccine for Covid-19 (SARS-CoV-2) Developed from Analysis of its General Method of Action for Infectivity', QRB Discovery, Volume 1, 29 May 2020.

330. A full set of network diagrams outlining all of IVM's institutional linkages based off of joint publications and grant awards can be found in Annex J. All data was collected using the automated search and knowledge representation capabilities of Data Abyss.
https://www.dataabyss.ai/

331. For additional information, please see Ryan Clarke, Lam Peng Er, and Lin Xiaoxu, 'High-Risk Virology Research at the Chinese Academy of Medical Sciences and Peking Union Medical College', EAI Background Brief No. 1642, 24 March 2022.

well as international collaborators at UTMB in Galveston.[331] In July 2021, Qi and colleagues published a study on an experiment that involved direct intranasal inoculation of virus in the olfactory system of humanized mice[332] and demonstrated rapid viral replication, massive cell death, and neurological damage.[333] Although SARS-CoV-2 infections primarily impact the respiratory system (and the lungs in particular), olfactory dysfunction is actually one of the most predictive and common symptoms in COVID-19 patients. Therefore, this research has its unique merit to confirm that humanized mice is an appropriate model for further examine the mechanism for olfactory dysfunction upon COVID-19 infection.

However, the authorship of this publication indicated that the authors like Chen Qi and Cheng-Feng Qin are from Beijing Institute of Microbiology and Epidemiology (BIME), which appears to be civilian research institute. However, BIME is actually the same institute of Institute of Microbiology and Epidemiology under AMMS, Academy of Military Medicine. Therefore, the connection of this study to military research institution was covered up by using the name of BIME.

---

332. Humanized mice used in this study were mice that are genetically modified to have lungs that are genetically identical to humans. Humanized mice are used in multiple biomedical domains to most closely simulate how disease pathogenesis occurs in humans.

333. Qi Chen, et. al., 'SARS-CoV-2 infection in the mouse olfactory system', Cell Discovery, Vol. 7, No. 9, 2021.
   Please also see Qi Chen, Chao Shan, Shi Peiyong, et. al., 'Treatment of Human Glioblastoma with a Live AttenuatedZika Virus Vaccine Candidate', mBio, Vol. 9. Iss. 5, September/October 2018.

Therefore, it is important to question whether this study also has the potential of dual-use applications. For example, a key finding of this study is that SARS-CoV-2-infected humanized mice experienced a damaged olfactory system, degradation of immune cell function, and impaired olfactory function. Robust viral replication and direct antiviral responses were only detected in the olfactory systems of the infected humanized mice and not in other parts of the brain.[334] Then, the next step would be to further engineer or conduct serial passage of the viruses so that it will infect or only infect other parts of the brain, using the same humanized mice model.

In 2020, Qi and colleagues artificially created a 'pseudorabies virus (PRV)' that expressed the CD2v protein of African Swine Flu (ASFV) and evaluated its effectiveness and safety as a vaccine candidate in mice.[335] No similar experiment has been conducted outside of China and it was well established for over a decade that the CD2v protein actually plays a key role in enhancing the replicability and transmissibility of ASFV virus in pigs.[336] The virulent effect of CD2v was tested by lethality, tissue pathology, expression of inflammatory factors and tissue inflammation in

---

334. Qi Chen, et. al., 'SARS-CoV-2 infection in the mouse olfactory system', Cell Discovery, Vol. 7, No. 9, 2021.

335. Qi Chen, at. al., 'The recombinant pseudorabies virus expressing African swine fever virus CD2v protein is safe and effective in mice', Virology Journal, Vol. 17, No. 180, 16 November 2020.

336. For example, please see Daniel Pérez-Núñez, et. al., 'CD2v Interacts with Adaptor Protein AP-1 during African Swine Fever Infection', PLOS ONE, 27 April 2015.
Rebecca Rowlands, et. al., 'The CD2v protein enhances African swine fever virus replication in the tick vector, Ornithodoros erraticus', Virology, Vol. 393, Iss. 2, October 2009.

the mice infected with various artificially created PRV strains. The viral genome DNA was detected in all tissues in PRV-infected mice while viral nucleic acid was detected in the brain and lungs of mice infected with certain PRV strains.[337] Qi and team also stated that specific PRV strains have the now-demonstrated ability to reduce immune system function in the early stages of infection, specifically the initial generation and proliferation of adequate T-cells. One key conclusion of this study by these scientists is that this experiment proves that CD2 is actually safe for use in mice and is therefore a viable component of a vaccine candidate. It should be noted that all mice in this study that were directly infected with any of the artificial PRV strains died. [338]

Qi and colleagues did not address any other unique reason why mice were chosen for study of a swine virus AFSV; besides it is more convenient to handle mice in the lab conditions for vaccine study. Qi has also previously conducted experiments on pigs to study the Porcine Deltacoronavirus.[339] Therefore, Qi's lab did have the capacity to study AFSV directly on pigs. How did they address the concerns that the experiment of AFSV in mice might make the virus adapted to be transmitted in mice and create an

---

337. Qi Chen, at. al., 'The recombinant pseudorabies virus expressing African swine fever virus CD2v protein is safe and effective in mice', Virology Journal, Vol. 17, No. 180, 16 November 2020.

338. Qi Chen, at. al., 'The recombinant pseudorabies virus expressing African swine fever virus CD2v protein is safe and effective in mice', Virology Journal, Vol. 17, No. 180, 16 November 2020.

339. For example, please see Qi Chen, et. al., 'Pathogenicity and pathogenesis of a United States porcine deltacoronavirus cell culture isolate in 5-day-old neonatal piglets', Virology, Vol. 482, August 2015.

additional animal reservoir for this virus, a dangerous virus that causes hemorrhagic disease of swine? The decision to experiment with the CD2v protein is also curious. CD2v has the proven primary function of increasing viral load and transmissibility of the AFSV virus. Therefore, any experimentation of the type that Qi and colleagues conducted would facilitate the emergence of AFSV strains with enhanced pathogenic functions or host range expansion. The 'discovery' of vaccine-related utility (if any) of CD2v would be a secondary discovery at best.

Additional Transnational Linkages Between AMMS and UTMB in Galveston, Texas[340]

In a 2018 study, UTMB's Chao Shan and Shi Peiyong (and others) worked with Qi Chen (AMMS) to describe using a live attenuated Zika virus vaccine candidate (ZIKV-LAV) to treat Glioblastoma (GBM), a brain tumor. [341] The wild-type zika virus strain (ZIKV) used in this study was originally isolated from a Chinese patient returning from Venezuela in 2016 and then transferred into mice. The live attenuated vaccine strain of ZIKV (ZIKV-LAV)

---

340. A full set of network diagrams outlining all of AMMS's institutional linkages based off of joint publications and grant awards can be found in Annex G. All data was collected using the automated search and knowledge representation capabilities of Data Abyss.
https://www.dataabyss.ai/

341. Qi Chen, Chao Shan, Shi Peiyong, et. al., 'Treatment of Human Glioblastoma with a Live Attenuated
Zika Virus Vaccine Candidate', mBio, Vol. 9. Iss. 5, September/October 2018.

342. Qi Chen, Chao Shan, Shi Peiyong, et. al., 'Treatment of Human Glioblastoma with a Live Attenuated
Zika Virus Vaccine Candidate', mBio, Vol. 9. Iss. 5, September/October 2018.

was generated by reverse genetic engineering technology.[342] It should be noted that current state of the art reverse genetic engineering technology, of which China is an established world leader, can render it impossible to determine whether a virus in question is natural or synthetic in origin. [343]

Qi, Chao, and Shi conducted intracerebral injections of ZIKV-LAV into mice and claim that ZIKV-LAV demonstrated efficacy against GBM by selectively killing glioma stem cells within the tumor. They also claim that ZIKV-LAV exhibited an 'excellent safety profile upon intracerebral injection into the treated animals' thereby making ZIKV-LAV a potential candidate for combination with the current treatment regimen for GBM therapy. [344]

Interestingly, in the same study Qi, Chao, and Shi state that recent epidemics of ZIKV in the Americas have generated a global public health emergency due to ZIKV's causal link to microcephaly and other congenital diseases in fetuses from infected pregnant women. They note that ZIKV preferentially infects neural progenitor cells, causing cell death and reduced proliferation, which results in impaired brain development in the fetus. [345] Seemingly to at least implicitly acknowledge the risks of

343. Ryan Clarke, 'Emerging Global Pandemic Risks Come from Engineered Viruses in Chinese Labs, Not the Jungle or Bat Caves', Epoch Times, 4 September 2021.

344. Qi Chen, Chao Shan, Shi Peiyong, et. al., 'Treatment of Human Glioblastoma with a Live Attenuated
Zika Virus Vaccine Candidate', mBio, Vol. 9. Iss. 5, September/October 2018.

345. Qi Chen, Chao Shan, Shi Peiyong, et. al., 'Treatment of Human Glioblastoma with a Live Attenuated
Zika Virus Vaccine Candidate', mBio, Vol. 9. Iss. 5, September/October 2018.

this research, they state that applying this oncolytic virotherapy to clinical treatment requires wild-type ZIKV to be modified to reduce neurovirulence to ensure that GBM patients do not have their brains directly infected by ZIKV. They also note that ZIKV-LAV should only retain its infectivity and oncolytic activity against glioma cells. In this study, Qi, Chao, and Shi claim to have demonstrated how to achieve these two endpoints in mice. [346]

On the opposite end of the biomedical spectrum, in one 2020 PNAS study, Chao, Shi and colleagues took a pre-epidemic Asian Zika virus strain (FSS13025 isolated in Cambodia in 2010) and inserted the 'E-V473M' substitution that significantly increased neurovirulence in neonatal mice and produced higher viral loads in the placenta and fetal heads in pregnant mice.[347] This E-V473M mutant strain was further studied in competition experiments in cynomolgus macaques. The results showed that this mutation increased Zika's fitness for viral generation in macaques, a clear demonstration of GoF results for Zika virus. It also indicated that these Chinese researchers were trying to find

---

346. Qi Chen, Chao Shan, Shi Peiyong, et. al., 'Treatment of Human Glioblastoma with a Live Attenuated Zika Virus Vaccine Candidate', mBio, Vol. 9. Iss. 5, September/October 2018.

347. Chao Shan, et. al., 'A Zika virus envelope mutation preceding the 2015 epidemic enhances virulence and fitness for transmission', PNAS, Vol. 117, No. 33., 18 August 2020.

348. Chao Shan, et. al., 'A Zika virus envelope mutation preceding the 2015 epidemic enhances virulence and fitness for transmission', PNAS, Vol. 117, No. 33., 18 August 2020.

For additional GoF work conducted by Galveston/UTMB's Pei-Yong Shi and colleagues at AMMS involving Zika viruses in mice, please see Ling Yuan, et. al., 'A single mutation in the prM protein of Zika virus contributes to fetal microcephaly', Science, Vol. 17, No. 358, 17 November 2017.

more application of reverse genetics techniques to conduct GoF research for a wide range of dangerous pathogens. [348]

August 2022 LayV Outbreak: PLA in Command (Via Front Organizations), Anomalous Infection Patterns

The discovery of Langya Henipavirus (LayV) in Shandong and Henan provinces of China has quickly attracted the attention of medical experts around the world.[349] LayV is a type of zoonotic henipavirus and 35 people have been identified to be infected with this pathogen since 2019 in these two provinces in China. Among all the patients, 26 people were infected with LayV only while nine others were co-infected with other pathogens at the same time. All 26 patients with the LayV infection have experienced fever with their probability of suffering from anorexia, coughing, weakness, muscle pain and leukopenia are as great as 50 percent. In addition, liver function impairment, thrombocytopenia, and headaches are also common symptoms of LayV infection. [350]

This report also mentioned that a live LayV sample was isolated from an infected patient and that the full genome sequence was

---

349. 'A new virus that can infect people has been discovered', Health Commission of Hebei Province, 9 August 2022.http://wsjkw.hebei.gov.cn/wbcz/390125.jhtml
Wang, Linfa, Wei, Liu, et. al, 'A Zoonotic Henipavirus in Febrile Patients in China', New England Journal of Medicine, Vol. 387, 4 August 2022.

350. Wang, Linfa, Wei, Liu, et. al, 'A Zoonotic Henipavirus in Febrile Patients in China', New England Journal of Medicine, Vol. 387, 4 August 2022.

characterized. The phylogenetic analysis based on the L gene homology indicated that LayV was more closely related to the Mojiang Virus, not Nipah or Hendra virus, the two more commonly known henipaviruses.[351] This surprised and confounded many experts.

The Mojiang virus was found in an infamous abandoned mine in Mojiang County in China's Southwestern Yunnan Province. This mine in Yunnan first attracted attention in 2012 when six miners working inside it contracted severe pneumonia of unknown origin and three of them died. [352] Researchers at the time claimed that the Mojiang Virus originated from rats in the mine.[353] In 2013, Shi Zhengli from WIV discovered the coronavirus RaTG13 from bats in the Mojiang mine, which is the official closest known relative to the new coronavirus SARS-CoV-2 (with a 96 percent genetic similarity between the two) and the Mojiang mine gained additional attention from researchers in China and their international collaborators. [354]

This mine in Mojiang resembles a 'cave of viruses' harboring these two dangerous viruses in different hosts: Coronaviruses in

351. Wang, Linfa, Wei, Liu, et. al, 'A Zoonotic Henipavirus in Febrile Patients in China', New England Journal of Medicine, Vol. 387, 4 August 2022.
352. Xavier Fernández-Aguilar, et. al., 'Novel Henipa-like Virus, Mojiang Paramyxovirus, in Rats, China, 2012', Emerging Infectious Diseases, Vol. 20, No. 6, June 2014.
353. Diego Cantoni, et. al., 'Pseudotyped Bat Coronavirus RaTG13 is efficiently neutralised by convalescent sera from SARS-CoV-2 infected patients', Communications Biology, Vol. 5, No. 409, 3 May 2022.
354. Joanna, Mazet, Peter, Daszak, Shi, Zheng-Li, et. al., 'Isolation and characterization of a bat SARS-like coronavirus that uses the ACE2 receptor', Nature, Vol. 503, No. 28, November 2013.

bats and Mojiang Virus in rodents. However, there are still many questions that remain unanswered about this mysterious cave: what happened to the other three miners who had unknown pneumonia but did not die? Did they have any other coinfection with other viruses? After the Mojiang Virus was identified, did those miners' samples get retested for any potential zoonotic infection from the Mojiang Virus? What is unique in this cave that makes it such a unique hub of emerging pathogens?

Another material issue related to the discovery of LayV in this recent study is the involvement of PLA medical entities. The two key Chinese scientists that have taken the lead in the analysis of LayV are Dr. Li-Qun Fang and Dr. Wei Liu, both of whom are part of the Beijing Institute of Microbiology and Epidemiology (BIME). However, BIME is actually the same entity of Institute of Microbiology and Epidemiology under AMMS and, by extension, the PLA. In addition, Supplementary materials related to this study clearly indicated that the PLA's 990 Military Hospital in Henan province was involved in this study. Interestingly, BIME reporting has indicated that 34 out of the 35 LayV patients were local farmers.[355] Why were the farmers' samples analyzed in a military hospital as a sentinel surveillance program?

BIME has also indicated that those 35 patients infected with LayV were identified during sentinel febrile illness surveillance (i.e., routine infectious disease surveillance) in 2020. Given the nature

---

355. Supplementary Appendix to Wang, Linfa, Wei, Liu, et. al, 'A Zoonotic Henipavirus in Febrile Patients in China', New England Journal of Medicine, Vol. 387, 4 August 2022.

of LayV, it is very unusual to report the discovery and isolation of a live henipavirus with significant delay of three years. A new henipavirus is highly epidemiologically significant and should have been publicly reported in 2019 as soon as it was discovered. Meanwhile, among the 35 patients, 6 patients were found to be co-infected with Severe Fever with Thrombocytopenia Syndrome Virus (SFTSV) while 2 patients were found to be co-infected with Hantavirus. [356]

The SFTSV and Hantavirus are highly infectious viruses that could lead to severe viral hemorrhage and their outbreaks in China are relatively rare events. So, in this so-called 'sentinel febrile illness surveillance', this group of military scientists identified three dangerous pathogens at one time with some patients being co-infected with two rare pathogens. How likely would this happen in a natural situation? Also, in regular sentinel febrile illness surveillance, these viruses would not be included in the regular screening under normal circumstances.

LayV, SFTSV and Hantaviruses can also all infect rodents. SFTSV is a novel phlebovirus (in the Bunyaviridae family) and certain tick species have been demonstrated as a competent vector of SFTSV by experimental transmission study and field study.[357] Further, LayV and Hantavirus can infect humans if

---

356. Supplementary Appendix to Wang, Linfa, Wei, Liu, et. al, 'A Zoonotic Henipavirus in Febrile Patients in China', New England Journal of Medicine, Vol. 387, 4 August 2022.

357. Yuan-Yuan Hu, et. al., 'Role of three tick species in the maintenance and transmission of Severe Fever with Thrombocytopenia Syndrome Virus', PLOS Neglected Tropical Diseases, Vol. 14, No. 6, 10 June 2020.

people encounter rodent droppings or feces. So, in order for the patients to be co-infected with SFTSV and LayV, the rodents need to be infected by the ticks first to get SFTSV, and also their droppings and feces need to be touched by those farmers. How 'lucky' these scientists were to find all of these exceedingly rare co-infection cases from a single field case study under an official sentinel surveillance framework.

Although SFTSV and Hantavirus infections have become endemic in Shandong or Henan Provinces in recent years, it is still very unusual to see patients co-infected with these dangerous pathogens. In the BIME study, no patient died even though SFTSV and Hantavirus normally high mortality rates. Given these dynamics, his study appears to be a targeted surveillance project to look for certain pathogens' zoonotic infection risk to humans via transmission by rodents (with screening of different species of rodents).

Would it be possible that this study was a test of these dangerous pathogens and see which one was more prone to cause human infection? With the involvement of a military hospital and scientists from the PLA, would it be possible that this was a field release of multiple dangerous pathogens followed by field screening of rodents and potential human infections caused by infected rodents? The answer to this question is beyond the scope of this specific book, but these questions are reasonable speculation and should serve as an alarm for national security experts.

CHAPTER SEVEN

Chinese Center for Disease Control and Prevention
Emergency Responder at Home, Major
CCP Export Abroad?

- Current Structure and Leadership
- Key Domestic Functions
- WIV-Like Live Bat Colony at Wuhan CDC, Close Proximity to the Huanan Seafood Market
- Transnational Linkages
- Africa CDC – The Next Frontier for Chinese CDC?
- Summary

CHAPTER 7

Chinese Center for Disease Control and Prevention Emergency Responder at Home, Major CCP Export Abroad?

Current Structure and Leadership

Chinese CDC is China's nationwide infectious disease surveillance and control agency that also has its own network of BSL3 labs. Unlike WIV, HVRI, CAMS, GIRH, and AMMS, Chinese CDC's main focus is operational with the early detection and control of emerging epidemics/pandemic being the priority with all laboratory and other research infrastructure playing a supporting and enabling role. Chinese CDC field teams will incorporate specific personnel for other Chinese virology research institutes, but under Chinese CDC operational structures and protocols. Like CAMS, Chinese CDC officially reports to the NHC and is headquartered in Beijing.

A key observation of Chinese CDC's role in China's overall COVID-19 pandemic response is that it does not appear to be the lead coordinating agency despite its official nationwide

Figure 7: Chinese CDC Organizational Structure

Source: 'About Us: Organizational Chart', Chinese Center for Disease Control and Prevention. https://www.chinacdc.cn/en/

footprint. This is in contrast to Chinese CDC's leading domestic role in the response to the SARS-CoV-1 outbreak in 2002 and 2003. Chinese CDC was also the main point of contact with its American counterparts at US CDC and the main provider of public health-related information. Chinese CDC now appears to have become more of 'one among many' in China's increasingly large and geographically dispersed virology research system.

The Director of Chinese CDC is Dr. Gao Fu (also known as George Gao) although he has recently announced that he is stepping down from his role. Dr. Gao is one of China's most high-profile scientists and is known for his contributions to the study of inter-species pathogen transmission.[358] Dr. Fu also publicly endorsed EcoHealth Alliance's Global Virome Project in 2018, while he was at the Institute of Microbiology (CAS). [359] In August 2022, it was announced that Dr. Feng Zijian will become the new Director of Chinese CDC. Dr. Feng was previously the Director of China CDC's Public Health Emergency Center and has conducted joint national assessments with United States Centers for Disease Control and Prevention (US CDC).[360] Dr. Feng's promotion to Director of Chinese CDC seems to fit the pattern of appointing scientists who have direct experience with the West, and the United States in particular.

Dr. Gao and his successor Dr. Feng along with fellow scientist Dr. Xiaofeng Liang are the only scientists on the Chinese CDC leadership team. The remainder of the Chinese CDC leadership consists of a CCP Party Secretary, personnel from CCP Secretary of the Inspection Commission, and other CCP-affiliated personnel.[361] This CCP oversight and control is also consistent with WIV, HVRI, CAMS, GIRH, and AMMS.

358. 'George F. Gao', Chinese Center for Disease Control and Prevention. https://www.chinacdc.cn/en/aboutus/leadership/201603/t20160324_128015.html

359. See, for example, Gao, George, Mazet, Joanna, Daszak, Peter, et. al., 'The Global Virome Project', Science, 359: 6378 (23 February 2018).

360. 'Promoting global public health security, U.S. CDC and China CDC conduct a national assessment', United States Centers for Disease Control and Prevention, 6 October 2017. https://www.cdc.gov/globalhealth/countries/china/stories/health-security.htm

361. 'Leadership', Chinese Center for Disease Control and Prevention. https://www.chinacdc.cn/en/aboutus/leadership/

Key Domestic Functions

The Chinese CDC operates as the key public health emergency response scientific and technical capability in China. However, in May 2021 the formation of the National Administration of Disease Prevention and Control in Beijing was announced.[362] It remains unclear as to how this new agency will interact with Chinese CDC as well as other officially civilian Chinese virology research institutes. Regardless, Chinese CDC has a nationwide infrastructure of epidemiological intelligence surveillance teams, reference and analytical labs (including a BSL3 lab in Wuhan), emergency response teams, and program administrators across all major cities in China, including Hong Kong.

In addition to Wuhan, Chinese CDC has operational and research infrastructure in Harbin, Shanghai, Kunming, and Guangzhou. Given this co-location, it is reasonable to assess that Chinese CDC personnel in these locations (including Beijing) directly interact with their counterparts from WIV, HVRI, CAMS, GIRH, and AMMS. Interestingly, Chinese CDC publishes 13 different journals across multiple fields of virology, vaccinology, and environmental sciences but only makes this information available in Chinese, a stark contrast from the other institutions that have been analyzed. [363]

---

362. 'China Focus: China inaugurates national administration of disease prevention and control', Xinhua, 13 May 2021.
http://www.xinhuanet.com/english/2021-05/13/c_139943875_2.htm

363. 'Publication', Chinese Center for Disease Control and Prevention.
https://www.chinacdc.cn/en/publication/fms/

WIV-Like Live Bat Colony at Wuhan CDC, Close Proximity to the Huanan Seafood Market

Given Chinese CDC's status as an official government organization, its Wuhan-based researchers do not regularly surface in scientific literature (in Chinese or English) related to high-risk pathogen research. Most of the identified Chinese CDC research appears to be descriptive and analytical as opposed to being related to experimentation, cloning, and/or any other high-risk methods. However, it should be noted that Wuhan CDC has a BSL3 lab roughly 200 yards from the Huanan Seafood Market, the still-official point of origin of the COVID-19 pandemic according to the CCP. Like WIV, Wuhan CDC also has a live bat colony where bats that have been captured in high-risk locations, such as Yunnan, are brought back over 1,000 miles in some cases back to Wuhan. [364]

This core scientific infrastructure on-site and the associated supply chain that enables bats to be captured and transported to Wuhan CDC would objectively enable to this Chinese CDC

---

364. Aylin Woodward, 'A 2019 video shows scientists from the Wuhan CDC collecting samples in bat caves — but the agency hasn't revealed any findings', Business Insider, 9 June 2021.
https://www.businessinsider.com/chinese-scientists-bat-caves-video-2021-6
Eva Dou and Lily Kuo, 'A scientist adventurer and China's 'Bat Woman' are under scrutiny as coronavirus lab-leak theory gets another look', Washington Post, 3 June 2021.
https://www.washingtonpost.com/world/asia_pacific/coronavirus-bats-china-wuhan/2021/06/02/772ef984-beb2-11eb-922a-c40c9774bc48_story.html
曠野青春 | 隱形防綫（英文字幕版）, China Science Communication, Broadcasted on CCTV on 10 December 2019
https://www.youtube.com/watch?v=ovnUyTRMERI

division to conduct similar high-risk research as WIV and/or coordinate on specific projects. While there are presently no discoverable joint publications between WIV and Wuhan CDC researchers in the bat coronavirus GoF domain, this multi-layered convergence of capability in one specific city in China can be assessed to be noteworthy.

Transnational Linkages [365]

With regards to the West, Chinese CDC appears to play more of a coordination function through the provision of information to its counterparts. However, Chinese CDC does have ongoing scientific and technical assistance programs in several Belt and Road Initiative (BRI) countries, particularly in Africa. Some of this work is funded by the Bill and Melinda Gates Foundation and the United Kingdom Department for International Development.[366] It is unclear why the Chinese CDC would require external, particularly Western, funding to manage these projects.

The Bill and Melinda Gates Foundation also provided another US$600,000 grant to Chinese CDC in May 2020 for the official purpose of 'to support emergency response and evaluation, and prepare China for the potential pandemic, which will not only

---

365. A full set of network diagrams outlining all of CAMS/PUMC's institutional linkages based off of joint publications and grant awards can be found in Annex L. All data was collected using the automated search and knowledge representation capabilities of Data Abyss.
https://www.dataabyss.ai/

366. 'About Us – Global Public Health', Chinese Center for Disease Control and Prevention'.
https://www.chinacdc.cn/en/

help disease control and containment but contribute China's experience to global health'.[367] Given Chinese CDC's status as a top government-funded institution with world-leading domestic capabilities, it is also unclear as to why Chinese CDC would require a US$600,000 grant from an American foundation.

Chinese CDC BRI-related work in Africa and merits some analysis. EcoHealth Alliance appears to be active in a very similar set of countries, specifically in West Africa.[368] Given EcoHealth Alliance's well-established relationship with Chinese CDC, and Dr. Fu in particular, this geographic overlap in West Africa is unlikely to be coincidental. As has been demonstrated in this Chapter and Chapter Three, there is also a funding overlap between Chinese CDC and EcoHealth Alliance in the form of the Bill and Melinda Gates Foundation. EcoHealth's mainstream operation as well as its Global Virome Project[369] have increasingly become focused on going into isolated geographies

---

367. 'China CDC', Bill and Melinda Gates Foundation, May 2020.
    https://www.gatesfoundation.org/about/committed-grants/2020/05/inv005832
368. 'EcoHealth Alliance Scientists Discover the Deadly Zaire Ebola Virus in West African Bat', EcoHealth Alliance, 24 January 2019.
    https://www.ecohealthalliance.org/2019/01/ecohealth-alliance-scientists-discover-the-deadly-zaire-ebola-virus-in-west-african-bat
    Peter Dazsak, Jonathan Epstein, et. al., 'Understanding One Health through biological and behavioral risk surveillance in Liberia: a cross-sectional study', The Lancet, Global Health, Meeting Abstracts, Volume 10, Special Issue 22, 1 March 2022.
369. For example, see 'Our Goals', Global Virome Project.
    https://www.globalviromeproject.org/our-goals
    'Why GVP is Needed', Global Virome Project.
    https://www.globalviromeproject.org/our-approach
    'Spillover: Visual Risk Ranking', Global Virome Project.
    https://www.globalviromeproject.org/spillover

that have sparse or no human interaction. The declared focus of this work is to discover new viruses in nature or to procure new samples of viruses that rarely infect humans. [370]

While this field-based work does not involve overt GoF work (at least not in-region) it does involve what is referred to as Gain-of-Opportunity. Both Chinese CDC and EcoHealth Alliance personnel are deliberately seeking out viruses and other pathogens that have had minimal or no human interaction for thousands of years and bringing these novel pathogens into laboratory settings. In the lab, these pathogens are free from any of the naturally developed constraints that they were under in their previous environment that prevented them for infecting humans in the first place. Also, as humans have had little to no interaction with many of these novel pathogens, population-level innate immunity is minimal to non-existent. By engaging in these field-based activities, both Chinese CDC and EcoHealth Alliance are generating new risks through their own direct intervention that would be highly unlikely to emerge under natural conditions otherwise.

Africa CDC – The Next Frontier for Chinese CDC?

The new Chinese-funded African Centers for Disease Control

---

370. For example, see 'Monitoring the Deadly Nipah Virus – Program Info', EcoHealth Alliance.
https://www.ecohealthalliance.org/program/monitoring-the-deadly-nipah-virus
'Emerging Disease Hotspots – Program Info', EcoHealth Alliance.
https://www.ecohealthalliance.org/program/emerging-disease-hotspots
'Project Deep Forest – Program Info', EcoHealth Alliance.
https://www.ecohealthalliance.org/program/project-deep-forest

and Prevention (Africa CDC) is being developed in Addis Ababa, the capital of Ethiopia. It should be noted that the current Director General of the World Health Organization, Dr. Tedros Adhanom Ghebreyesus, is also from Ethiopia and has coordinated closely with the CCP over the course of COVID-19 pandemic. Interestingly, China has also constructed the African Union (AU) headquarters in Addis Ababa at the cost of US$200 million. [371]

The project is being led by China Civil Engineering Construction Corporation (CCECC) and is claimed to be on schedule to be completed by the end of 2022 at the cost of US$80 million. Africa CDC will have an emergency operation center, its own data center, laboratories of unspecified types, training and conference centers, briefing rooms, and accommodation for foreign experts and visitors. [372]

The origins of the Africa CDC project are in an April 2015 agreement between the United States and the AU. Under this agreement, the United States agreed to provide technical expertise and to second US CDC staff members to Africa CDC.

---

371. Jevans Nyabiage, 'Why China is building gleaming new government facilities in Africa', South China Morning Post, 23 May 2021.
https://www.scmp.com/news/china/diplomacy/article/3134224/why-china-building-gleaming-new-government-facilities-africa?module=inline&pgtype=article

372. Jevans Nyabiage, 'How the US lost Africa to China over new disease control centre in Addis Ababa', South China Morning Post, 13 August 2022.
https://www.scmp.com/news/china/diplomacy/article/3188010/how-us-lost-africa-china-over-new-disease-control-centre-addis
'Interview: China-aided Africa CDC project running smoothly with "full force," says expert', Xinhua, 6 June 2021.
http://www.xinhuanet.com/english/africa/2021-06/06/c_139992119_2.htm

In 2018, the AU and China determined that the Chinese would construct the Africa CDC buildings. Funding has also been provided by the Bill and Melinda Gates Foundation, including in September 2020. [373]

While there have not been any publicly released official communications regarding the involvement of Chinese CDC in the Africa CDC project, it is not unreasonable to assess that Chinese CDC will be involved in the operationalization of key Africa CDC divisions and laboratory environments. In such a scenario, Africa CDC can emerge as a key convergence point for the high-risk, field-based pathogen research that is being conducted by Chinese CDC-linked organizations such as the EcoHealth Alliance. It should be noted that Chinese virology research institutes have already begun the process of internationalization with WIV recently establishing a joint laboratory with the Defense Science and Technology

373. Jevans Nyabiage, 'How the US lost Africa to China over new disease control centre in Addis Ababa', South China Morning Post, 13 August 2022.
https://www.scmp.com/news/china/diplomacy/article/3188010/how-us-lost-africa-china-over-new-disease-control-centre-addis
'Gates Foundation Honors Director of Africa CDC With 2020 Global Goalkeeper Award', Bill and Melinda gates Foundation, 21 September 2020.
https://www.gatesfoundation.org/ideas/media-center/press-releases/2020/09/gates-foundation-honors-director-of-africa-cdc-with-2020-global-goalkeeper-award
374. Ryan Clarke, 'The International Frontier of the CCP's Bioweapons Program: Wuhan Institute of Virology, Chinese Academy of Medical Sciences, and the Pakistan Army's Defence Science and Technology Organization', The Klaxon, 14 April 2022.
https://static1.squarespace.com/static/5de08d699f40c13aa68de2ee/t/6257ac00eb8d8d7ccddc5eba/1649912833748/The+Emerging+Frontier+of+the+CCP+Bioweapons+Program+-+Dr+Ryan+Clarke.+14+April+2020.pdf

Organization (DESTO), which is run by the Pakistan Army in Rawalpindi.[374] Once the Africa CDC laboratories are fully operational (presumably under Chinese stewardship), a new set of variables related to high-risk pathogen research in lab settings have the potential to emerge as well.

Summary

While the Chinese CDC appears to have experienced a domestic degradation of its status from its high point in 2002-2003, its operational focus and experience augmented by laboratory and field-based pathogen research makes Chinese CDC a high-value export to Africa. The Africa CDC project provides a clear structural opportunity for Chinese CDC to converge its own activities in Africa (specifically BRI countries) and the activities of partner organizations such as EcoHealth Alliance. Chinese CDC would be entering an environment which is heavily influenced (if not controlled entirely) by the CCP and would have a substantial degree of freedom of action, especially in the initial phases.Once Chinese CDC has established a strong base of operations at Africa CDC Headquarters in Addis Ababa, individual country-level programs could also be built out under a 'hub and spokes' model.

CHAPTER EIGHT

Net Assessment

- China's High-Risk Virology Research Ecosystem: More Domestically Diversified with Narrowing Transnational Linkages?

- Strategic Implications and Near-Term Directions

CHAPTER 8

Net Assessment

China's High-Risk Virology Research Ecosystem: More Domestically Diversified with Narrowing Transnational Linkages?

While CAMS/PUMC is not formally organized under the PLA, its high-risk pathogen research network is demonstrably more diversified than even AMMS in terms of pathogen types and both its domestic and transnational linkages, specifically to UTMB in Galveston. CAMS/PUMC also has demonstrated high-risk pathogen research capabilities that are at least on par with WIV and may actually exceed them at this stage. CAMS/PUMC is now a world leader in the development of synthetic viruses in the lab, including SARS-CoV-2 viruses. This marks a major development in that CAMS/PUMC has the independent capability to engineer a range of viruses for various applications after learning from the West. The significance of CAMS and its institutes like IMB and IPB is that they are rapidly developing China into a 'great virology power'. In a COVID-19 global pandemic world and its aftermath, China is steadily emerging as a comprehensive great power with an independent ability to conduct cutting-edge virology research.

Through CML (CAMS) and its associated Gabriel Network, IPB has considerably more publicly surfaced transnational linkages than AMMS or GIRH/Huyan Institute. Despite having more transnational linkages, CML does not have the same level of track record in high-risk pathogen research as AMMS. However, there is some recent evidence that this may not represent a static situation, namely the 2021 study in Virologica Sinica in which scientists in CML developed a synthetic 'SARS-CoV-2-GFP replicon'. [375]

While it is important to not over extrapolate from one specific study, it nonetheless demonstrates that this level of advanced capability and intent exist within this Lab. CML also has a declared partnership with ILAS, also under CAMS. ILAS has a track record of high-risk pathogen research that often mirrors the work being done at AMMS. ILAS is also home to Bao Linlin, who conducts GoF research on avian viruses that is banned in the West.[376] At present there is no available evidence of a crossover between ILAS and CML but there is an objectively observable structural opportunity for such an event to occur.

Interestingly, despite having extensive overt links with the CCP,

375. Bei Wang, Chongyang Zhang, Xiaobo Lei, Lili Ren, Zhendong Zhao and He Huang, 'Construction of Non-infectious SARS-CoV-2 Replicons and Their Application in Drug Evaluation', Virologica Sinica, Vol. 36, No. 5, October 2021. https://www.ncbi.nlm.nih.gov/pmc/articles/PMC8034055/

376. For examples of Bao Lin Lin's high-risk pathogen research conducted at ILAS, please see Linlin Bao, et. al., 'Novel Avian-Origin Human Influenza A(H7N9) Can Be Transmitted Between Ferrets via Respiratory Droplets', Journal of Infectious Diseases, Vol. 209, Issue 4, 15 February 2014.
Linlin Bao, et. al., 'Transmission of H7N9 influenza virus in mice by different infective routes', Virology Journal, Vol. 11, Article No. 185, 2014.

open-source data suggests that GIRH/Huyan Institute does not appear to be engaged in GoF or other high-risk pathogen research projects. GIRH\Huyan instead appears to focus more strongly on clinical activity, acute patient care, and, through Zhong Nanshan, public health communication and engagement. While IPB appears to be engaging in some high-risk virology research, publicly available information demonstrates that AMMS is more active than GIRH across multiple virus types (Zika, AFSV, Ebola, and SARS-CoV-2) and high-risk methods such as serial passaging and the use of humanized mouse models.

Both Chen Wei and Qi Chen at AMMS have a well-established track record of working with some of the world's most dangerous pathogens under questionable biomedical rationales. Qi has more publicly available research, in particular with Shi Peiyong and Chao Shan from UTMB on Zika GoF experiments. However, it is unclear as to whether this indicates that Qi is indeed more active than Chen or if much of Chen's research has remained confidential. Within the AMMS organizational structure, Chen is clearly a more strategic leader than Qi.

Chen's established linkages with Qiu Xiangguo (formerly of NML) are significant, especially in the domain of Henipah/Nipah virus. Henipah virus has not been clinically detected in China and there are already adequate diagnostics available in the market. As this virus has only been clinically detected in Malaysia, Singapore, India, and Bangladesh and is characterized by irregular and short-duration outbreaks, there is not a viable market for a vaccine either. Even in the event that a Henipah/Nipah virus vaccine was claimed to have been developed in China, it would be unlikely to have a substantial uptake in these countries.[377] Given these epidemiological and market conditions, why would Major General Chen Wei be sourcing these viral samples from Qiu at NML in Winnipeg?

Another key observation is that AMMS has continued its high-risk research on the SARS-CoV-2 virus even during the most acute phases of the global COVID-19 pandemic. None of this research, including the serial passaging experiments, have been credibly attributed to any new biomedical breakthrough. Similarly, the artificial creation of a pseudorabies virus to treat ASFV is also dangerous and lacking a clearly linked positive biomedical outcome. Further, much of the high-risk pathogen research at AMMS appears to be done 'in-house' or with a narrowly-defined set of transnational partners. As self-reliance in the virology domain is the overtly stated aim of Chen Wei, AMMS is likely on the pathway to a nearly complete domestic orientation. A similar trend has been observed with other Chinese virology research institutes such as WIV, Harbin Veterinary Research Institute (HVRI)[378], and CAMS [379] .

---

377. For examples of a lack of trust in Chinese-manufactured vaccines, please see Michael Yong, 'People who got Sinovac vaccine nearly 5 times more likely to develop severe COVID-19 than Pfizer: Singapore study', ChannelNewsAsia, 14 April 2022.
'Hundreds of Thai medical workers infected despite Sinovac vaccinations', Reuters, 11 July 2021.
Teresa Wong, 'Covid: Is China's vaccine success waning in Asia?', BBC, 19 July 2021.
378. For analysis on WIV and HVRI, please see Ryan Clarke and Lam Peng Er, 'Coronavirus Research Networks in China: Origins, International Linkages and Consequences', Center for Non-Traditional Security Studies, May 2021, Singapore.

However, it is more pronounced in the case of AMMS.

As other Chinese institutes such as WIV, HVRI, and AMMS come under increased international scrutiny (in December 2021 AMMS was put on the Export Control Blacklist by the U.S. Commerce Department)[380] IPB's relatively greater international connectivity via CML could assume enhanced relevance. While China has established itself as a world leader in high-risk pathogen research, transnational linkages will still remain relevant. These linkages would enable immediate access to new methods and technologies and to maintain an up-to-date awareness of what represents state of the art in other key competitor countries, especially the United States.

Strategic Implications and Near-Term Directions

All Chinese biomedical research institutions fall under the control of the CCP and the Civil-Military Fusion Law. As such, there is a possibility that any institution can be repurposed and directly controlled by the Chinese government under specific contingencies, including lab accidents.[381] The Civil-Military Fusion Law is an overarching legal framework within which all biomedical institutions must operate. However, despite this uniform structure, CAMS/PUMC and AMMS have nonetheless

---

379. For analysis on CAMS, please see Ryan Clarke, Lam Peng Er, and Lin Xiaoxu, 'High-Risk Virology Research at the Chinese Academy of Medical Sciences and Peking Union Medical College', EAI Background Brief No. 1642, 24 March 2022.
380. Michael Vernick and Marta Thompson, 'Prominent Chinese Academy of Military Medical Sciences is Added to Export Control Blacklist', Akin Gump, 28 December 2021.

emerged as primary nodes in the Chinese virology research network. AMMS carries out high-risk experiments in its own right while also enabling other nominally civilian institutions in China. Displaced high-risk research that was previously conducted at other institutes, such as WIV, would have 'top cover' protection to be conducted, especially given Major General Chen Wei's status within the highest levels of the CCP. It should be noted that the 2021 SARS-CoV-2 GoF serial passaging study also involved Shi Zhengli from WIV.[382] This is unlikely to be purely coincidental.

CAMS/PUMC meanwhile conducts nearly identical high-risk pathogen research that has been observed at WIV and HVRI while avoiding international scrutiny even as the respective capabilities of its constituent units IMB, IPB, CML, and ILAS accelerate. While CAMS/PUMC is not formally organized under the PLA, its high-risk pathogen research network is demonstrably more diversified than even AMMS in terms of pathogen types and both its domestic and transnational linkages, specifically to UTMB in Galveston. CAMS/PUMC also has demonstrated high-risk pathogen research capabilities that are at least on par with WIV and may actually exceed them. This has been accomplished

381. For additional analysis of the Civil-Military Fusion Law, please see 'Alibaba and Ant Group: Involvement in China's Military-Civilian Fusion Initiative', RWR Advisory Group, 2 October 2020.
https://www.rwradvisory.com/wp-content/uploads/2020/10/RWR-Report-Ant-MilCiv-Fusion-10-2020.pdf
For a more in-depth discussion, please see Ryan Clarke, 'Emerging Global Pandemic Risks Come from Engineered Viruses in Chinese Labs, Not the Jungle or Bat Caves', Epoch Times, 4 September 2021.
382. Zheng-Li Shi, Ben Hu, et. al., 'Genetic Mutation of SARS-CoV-2 during Consecutive Passages in Permissive Cells', Virologica Sinica, Vol. 26, 2021.

while avoiding international attention almost entirely.

The aggregated capabilities of CAMS/PUMC (including IPB, ILAS, and CML), AMMS, GIRH/Huyan Institute, WIV, and HVRI demonstrate an ambitious and increasingly domestically-driven high risk pathogen research ecosystem. Unlike prior generations, these Chinese pathogen research institutes will maintain specific transnational linkages under CCP direction to ensure that China remains the world leader with an ever-increasing gap between 1st and 2nd place. The inherent dual-use nature of these experiments on SARS-CoV-2, ASFV, Zika, Henipah/Nipah virus have geostrategic implications. Any nation that can be the first to identify an emerging pandemic and take specific measures to protect its population will inevitably have strategic advantages over nations that do not. [383]

---

383. For example, please see Ryan Clarke, 'Is China Converting COVID-19 Into a Strategic Opportunity?', EAI Background Brief No. 1545, 9 July 2020.

CHAPTER NINE

The Future of the Chinese Military-Civilian Virology Complex: China as Number One?

- China's New Virology Frontier: Advanced BSL3 Lab Infrastructure in Every Province
- Chinese Virology Labs: Greater Self-Reliance Amid US-Chinese 'Decoupling'?
- China's New Biosafety Law and 14th 5-Year Plan: Improving and Strengthening Labs?
- Pandemic Readiness and Geopolitical Impact: Underscore Importance of Virology Labs

CHAPTER 9

The Future of the Chinese Military-Civilian Virology Complex: China as Number One?

China's New Virology Frontier: Advanced BSL3 Lab Infrastructure in Every Province

In May 2020 China's NDRC issued a plan for every Chinese province to have at least one BSL3 lab. The NDRC cited the recent COVID-19 outbreak as the catalyst to this new initiative.[384] It should be noted that for some of the more sensitive, high-risk analytical tasks and experiments, there is often an unclear line between BSL3 and BSL4 labs. For example, Dr. Shi Zhengli is believed to have conducted some of her bat coronavirus bioengineering experiments in a BSL3 lab at the WIV.

Earlier in 2004, China launched a national BSL program that

---

384. Global Times, 'All provinces in China are asked to set up P3 lab: ministries', 20 May 2020.
https://www.globaltimes.cn/content/1188916.shtml

accredited 42 BSL3s.[385] In addition, four mobile BSL-3 laboratories were imported from the Labover company (headquartered in Montpellier, France) and distributed to institutes in Beijing, Shanghai, and Guangdong. These imported labs were intended to enable mobile nationwide surveillance of pathogens and to support emergency response operations. [386] Both Beijing and the southern Chinese province of Guangdong will serve as two key nodes of this nationwide BSL3 rollout. Guangdong may build up to 30 BSL3 labs and one BSL4 lab (which would be China's third official BSL4 lab). Under this initiative, Beijing will also build out its first BSL3 permanent (non-mobile) lab. [387]

This rapid proliferation of BSL3 labs, if executed in line with NDRC directives, will fundamentally alter the scale, scope, and structure of virology research in China. Given China's one-party state bureaucracy, one potential emergent structure could take shape in which every provincial BSL3 lab would come under CAS or CAAS governance with the CCP on the management board. This would also involve close collaboration with city- and provincial-level governments given the strong localism witnessed even in the centralized one-party state in China. Under

---

385. The majority of these BSL3 labs are located in key Chinese cities such as Beijing, Shanghai, and Guangzhou.
386. Yuan, Zhiming, 'Current status and future challenges of high-level biosafety laboratories in China', Journal of Biosafety and Biosecurity, 1:2 (September 2019).
387. Zhang, Phoebe, 'Top-grade biosafety lab building spree planned in southern China', South China Morning Post, 25 May 2020. See also Global Times, 'Beijing to build P3 laboratory', 18 May 2020. https://www.globaltimes.cn/content/1188638.shtml, and Lei, Li, 'Visiting the mobile P3 lab that contributed to curbing COVID-19 in Beijing', Global Times, 12 July 2020.

this structure, WIV, HVRI, CAMS/PUMC (including IPB, ILAS, and CML), AMMS, GIRH/Huyan Institute and their respective research activities and operational structures would be frames of reference for these more numerous BSL3 (and possibly BSL4) labs with strong provincial links that nonetheless fall under CCP oversight via CAS or CAAS management.

Chinese Virology Labs: Greater Self-Reliance Amid US-Chinese 'Decoupling'?

China today possesses world-class pathogen expertise. China is now capable of training its own future generations of virologists onshore. In the years ahead, China need not send large numbers of its students to the West for virology training as has been the case with previous generations. Conceivably, China can opt out of any future global governance frameworks pertaining to GoF or other virology research at little or no cost to China itself.

However, driven by the desire to remain close to cutting edge developments outside of China, key labs will continue collaborating with international virology networks. While Chinese virologists have previously had open and free access to research and educational opportunities in key Western countries, and the United States in particular, this trend may not continue. The broader context of Sino-US decoupling across multiple areas of trade, technology, capital markets, and other strategic matters is likely to inhibit transnational collaboration. China then will have greater incentive to boost virology research on its own efforts.

China's New Biosafety Law and 14th 5-Year Plan: Improving and Strengthening Labs?

On 17 October 2020, the Standing Committee of the National People's Congress (NPC) passed a Biosecurity Law which took effect on 15 April 2021. Under this new legislation, the country will roll out 11 basic systems for biosafety risk prevention and control which includes a risk monitoring and early warning system, an information sharing and release system, an emergency response system, and an investigation and traceability system.[388] This new law follows up on an authoritative Party Directive issued in February 2020 which declared a 'People's War' on the COVID-19 virus and gave clear instructions to avoid theft, leakage, and misplacement of biological samples.[389]

This Biosafety Law emphasizes the responsibilities of relevant local authorities at all levels in the building and improvement of the biosafety systems, with administrative penalties and fines to be imposed for failure to adhere to the law. The Biosafety Law warned that medical institutes and their staff who conceal, falsely inform, delay or omit the reports of infectious diseases, animal or plant epidemics, or diseases of unknown causes, will be reprimanded and directors of the institutes will be sanctioned and

---

388. Lin, Wan, 'China passes first biosafety law following COVID-19 epidemic, raises level to national security', Global Times, 18 October 2020.
389. Party Committee of the Beijing Municipal Center for Disease Control and Prevention, 'Beijing CDC Party Committee issued a wartime status order to suspend or remove middle-level cadres that cause major adverse effects on prevention and control', 13 February 2020.
http://t.m.china.com.cn/convert/c_k5AE9Pn8.html

have their professional certificates suspended. [390]

If the Biosafety Law and its accompanying epidemiological information/intelligence infrastructure are effectively implemented alongside a rapidly expanding BSL3 and BSL4 network, China will likely have one of the biggest infectious disease surveillance and study systems in the world. It should be noted that China already possessed an advanced infectious disease surveillance system even prior to the COVID-19 outbreak. One key implication of these developments is that the PRC would likely be the most prepared country for the next major pandemic and would be able to identify and contain any threats ahead of other advanced Western countries and Japan. The critical issue then is whether and when the CCP would choose release life-saving information to the world and to its own people. The political stability of the CCP is always set as top priority and public health data are always treated as state secrets under CCP regulations. What specific data will be released or whether any data will be released at all represents a purely political determination. Human life and public safety are secondary considerations and could even be viewed as acceptable collateral damage by the CCP.

In March 2021, the NPC passed the 14th Five Year Plan with a vision for a technologically advanced and self-reliant China. This Plan targets a 7% annual growth in R&D. The latest Five-Year Plan identified seven 'frontier' technological fields in which the

---

390. Lin, Wan, 'China passes first biosafety law following COVID-19 epidemic, raises level to national security', Global Times, 18 October 2020.

state should cultivate domestic capabilities:

- New generation artificial intelligence,
- Quantum information,
- Integrated circuits (semiconductors),
- Neuroscience and 'brain-inspired' research,
- Genetics and biotechnology,
- Clinical medicine and health,
- Deep sea, deep space and polar exploration.

Simply put, the PRC seeks to be more technologically advanced and self-reliant. Presumably, this grand strategy will also apply to the country's ambitious virology R&D. Though the latest Five-Year Plan did not explicitly elaborate on the future of Chinese pathogen research, we can surmise that this multidisciplinary field falls within the broad categories of 'genetics and biotechnology' and 'clinical medicine and health'. It can be anticipated that more money and human resources will be channeled to virology research under the 14th Five Year Plan.

Pandemic Readiness and Geopolitical Impact: Underscore Importance of Virology Labs

The enhancement of top Chinese laboratories to cope with future pandemics is necessary for China's geopolitical interests. That the COVID-19 pandemic temporarily disrupted the military operations of some countries (including the United States) was a salutary lesson for many and presumably for the PLA too. A Chinese proverb says: 'crisis is opportunity'. A case can be made that the PLA and Chinese Coast Guard were more assertive since the COVID-19 pandemic broke out in December 2019. When a few of Beijing's maritime rivals were reeling from the pandemic, the PLA and the Chinese Coast Guard were able to flex their muscles. Beijing was able to do this because the country was 'first in, and first out' of this pandemic. (To be sure, Chinese foreign policy was already more assertive over maritime disputes before the COVID-19 pandemic).

Table 5 below lists the key decisions and actions taken by Beijing in the Indo-Pacific in 2020. This supports the argument that China was opportunistic and emboldened to act during the global pandemic crisis.

Table 5: Key Chinese Decision Table

Date	Decision/Action	Regional Implications	Domain
9-30 March 2020	Chinese Coast Guard Vessels were spotted multiple times in and around the disputed Mischief Reef, Second Thomas Shoal, First Thomas Shoal, and Half-Moon Shoal.	South China Sea	Strategic
30 March 2020	10 Chinese speedboats entered Taiwanese waters and attacked a Taiwanese vessel that was clearing illegal Chinese fishing nets	Taiwan	Strategic
2 April 2020	A Japanese destroyer was damaged in East China Sera after it was rammed by a Chinese 'fishing boat'	East China Sea	Strategic
10 April 2020	A Vietnamese fishing boat was sunk near the Paracel Islands	South China Sea	Strategic

11 April 2020	An 'unspecified number' of PLA H6 bombers, J11 fighters, and KJ-500 airborne early warning and control aircraft flew over the Bashi Channel (just southwest of Taiwan) between Taiwan and the Philippines before circling back to an unspecified base in China. Taiwan scrambled fighter jets to warn off the PLA aircraft. China officially acknowledged that this 'far sea long-range drill' has taken place at least four times since January 2020 and is now a regular component of PLA activity. Taiwan claimed that this was the 6th occasion just in 2020 when PLA aircraft operated close to Taiwanese airspace.	Taiwan	Strategic
16 April 2020	When a US Navy Destroyer was transiting Taiwan the PLA staged aggressive military exercises in the Taiwan Strait without any prior announcement or warning.	Taiwan	Strategic
18 April 2020	China deployed a 'research vessel' clearly within Malaysia's EEZ	South China Sea	Strategic
22 April 2020	China's State Council's official declares that the city of Sansha in Hainan now has two new administrative districts to 'administer waters in the South China Sea' In addition to these specified events, there have been multiple confirmed instances of sporadic standoffs between the US Navy and the PLAN, Chinese Coast Guard, and suspected members of China's Maritime Militia.	South China Sea	Diplomatic/ Strategic

5 May 2020	Xinhua reports that Xi Jinping, while referencing China's response to the COVID-19 outbreak, states 'Crises and opportunities always exist side by side. Once overcome, a crisis is an opportunity'	Pan-Asia	Strategic
5 May 2020	After a series of previous failures, China successfully launches its Long March-5B rocket that is officially part of China's Moon/Mars/Tiangong Space Station mission ambitions.	International – Space	Diplomatic/ Strategic
26 May 2020	Multiple skirmishes occur between the PLA and Indian troops at multiple locations around the Line of Actual Control, a disputed border region consisting of roughly 120,000 square kilometers of disputed territory	South Asia	Strategic
28 May 2020	Xi Jinping orders the PLA to increase its combat readiness citing increased threats from 'Taiwan independence forces' and in recognition that 'epidemic control efforts have been normalized'.	Taiwan	Strategic
29 May 2020	Beijing promulgates Hong Kong National Security Law	Special Autonomous Region / Domestic	Strategic
1 June 2020	Li Zuocheng, Chief of the Joint Staff Department and Member of the Central Military Commission, openly stated that China will use force against Taiwan if there is no other way to prevent Taiwan from becoming independent.	Regional – Taiwan	Strategic

2 June 2020	Information begins to circulate that China is planning to attempt to impose an Air Defense Identification Zone (ADIZ) in the South China Sea similar to Beijing's actions of establishing in ADIZ in the East China Sea in 2013.	South China Sea	Strategic
	China's Ministry of National Defense announces that its first domestically-built aircraft carrier, CNS Shandong, is carrying out sea trials in preparations for deployment.	South China Sea and/or East China Sea	Strategic

Source: Ryan Clarke, 'Is China Converting COVID-19 Into a Strategic Opportunity?', EAI Background Brief No. 1545, East Asian Institute, National University of Singapore, 9 July 2020.

The first confirmed COVID-19 case in the United States was on January 21, 2020 in Washington State. By April 2021 the US had suffered more than half a million fatalities.[391] Many states and cities were locked down. The US Navy had to rapidly withdraw many assets including the aircraft carriers USS Theodore Roosevelt and USS Ronald Reagan, from the Asia-Pacific due to COVID-19 infection risks.[392] However, in June the same year, the US deployed an unprecedented three aircraft carrier fleets in a show of strength and resolve.

China deployed the Liaoning Aircraft carrier naval battle group[393] through the international waters of the Miyako Strait

---

391. As a point of reference, total American casualties during the Vietnam War totaled 47,424.

392. Crews from a total of five US aircraft carriers tested positive for COVID-19.

393. The Liaoning Aircraft carrier naval battle group also consisted of two destroyers, two frigates, and one combat support ship

off the coast of Taiwan on the immediate tails of the US Navy's temporary withdrawal. Chinese naval activities coincided with China's State Council's official declaration on April 18, 2020 that the prefectural-level city of Sansha (under Hainan province and located on Yongxing Island in the South China China) now 'administers waters in the South China Sea'. Presumably, Beijing perceived an opportunity to strike amid the COVID-19 outbreak when other claimant states were distracted. In the scenario of a future global pandemic outbreak, it is not inconceivable that the PLA and the Chinese Coast Guard may take advantage of a strategic vacuum again when the maritime forces of its geostrategic rivals are disrupted by a lethal and contagious virus. In this regard, highly capable Chinese virology labs will have a dual civilian-military function: protecting both the general civilian population and enabling the military (to exercise its strategic and tactical options).

Conclusion

This book has identified and analyzed some of the key institutions and top researchers that are engaged in dangerous pathogen studies, especially with GoF studies. This book has mapped out the networks of international collaboration related to these studies or researchers in order to generate clarity regarding the scale and flow of the operations and greater precision regarding specific imminent dangers.

These dangerous studies have been glorified by their proponents as a way to better understand pathogens and develop vaccines and drugs. However, during the process, these scientists have created more dangerous pathogens that further threaten the health of humans and animals both within China and internationally. An outbreak of a dangerous pathogen, whether from natural zoonotic infection, laboratory leak incident, or a release of a biological weapon, has the recently-demonstrated propensity to become a major global disaster. Therefore, we need to be more stringent in monitoring, controlling or prohibiting such dangerous research. In the process of promoting the development of biotechnology, we must first guard the most basic medical ethics and the ethics of researchers.

We can have an open mind to embrace international collaboration in the scientific, medical or public health research arena. However, at the same time, we cannot be naive to assume that nobody or no government has maligned intentions and objectives. A layer of national or international security needs to be established to have better oversight, which is particularly needed when dealing with a dictatorship with hostile global ambitions like the CCP.

ANNEX

Annex A: The Data Abyss Platform - Identifying Emerging Threats and Security Risks

Annex B: WIV Transnational Linkages Network Graph

Annex C: Transnational Linkages of HVRI

Annex D: Aggregated Institutional Linkages of the Chinese Academy of Medical Sciences and Peking Union Medical College (CAMS/ PUMC)

Annex E: Aggregated Institutional Linkages of the Institute of Pathogen Biology

Annex F: Overall Institutional Linkages of the Institute of Pathogen Biology's Christophe Merieux Lab (CAMS/PUMC)

Annex G: ggregated Institutional Linkages of the Guangzhou Institute of Respiratory Health/Huyan Institute

Annex H: Aggregated Institutional Linkages of the Academy of Military Medical Sciences

Annex I: Surfaced High-Risk Linkages of the Academy of Military Medical Sciences

Annex J: Keywords Cloud of Strategic Academy of Military Medical Sciences Partner Organizations Based on Joint S&T Publications and Joint Grant Awards

Annex K: Overall Institutional Linkages of Institute of Virology and Microbiology (AMMS)

Annex L: All Key Institutional Linkages Between the UTMB Galveston and Chinese Virology Research Institutes

Annex M: Overall Institutional Linkages of Chinese CDC

Annex N: Strategic-Level Organizational Diagram of Chinese Domestic High-Risk Pathogen Research Institutes

Annex A: The Data Abyss Platform - Identifying Emerging Threats and Security Risks

Data Abyss (https://www.dataabyss.ai/) is our strategic intelligence and knowledge representation capability for assessing China's science and technology roadmaps and China's technology ecosystem. Data Abyss delivers an advanced analytics search experience for all users through the world's only search-based scientific intelligence platform for Chinese science and technology intelligence. The Data Abyss Platform is the powered by the Data Abyss Science and Technology Data Model, it coherently blends:

- Full-text search with support for misspellings, phonetics, relevance ranking, highlighting and more
- Business intelligence and scientific visualizations
  Relational set-to-set navigation and drilldowns: pivot operation across connected big datasets
- Link analysis allows you to explore the connections in your data
- Geo/Temporal analysis to allow multi-layer, interactive maps and time analysis

Data Abyss tags entities with risk and impact indicators that are associated with known and potentially unknown risky and impactful entities. Data Abyss identifies risk by leveraging reference data sets of entities from U.S. Department of Commerce-tracked Military End Users (MEU) & Entity Lists (EL), Federal Communications Commission's Covered Lists (CL), and entities tracked by the Australia Strategic Policy Institute (ASPI). Data Abyss leverages Artificial Intelligence-assisted processing techniques to track down PLA affiliates and linked transnational entities. Very High-Risk entities are tagged to track the entities' connections with already-tracked entities by the U.S. Department of Commerce, Federal Communications Commission, and ASPI. Extreme Risk entities are tagged to track the entities' connections to PLA military units. Extreme Risk entities are marked with a deep purple node which denotes entities connections to PLA military units. This key is leveraged in the graphs to highlight these distinctions between Extreme Risk and Very High-Risk entities.

These holistic views of the organizational targeting spectrum allow for in-depth analysis and understandings of:
- Active recruitment of American virologists and other related scientists by Chinese entities
- Chinese research on reverse engineering research for virology-related technologies
- American corporate and university research with sanctioned Chinese state-owned enterprises
- Unidentified Chinese virology organizations and associated research partnerships with sanctioned Chinese state-owned enterprises
- The increasing dual-use virology capabilities in China, including both state and non-state actors, and the demonstrated willingness of these parties to collaborate or transact with each other

Powered by Elasticsearch, Data Abyss offers a strong foundation for unstructured Chinese science and technology intelligence content search and analysis, including visual topic clustering. The exploration happens in real time (with no pre-processing) and works effectively on live streaming data and investigation-specific content subsets such as science and technology intelligence-related organizations, keywords, authors/inventors, topics, and/or grant funding information.

Data Abyss allows technology analysts, operators, and researchers to identify opportunities and challenges across any technology specialty or scientific domain to include robotics, space, blockchain, mobile networks, software supply chain, biotechnology, and microelectronics. The platform leverages natural language processing, advanced search queries and capabilities, statistics, and unsupervised machine learning-driven anomaly and outlier detection. The unsupervised machine learning within Data Abyss helps users find patterns in scientific data and use time series modeling to detect anomalies in the data and forecast trends based on historical data. Data Abyss also enables specified analysis on outlier data points that stray from the rest.

For this book, Data Abyss developed analytical methodologies, algorithms, and software platforms to aggregate, label, and synthesize information on Chinese high-risk pathogen research institutes at scale. This process allows for the aggregation of related metadata on people, places, publications, organizations, funding awards and/or grants, risk, and social media profiles to be aggregated on these entities over time-series formatting.

The result is the ability to perform in-depth time-oriented analysis and understanding of the relationships and meaningful correlations that exist across organizational networks. These network graphs have been aggregated and are searchable per specific science and technology domains, topics, components, algorithms, approaches, methodologies, or scientific terms.

The foundational processing to derive these relationships includes science and technology journal publications, research articles, achievements/awards, book chapters, and other collaborative scholarly literature that is processed at scale to derive authors, organizations, technologies, funding names, award numbers, email addresses, web domains, URLs, dates, risk, and other data to derive specific meaning on the scientific articles across the Chinese and English internet and languages. The metadata of these documents was parsed and cleaned before it was extended to other processors that could add value as new datasets. Affiliation name cleaning as well as other cleaners allowed for precision aggregation techniques once that data is ready to be augmented. These organization affiliations allow for holistic views across the entire science and technology spectrum to:

- Map corporate networks to mitigate direct/indirect foreign influence
- Map research networks to surface organizational relationships that are involved in high-risk virology research
- Cross-reference PLA-affiliated via open-source publications

- Identify undisclosed links to foreign military, intelligence, and recruitment programs

Once the article processing and aggregation functions are completed, the articles, organizations, and associated metadata are then aggregated at scale, with an in-memory representational graph approach. This graph derives the relationships across documents and time from Chinese-language open-source data. This massive scale process allows for the generation of a near-complete aggregated picture of every Chinese entity relationship across the entire science and technology spectrum. This entity representation of every relationship describes the current state organizational network. This computationally intensive process would be nearly impossible for analyst teams to manually derive as the relationships across Chinese strategic science and technology organizations contain up to billions of connections. The net result of this approach is that all entities' relationships can be automatically known over a specific time-series. Through the Data Abyss analytical platform, an analyst can quickly query (for example) AMMS, which gives analysts the results of every author, coauthor, organizational affiliation, article title, date, keyword, known high-risk relationships, grant funds, and other data that has ever been directly associated with AMMS. This results in thousands of data points per organization.

Annex B: Overall Institutional Linkages of Wuhan Institute of Virology

Domestic Linkages of the Wuhan Institute of Virology

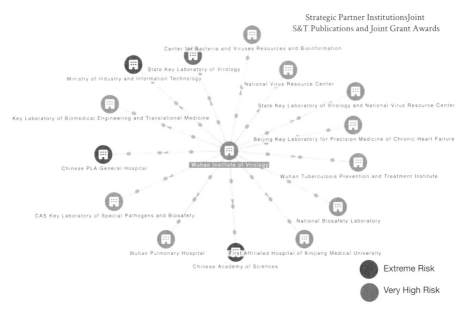

The top identified domestic WIV-affiliated organizations by count metrics are as follows:

University of Chinese Academy of Sciences	1st
Center for Biosafety Mega-Science	2nd
Beijing Key Laboratory for Precision Medicine of Chronic Heart Failure	3rd
CAS Key Laboratory of Special Pathogens and Biosafety	4th
Center for Bacteria and Viruses Resources and Bioinformation	5th
Chinese PLA General Hospital	6th
Key Laboratory of Biomedical Engineering and Translational Medicine	7th

Transnational Linkages of Wuhan Institute of Virology

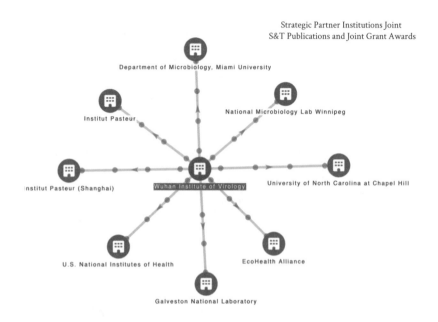

The top identified transnational WIV-affiliated organizations by count metrics are as follows:

Institut Pasteur (Shanghai)	1st
National Microbiology Lab (Winnipeg)	2nd
University of North Carolina at Chapel Hill	3rd
Institut Pasteur (Paris)	4th
EcoHealth Alliance	5th
U.S. National Institutes of Health	6th
Galveston National Laboratory	7th
Department of Microbiology, Miami University	8th

Annex C: Overall Institutional Linkages of Harbin Veterinary Research Institute

Domestic Linkages of Harbin Veterinary Research Institute

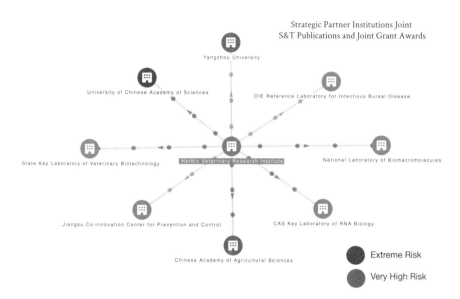

The top identified domestic HVRI-affiliated organizations by count metrics are as follows:

State Key Laboratory of Veterinary Biotechnology	1st
Chinese Academy of Agricultural Sciences	2nd
CAS Key Laboratory of RNA Biology	3rd
University of Chinese Academy of Sciences	4th
Yangzhou University	5th
National Laboratory of Biomacromolecules	6th
OIE Reference Laboratory for Infectious Bursal Disease	7th
Jiangsu Co-innovation Center for Prevention and Control	8th

Transnational Linkages of Harbin Veterinary Research Institute

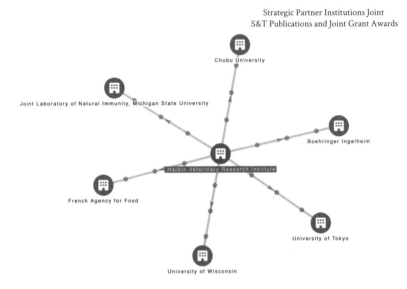

The top identified transnational HVRI-affiliated organizations by count metrics are as follows:

Chubu University	1st
Joint Laboratory of Natural Immunity, Michigan State University	2nd
University of Wisconsin	3rd
University of Tokyo	4th
Boehringer Ingelheim	5th
French Agency for Food	6th

Annex D: Overall Institutional Linkages of the Chinese Academy of Medical Sciences and Peking Union Medical College (CAMS/PUMC)

Domestic Linkages of the Chinese Academy of Medical Sciences

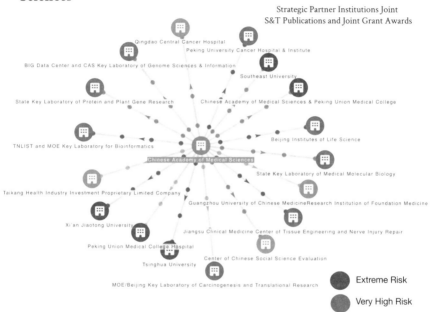

The top identified domestic CAMS-affiliated organizations by count metrics are as follows:

Peking Union Medical College	1st
Peking Union Medical College, Institute of Medical Information, CAMS	2nd
Department of Biomedical Engineering, Institute of Basic Medicine, CAMS	3rd
TNLIST and MOE Key Laboratory for Bioinformatics	4th
Tsinghua University	5th

Xi'an Jiantong University	6th
Peking University Cancer Hospital & Institute	7th
Beijing Institute of Lifeomics	8th
Institute of Military Cognition and Brain Sciences, Academy of Military Medical Sciences	9th
State Key Laboratory of Protein and Plant Gene Research	10th
Southeast University	11th
Big Data Center and CAS Key Laboratory of Genome Sciences & Information	12th
State Key Laboratory of Medical Molecular Biology	13th
National Cardiovascular Center, CAMS	13th
Jiangsu Clinical Medicine Center of Tissue Engineering and Nerve Injury Repair	14th

Transnational Linkages of the Chinese Academy of Medical

Sciences
The top identified transnational CAMS-affiliated organizations by count metrics are as follows:

Johns Hopkins University	1st
Columbia University	2nd
Saint Louis University	3rd
University of Delaware	4th
University of Texas Medical Branch at Galveston	5th
Christophe Merieux Laboratory	6th
CML GABRIEL Network	7th
Erasmus University of Holland	8th
Oxford University	9th
University of Queensland	10th
United States Army Medical Research and Materiel Command, Fort Detrick	11th

Annex E: Overall Institutional Linkages of the Institute of Pathogen Biology

Domestic Linkages of the Institute of Pathogen Biology

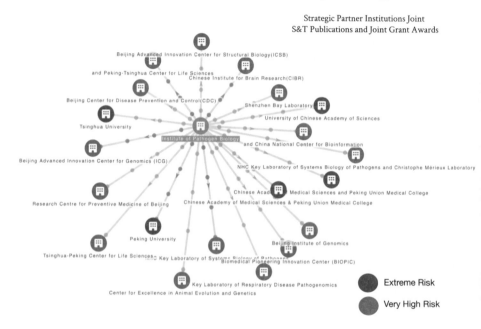

The top identified domestic Institute of Pathogen Biology-affiliated organizations by count metrics are as follows:

Chinese Academy of Medical Sciences and Peking Union Medical College	1st
Beijing Advanced Innovation Center for Genomics (ICG)	2nd
Beijing Advanced Innovation Center for Structural Biology (ICSB)	3rd
Beijing Center for Disease Prevention and Control (China CDC)	4th
Beijing Institute of Genomics	5th
Center for Excellence in Animal Evolution and Genetics	6th
Chinese Institute for Brain Research (CIBR)	7th

Collaborative Innovation Center for Diagnosis and Treatment of Infectious Diseases	8th
Key Laboratory of Respiratory Disease Pathogenomics	9th
Ministry of Health Key Laboratory of Systems Biology of Pathogens	10th
National Health Commission Key Laboratory of Systems Biology of Pathogens	11th
Chinese Academy of Sciences Key Laboratory of Zoological Systematics and Evolution, Institute of Zoology	12th
Chinese Academy of Sciences Center for Biosafety Megascience	13th

Transnational Linkages of the Institute of Pathogen Biology

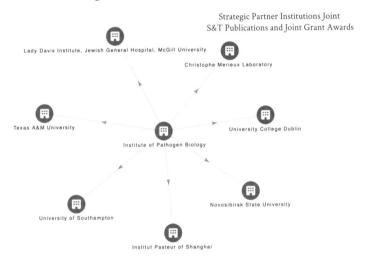

The top identified transnational Institute of Pathogen Biology-affiliated organizations by count metrics are as follows:

Christophe Merieux Laboratory	1st
Institut Pasteur of Shanghai	2nd
University of Southampton	3rd
Lady David Institute, Jewish General Hospital, McGill University	4th
Texas A&M University	5th
Novosibirsk State University	6th
University College Dublin	7th

Annex F: Overall Institutional Linkages of the Institute of Pathogen Biology's Christophe Merieux Lab (CAMS/PUMC)

Domestic Linkages of Christophe Merieux Laboratory, Institute of Pathogen Biology (CAMS)

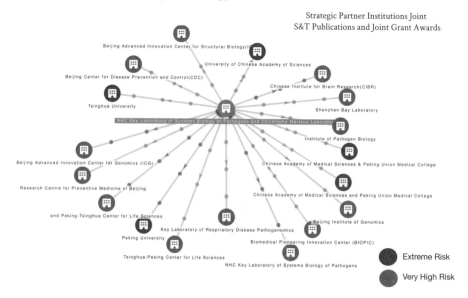

Strategic Partner Institutions Joint
S&T Publications and Joint Grant Awards

Extreme Risk

Very High Risk

The top identified domestic Christophe Merieux Laboratory-affiliated organizations by count metrics are as follows:

Beijing Advanced Innovation Center for Genomics (ICG)	1st
Beijing Advanced Innovation Center for Structural Biology (ICSB)	2nd
Beijing Center for Disease Prevention and Control (CDC)	3rd
Beijing Institute of Genomics	4th
Center for Excellence in Animal Evolution and Genetics	5th
Chinese Institute for Brain Research (CIBR)	6th
Key Laboratory of Respiratory Disease Pathogenomics	7th
NHC Key Laboratory of Systems Biology of Pathogens	8th
Biomedical Pioneering Innovation Center (BIOPIC)	9th

China National Center for Bioinformation	10th
Shenzhen Bay Laboratory	11th
Chinese Academy of Medical Sciences & Peking Union Medical College	12th

Transnational Linkages of the Christophe Merieux Lab, Institute of Pathogen Biology (CAMS)

The top identified transnational Christophe Merieux Laboratory-affiliated organizations by count metrics are as follows:

Rodolphe Merieux Laboratory	1st
Institut Pasteur of Shanghai	2nd
Aix-Marseille University	3rd
University of Southampton	4th
King George's Medical University (Lucknow, India)	5th
Lao Tropical Public Health Institute	6th
Instituto Oswaldo Cruz (Rio De Janeiro, Brazil)	7th
Institute of Tropical Medicine, University of Sao Paulo	8th
Centre d'Infectiologie Clinique Charles Merieux	9th

Annex G: Overall Institutional Linkages of the Guangzhou Institute of Respiratory Health/Huyan Institute

Domestic Linkages of the Guangzhou Institute of Respiratory Health

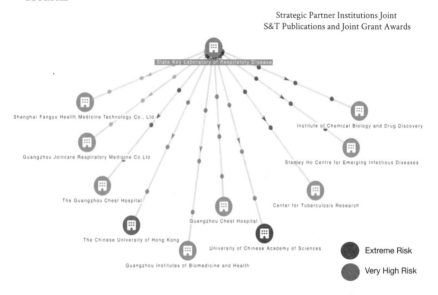

Strategic Partner Institutions Joint
S&T Publications and Joint Grant Awards

The top identified domestic Guangzhou Institute of Respiratory Health/Huyan Institute-affiliated organizations by count metrics are as follows:

Guangzhou Medical University	1st
Guangzhou Baiyunshan Hutchison Whampoa Chinese Medicine Co., Ltd.	2nd
Kunming Medical University	3rd
Wuhan Institute of Virology	4th
Ministry of Health Key Laboratory of Medical Virology and Viral Diseases, Institute of Viral Disease Control	5th
Chinese Center for Disease Control and Prevention (Chinese CDC)	6th

World Health Organization Western Pacific Region Measles/Rubella Reference Laboratory	7th
Department of Respiratory Medicine, 458th Hospital of the People's Liberation Army	8th
General Hospital of the Shenyang Military Region of the People's Liberation Army	9th
People's Liberation Army Organ Transplantation Institute, Eighth Medical Center, General Hospital of the People's Liberation Army (Beijing)	10th
Department of Respiratory Medicine, General Hospital of the Eastern Theater Command of the People's Liberation Army	11th
Shanghai Fangyu Health Medicine Technology Co., Ltd.	12th
Shanghai Frontier Health Pharmaceutical Technology Co., Ltd.	13th
Guangzhou Joincare Respiratory Medicine Co., Ltd.	14th

Transnational Linkages of the Guangzhou Institute of Respiratory Health

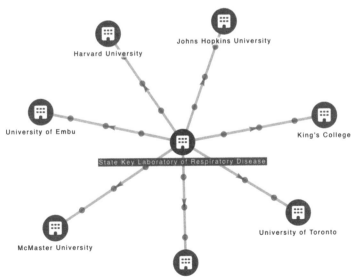

Strategic Partner Institutions Joint
S&T Publications and Joint Grant Awards

The top identified transnational Guangzhou Institute of Respiratory Health/Huyan Institute-affiliated organizations by count metrics are as follows:

Harvard University	1st
Johns Hopkins University	2nd
University of Embu (Nairobi, Kenya)	3rd
Stony Brook University - State University of New York	4th
King's College London	5th
University of Toronto	6th
Firestone Respiratory Health Research Institute (Hamilton, Canada)	7th
McMaster University (Hamilton, Canada)	8th

Annex H: Overall Institutional Linkages of the Academy of Military Medical Sciences

Domestic Linkages of the Academy of Military Medical Sciences

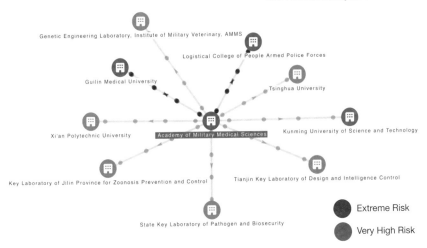

Strategic Partner InstitutionsJoint
S&T Publications and Joint Grant Awards

The top identified domestic AMMS-affiliated organizations by count metrics are as follows:

Academy of Military Medical Sciences (itself)	1st
Department of Virology, State Key Laboratory of Pathogen and Biosecurity, Beijing Institute of Microbiology and Epidemiology, AMMS	2nd
Genetic Engineering Laboratory, Institute of Military Veterinary, AMMS	3rd
Institute of Disease Control and Prevention, AMMS	4th
Key Laboratory of Jilin Province for Zoonosis Prevention and Control, Military Veterinary Institute, AMMS	5th
Military Veterinary Institute, AMMS	6th

| State Key Laboratory of Pathogen and Biosecurity, Beijing Institute of Microbiology and Epidemiology, AMMS | 7th |
| State Key Laboratory of Proteomics, Translational Medicine Center of Stem Cells, 307-Ivy Translational Medicine Center, Laboratory of Oncology, Affiliated Hospital, AMMS | 8th |

Transnational Linkages of the Academy of Military Medical Sciences

Strategic Partner InstitutionsJoint
S&T Publications and Joint Grant Awards

The top identified transnational links of the Academy of Military Medical Sciences-affiliated organizations by count metrics are as follows:

University of Texas Medical Branch (Galveston, Texas)	1st
University of Buffalo - The State University of New York	2nd
Department of Chemistry and Biochemistry - University of Texas at Austin	3rd
National Microbiology Lab (Winnipeg, Canada)	4th
Creighton University School of Medicine (Omaha, Nebraska)	5th
CanSino Biologics (Hong Kong)	6th
Biomedical Discovery Institute, Department of Microbiology, Monash University (Melbourne, Australia)	7th
Department of Anatomy and Physiology, College of Veterinary Medicine, Kansas State University	8th
United States Army Research Institute of Infectious Diseases	9th
Department of Biomedical Sciences, Mercer University School of Medicine (Macon, Georgia)	10th

Annex I: Surfaced High-Risk Linkages of the Academy of Military Medical Sciences

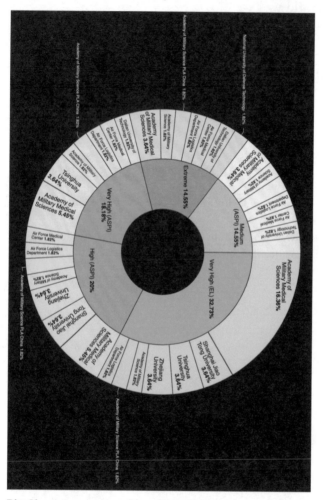

Pie Chart Annotation: Identified AMMS high-risk organizational relationships based on data provided by the U.S. Department of Commerce's Bureau of Industry and Security (BIS) Entity List and the Australian Strategic Policy Institute (ASPI). Natural Language Processing (NLP) techniques have been used to automatically identify PLA organizations derived from joint Science and Technology publications and joint grant awards which are tagged as extreme risks.

Annex J: Keywords Cloud of Strategic Academy of Military Medical Sciences Partner Organizations Based on Joint Science and Technology Publications and Joint Grant Awards

Keywords Cloud Annotation: The keyword cloud tracks specific domain areas that have been prioritized by the AMMS-subordinated organizations that are the most active in terms of Science and Technology publications and joint grant awards.

Annex K: Overall Institutional Linkages of Institute of Virology and Microbiology (AMMS)

Domestic Linkages of the Institute of Virology and Microbiology (AMMS)

Strategic Partner InstitutionsJoint
S&T Publications and Joint Grant Awards

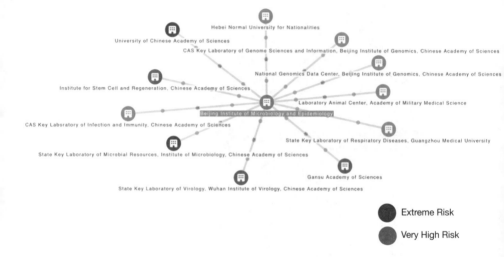

The top identified domestic Institute of Virology and Microbiology (AMMS)-affiliated organizations by count metrics are as follows:

State Key Laboratory of Pathogen and Biosecurity, Beijing Institute of Microbiology and Epidemiology	1st
Science and Technology on Parallel and Distributed Processing Laboratory	2nd
Beijing Genomics Institute -Shenzhen	3rd
Beijing Engineering Research Center of Protein and Antibody, Sinocelltech Ltd.	4th

Beijing Key Laboratory of Monoclonal Antibody Research and Development, Sino Biological Inc.	5th
CAS Key Laboratory of Genome Sciences and Information, Beijing Institute of Genomics, Chinese Academy of Sciences	6th
CAS Key Laboratory of Infection and Immunity, Institute of Biophysics, Chinese Academy of Sciences	7th
Laboratory Animal Center, Academy of Military Medical Science	8th
National Institute for Viral Disease Control and Prevention, Chinese Center for Disease Control and Prevention	9th
PLA Strategic Support Force Medical Center	10th
School of Computer Science National University of Defense Technology	11th
The Central Laboratory of Health Quarantine, Shenzhen Travel Healthcare Center, Shenzhen Entry-Exit Inspection and Quarantine Bureau	12th

Transnational Linkages of the Institute of Virology and Microbiology (AMMS)

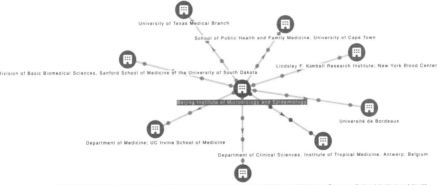

Strategic Partner Institutions Joint S&T Publications and Joint Grant Awards

University of Texas Medical Branch

School of Public Health and Family Medicine, University of Cape Town

Division of Basic Biomedical Sciences, Sanford School of Medicine of the University of South Dakota

Lindsley F. Kimball Research Institute; New York Blood Center

Beijing Institute of Microbiology and Epidemiology

Université de Bordeaux

Department of Medicine; UC Irvine School of Medicine

Department of Clinical Sciences, Institute of Tropical Medicine, Antwerp, Belgium

Biostatistics Research Branch, Division of Clinical Research, National Institute of Allergy and Infectious Diseases, National Institutes of Health

The top identified transnational links of Institute of Virology and Microbiology (AMMS)-affiliated organizations by count metrics are as follows:

University of Texas Medical Branch (Galveston, Texas)	1st
Lindsley F. Kimball Research Institute, New York Blood Center	2nd
Universite de Bordeaux	3rd
Biostatistics Research Branch, National Institute of Allergy and Infectious Diseases, National Institutes of Health	4th
Department of Medicine, UC Irvine School of Medicine	5th
School of Public Health and Family Medicine, University of Cape Town	6th
Division of Basic Biomedical Sciences, Sanford School of Medicine of the University of South Dakota	7th
Department of Clinical Sciences, Institute of Tropical Medicine (Antwerp, Belgium)	8th

Annex L: All Key Institutional Linkages Between the University of Texas Medical Branch at Galveston and Chinese Virology Research Institutes

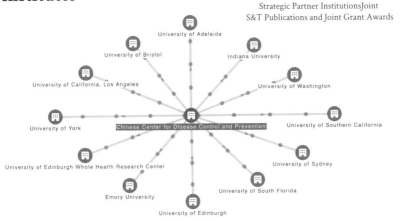

Strategic Partner Institutions Joint
S&T Publications and Joint Grant Awards

The top identified UTMB Galveston-affiliated organizations in China by count metrics are as follows:

Anhui Province Center for Disease Control and Prevention	1st
Department of Gastroenterology and Hepatology, Chinese PLA General Hospital	2nd
Department of Gastroenterology, Chinese Navy General Hospital	3rd
Department of Internal Medicine, Chinese PLA General Hospital	4th
Jinan Junqu Center for Disease Control and Prevention	5th
School of Public Health, Shandong University	6th
School of Pharmacy, Sun Yat-Sen University	7th
State Key Laboratory of Infectious Disease Control and Prevention China Center for Disease Control and Prevention Institute for Infectious Disease Control and Prevention	8th
Peking Union Medical College Hospital	9th
Department of Pathology, Zhongnan Hospital, Wuhan University	10th
Department of Pathogen Biology, Wuhan University School of Medicine	11th
Institute of Virology, School of Medicine, Wuhan University	12th

Annex M: Overall Institutional Linkages of Chinese CDC

Domestic Linkages of the Chinese CDC

The top identified domestic Chinese CDC-affiliated organizations in China by count metrics are as follows:

University of Chinese Academy of Sciences	1st
Wuhan University of Science and Technology	2nd
Wuhan University School of Basic Medical Sciences	3rd
Southeast University	4th
Changsha Center for Disease Control and Prevention	5th
Shandong Center for Disease Control and Prevention	6th
Peking University	7th
Shanghai Jiao Tong University School of Medicine	8th
Hubei Provincial Center for Disease Control and Prevention	9th
Yuelu District Center for Disease Control and Prevention	10th
Beijing Runbio Biotechnology Development Co.	11th
WHO Collaborating Center for Malaria	12th

Transnational Linkages of the Chinese CDC

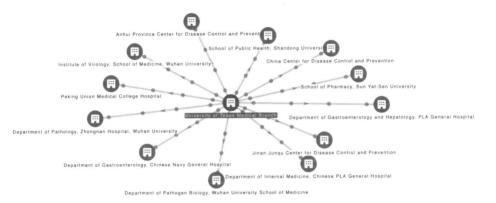

Strategic Partner InstitutionsJoint
S&T Publications and Joint Grant Awards

The top identified transnational Chinese CDC-affiliated organizations in China by count metrics are as follows:

University of Southern California	1st
Emory University	2nd
University of Adelaide	3rd
University of Edinburgh	4th
University of Bristol	5th
Georgia State University	6th
University of South Florida	7th
University of Sydney	8th
University of Washington	9th
Indiana University	10th
University of California, Los Angeles	11th
University of York	12th

Annex N: Strategic-Level Organizational Diagram of Chinese Domestic High-Risk Pathogen Research Institutes

Part I:

Part II:

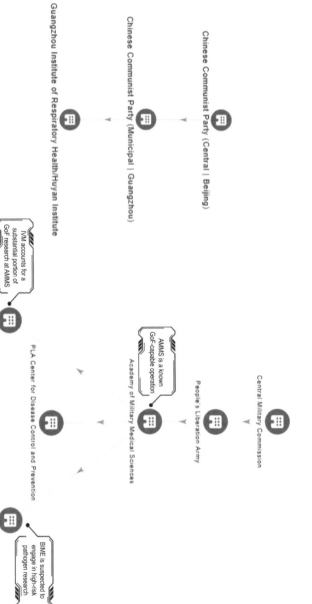

Selected Bibliography

Abouelkhair, Mohammed, 'Non-SARS-CoV-2 genome sequences identified in clinical samples from COVID-19 infected patients: Evidence for co-infections', *PeerJ*. 2 November 2020.

'About the Journal', Journal of Thoracic Disease, AME Publishing Company, Hong Kong.
https://jtd.amegroups.com/about

'About Us - Chinese Academy of Sciences', Chinese Academy of Sciences (CAS).
https://english.cas.cn/about_us/

'About Us – Global Public Health', Chinese Center for Disease Control and Prevention'.
https://www.chinacdc.cn/en/

'About Us - Harbin Veterinary Research Institute', Chinese Academy of Agricultural Sciences (CAAS).
http://www.hvri.ac.cn/en/aboutus/athvri/index.htm

'About Us, Institute of Medical Biology – Chinese Academy of Medical Sciences',
https://www.imbcams.ac.cn/en/aboutus
'About Us: Organizational Chart', Chinese Center for Disease Control and Prevention.
https://www.chinacdc.cn/en/

'About' and 'Organization' pages, Zhong Nanshan Medical Foundation of Guangdong Province, http://www.znsmf.org/jijinhuijianjie/
'Academic Committee,' State Key Laboratory of Respiratory Diseases, posted January 23, 2011, https://web.archive.org/web/20120311175913/http://www.gird.cn/sklrd/Article-144.aspx
'A Cohort of Researchers', State Key Laboratory of Respiratory Disease.
http://www.sklrd.cn/show.php?id=357

Adamson, Blythe, et. al., 'The Potential Cost-Effectiveness of HIV Vaccines: A Systematic Review', *PharmacoEconomics*, March 2017.

'Administration, Wuhan Institute of Virology – Chinese Academy of Sciences', Wuhan Institute of Virology (WIV)
http://english.whiov.cas.cn/About_Us2016/Administration2016/

'A delegation led by Ambassador of France in China visited Institut Pasteur of

Shanghai, CAS', Institut Pasteur-Chinese Academy of Sciences (IPS), 10 December 2020.
http://english.shanghaipasteur.cas.cn/IPIN2016/News2016/201912/t20191210_227526.html

Akst, Jef, 'Lab-Made Coronavirus Triggers Debate', The Scientist, 16 November 2015. Wain-Hobson, Simon 'An Avian H7N1 Gain-of-Function Experiment of Great Concern', mBio, Vol. 5, No. 5, September/October 2014.

Alexander, Harriet, 'Fauci and NIH defend giving $600K to Wuhan to study how viruses can transmit from bats to humans before COVID-19 outbreak - after being accused of funding 'gain of function' research in heated argument with Rand Paul', Mail Online, 26 May 2021.
https://www.dailymail.co.uk/news/article-9618623/Fauci-NIH-confirm-600-000-public-money-went-Wuhan-two-weeks-Rand-Paul-row.html

Allison, Graham, 'What Happened to the Soviet Superpower's Nuclear Arsenal? Clues for the Nuclear Security Summit', Faculty Research Working Paper Series RWP12-038, Harvard Kennedy School of Government, August 2012.

'All provinces in China are asked to set up P3 lab: ministries', Global Times, 20 May 2020.
https://www.globaltimes.cn/content/1188916.shtml

'Always follow the party for the masses' welfare,' Zhong Nanshan Medical Foundation of Guangdong Province, 4 August 2021.
http://www.znsmf.org/news/720.html

'An Introduction of Wu Jieping Fellow', Wu Jieping Medical Foundation,
https://www.wjpmf.org.cn/aboutwjp.html

'A new virus that can infect people has been discovered', Health Commission of Hebei Province, 9 August 2022.http://wsjkw.hebei.gov.cn/wbcz/390125.jhtml

Anthony, Simon, Daszak, Peter, et. al., 'Global patterns in Coronavirus diversity', Virus Evolution, Vol. 3, No. 1, 2017.

'Awardee of Medical Sciences and Materia Medica Prize: Feng Chuanhan', Holeung Ho Lee Foundation,
http://www.hlhl.org.cn/english/showsub.asp?id=414

' 中國醫學科學院病原生物學研究所 '.
中國醫學科學院病原生物學研究所 _ 百度百科 (baidu.com)

金奇（研究員。男，朝鮮族,）.
金奇（研究員。男，朝鮮族）_ 百度百科 (baidu.com)

'中國人民解放軍軍事醫學科學院 '.
中國人民解放軍軍事醫學科學院 _ 百度百科 (baidu.com)

Bao, Linlin, et. al., 'Novel Avian-Origin Human Influenza A(H7N9) Can Be Transmitted Between Ferrets via Respiratory Droplets', *Journal of Infectious Diseases*, Vol. 209, Issue 4, 15 February 2014.

Bao, Linlin, et. al., 'Transmission of H7N9 influenza virus in mice by different infective routes', *Virology Journal*, Vol. 11, Article No. 185, 2014.

Babu, Judy, 'Nepal allows late-stage trials for Chinese mRNA vaccine candidate – Xinhua', Reuters, 28 August 2021.
https://www.reuters.com/world/asia-pacific/nepal-allows-late-stage-trials-chinese-mrna-vaccine-candidate-xinhua-2021-08-27/

'Beijing CDC Party Committee issued a wartime status order to suspend or remove middle-level cadres that cause major adverse effects on prevention and control', Party Committee of the Beijing Municipal Center for Disease Control and Prevention, 13 February 2020.
http://t.m.china.com.cn/convert/c_k5AE9Pn8.html

'Beijing to build P3 laboratory', Global Times, 18 May 2020.
https://www.globaltimes.cn/content/1188638.shtml

'Bill & Melinda Gates Foundation Dedicates Additional Funding to the Novel Coronavirus Response', Bill & Melinda Gates Foundation, 5 February 2020.
https://www.gatesfoundation.org/ideas/media-center/press-releases/2020/02/bill-and-melinda-gates-foundation-dedicates-additional-funding-to-the-novel-coronavirus-response

Bioexpo – China 2021, 'The 4th China International BioPharma Conference & Exhibition', 19-21 September 2021.
http://www.cajc-china.com/?_l=en

Blackwell, Tom, 'Dismissal and investigation by RCMP of Winnipeg co-inventor of Ebola drug stuns colleagues', National Post, 16 July 2019.
https://nationalpost.com/news/canada/dismissal-and-investigation-by-rcmp-of-winnipeg-co-inventor-of-ebola-drug-stuns-colleagues

Blackwell, Tom, 'In mystery investigation of two Canadian scientists, a request for

Ebola, henipavirus from the Wuhan lab', National Post, 5 May 2020.
https://nationalpost.com/news/covid-19-pandemic-wuhan-institute-of-virology-ebola-national-microbiology-laboratory

Boehringer Ingelheim, 'Boehringer Ingelheim and Harbin Veterinary Research Institute set up 'industry-academia-research' exchange platform', 10 May 2019.
https://www.boehringer-ingelheim.com/press-release/new-exchange-platform-harbin-research-institute

Bo, Tang, 'Coronavirus Pandemic: Last assisting medical team leaves Wuhan', CGTN, 16 April 2020.
https://news.cgtn.com/news/34497a4e78514464776c6d636a4e6e62684a4856/index.html

Brazelton, Mary Augusta, 'Western Medical Education on Trial: The Endurance of Peking Union Medical College, 1949–1985'. Twentieth-Century China, Vol. 40, Issue 2, 2015.
'Brief introduction of Academician Zhong Nanshan', Guangzhou Institute of Respiratory Disease Academician Column, 2 August 2011, archived at https://web.archive.org/web/20120825010142/http://www.gird.cn/girdweb/Article-460.aspx
'Building leadership and establishing brand reputation, without forgetting the mission of serving people: Commemorating the first Party branch's pioneering deeds made by the Guangzhou Institute of Respiratory Health in the First Affiliated Hospital of GUANGZHOU Medical University', Guangzhou Institute of Respiratory Health, 5 June 2019.
http://www.gird.cn/show.php?id=62

Burke, Kelly, 'Australian CSIRO in Geelong linked to coronavirus 'bat laboratory' theory', 7 News, 28 April 2020.
https://7news.com.au/news/world/australian-csiro-in-geelong-linked-to-coronavirus-bat-laboratory-theory--c-1002195

Business Wire, 'Top Virologists of the Global Virus Network (GVN) Meet in China to Address Threats',12 May 2015.
https://www.businesswire.com/news/home/20150512006108/en/Top-Virologists-Global-Virus-Network-GVN-Meet

Cai, Jane, 'Shanghai needs food, not TCM Covid-19 medicine Lianhua Qingwen: medical experts', South China Morning Post, 20 April 2022.
https://www.scmp.com/news/china/science/article/3174746/shanghai-needs-food-not-tcm-covid-19-medicine-lianhua-qingwen

Cantoni, Diego, et. al., 'Pseudotyped Bat Coronavirus RaTG13 is efficiently neutralised by convalescent sera from SARS-CoV-2 infected patients', *Communications Biology*, Vol. 5, No. 409, 3 May 2022.

Cao, Zinan, 'Respiratory expert Zhong Nanshan's latest views on COVID-19', China Daily, 15 April 2020. https://covid-19.chinadaily.com.cn/a/202004/15/WS5e96cdbaa3105d50a3d16765_2. html

'CAS-NAS Workshop on Emerging Infections and Global Health Security Held', Beijing Institutes of Life Sciences, Chinese Academy of Sciences, 1 October 2015. http://english.biols.cas.cn/news/news/201701/t20170109_173250.html

Center for Infectious Disease Research and Policy (CIDRP), 'Dutch researcher resumes H5N1 transmission studies', University of Minnesota, 28 February 2013. https://www.cidrap.umn.edu/news-perspective/2013/02/flu-news-scan-resuming-h5n1-research-h7n3-mexico-fda-flu-strain-selections

Chakraborty, Sandeep, 'There was a simultaneous outbreak of the zoonotic Nipah henipavirus in Wuhan - 4 out of 5 patients have the virus in Jinyintan Hospital, along withSARS-Cov2, in their metagenome - which seems to have resolved by itself', OSF, 1 October 2020.

Chan, Alina and Ridley, Matt, *Viral: The Search for the Origin of COVID-19*, Harper, November 2021.

Chan, Minnie, 'How China's military took a frontline role in the coronavirus crisis', South China Morning Post, 17 March 2020. https://www.scmp.com/news/china/military/article/3075396/how-chinas-military-took-frontline-role-coronavirus-crisis

Chan, Minnie and Zheng, William, 'Meet the major general on China's coronavirus scientific front line', South China Morning Post, 3 March 2020. https://www.scmp.com/news/china/military/article/3064677/meet-major-general-chinas-coronavirus-scientific-front-line

Chen, Gui-Ling, et. al., 'Safety and immunogenicity of the SARS-CoV-2 ARCoV mRNA vaccine in Chinese adults: a randomized, double-blind, placebo-controlled, phase 1 trial', *The Lancet Microbe*, Vol. 3, Iss. 3, 1 March 2022.

' 在 ' 土地上 ' 默默耕耘的陳華癸 ' (Chen Huagui who works silently on the 'land; Zai Tu Di Shang Mo Mo Geng Yun De Chen Hua Gui)', Xinhua, 6 November 2018. http://www.xinhuanet.com/science/2018-11/06/c_137595169.htm

Chen, Hualan, Kawaoka, Yoshihiro, et. al., 'A Single-Amino-Acid Substitution in the NS1 Protein Changes the Pathogenicity of H5N1 Avian Influenza Viruses in Mice', *Journal of Virology*, Vol. 82, No. 3, February 2008.

Chen, Hualan, Kawaoka, Yoshihiro, et. al., 'A Duck Enteritis Virus-Vectored Bivalent Live Vaccine Provides Fast and Complete Protection against H5N1 Avian Influenza Virus Infection in Ducks', *Journal of Virology*, Vol. 85, No. 21, November 2011.

Chen, Hualan, et. al., 'H5N1 Hybrid Viruses Bearing 2009/H1N1 Virus Genes Transmit in Guinea Pigs by Respiratory Droplet', *Science*, Vol. 340, No. 6139, 21 June 2013.

Chen, Huanchun, et. al, The 100th *Anniversary of Mr. Chen Huakui's Birth Anthology*, China Science Publishing & Media Ltd. Beijing: 2014.

'Chen Rongchang', Guangzhou Medical University, 5 January 2022.
https://ygc.gzhmu.edu.cn/info/1121/1632.htm

Cheung, Tai Ming, *Fortifying China: The Struggle to Build a Dual-Use Economy*, Cornell University Press, 2019.

'China builds new plant for IMBCAMS COVID-19 vaccine -state media', Reuters, 9 June 2021.
https://www.reuters.com/world/asia-pacific/china-builds-new-plant-imbcams-covid-19-vaccine-state-media-2021-06-09/

'China CDC', Bill and Melinda Gates Foundation, May 2020.
https://www.gatesfoundation.org/about/committed-grants/2020/05/inv005832

'China flaunts French connection to Wuhan lab; Ambivalent on WHO probe into origin of coronavirus', Economic Times, 7 May 2020.
https://economictimes.indiatimes.com/news/international/world-news/china-flaunts-french-connection-to-wuhan-lab-ambivalent-on-who-probe-into-origin-of-coronavirus/articleshow/75600806.cms?utm_source=contentofinterest&utm_medium=text&utm_campaign=cppst

'China Focus: China inaugurates national administration of disease prevention and control', Xinhua, 13 May 2021.
http://www.xinhuanet.com/english/2021-05/13/c_139943875_2.htm

曠野青春 | 隱形防綫（英文字幕版）, China Science Communication, Broadcasted on CCTV on 10 December 2019.
https://www.youtube.com/watch?v=ovnUyTRMERI

'潛心苦鑽研 十年磨一劍：記我的同窗好友陳薇博士', 中國青年科技 [China Youth Science and Technology], Vol. 12, 2003.

'鐘南山', Chinese Academy of Engineering, 7 March 2017. https://web.archive.org/web/20170306224833/http:/www.cae.cn/cae/jsp/introduction.jsp?oid=20111231115352671145511

'組織機構', Chinese Academy of Medical Sciences. http://www.cams.ac.cn/yxgk/zzjg/index.htm

'Chinese Academy of Medical Sciences and Peking Union Medical College are seeking global talents', NatureCareers, 2022. https://www.nature.com/naturecareers/employer/79137

'非典科技向你宣戰（图', Chinese Academy of Sciences, 2 May 2003. https://www.cas.cn/zt/kjzt/fdgx/ggqy/200305/t20030502_1709485.shtml

'Chinese scientist Huang Kexue jailed for trade theft', BBC, 22 December 2011. https://www.bbc.com/news/business-16297237

'Christophe Merieux Laboratory', Merieux Foundation. https://www.fondation-merieux.org/en/what-we-do/enhancing-research-capabilities/research-laboratories/christophe-merieux-laboratories/

'Christophe Merieux Laboratory – Beijing, China', Gabriel Network. https://www.gabriel-network.org/laboratoires/christophe-merieux-laboratory/research-activities/?lang=en#menu

'科學家少將' 陳薇', CKNI. https://gb.global.cnki.net/KCMS/detail/detail.aspx?dbcode=CYFD&dbname=CYFD2018&filename=N2018050116001696&uniplatform=OVERSEAS_CHS&v=V5i7DO3LGB-oo9mDEsrJp_wtn8T2Es_CZ7DY4NJKvYbcMFdoZYDUJzVIP27riIINRYmREKBe-_M%3d

'不負時代 不辱使命', 中國新聞發布（實務版）, Vol. 3, 2022. https://gb.global.cnki.net/KCMS/detail/detail.aspx?dbcode=CJFD&dbname=CJFDAUTO&filename=XWSW202203008&uniplatform=OVERSEAS_CHS&v=EHfAJUoXF8U1iQASa4y9dcpgfgUlPTNMl6QZ5UW53tmXIjA_Yg4A3yPkhFSqgTRb

'兩會這一刻', 中國紀檢監察, Vol. 6, 2021. https://gb.global.cnki.net/KCMS/detail/detail.aspx?dbcode=CJFD&dbname=CJFDLAST2021&filename=JANC202106011&uniplatform=OVERSEAS_CHS&v=imqwiUDjtamw0hcW19_2vETH6LZEqhCQnDVSvj83SYzEx0-7LOQqE9ahHrmRdyS_

' 陳薇：軍中女英雄，國家棟梁才 ', 商業文化 , Vol. 19, 2021.
https://gb.global.cnki.net/KCMS/detail/detail.aspx?dbcode=CJFD&dbname=CJFD
LAST2021&filename=SYWH202119008&uniplatform=OVERSEAS_CHS&v=YHN-
_0PpaIaIF-MWvC1uVBjbEEjLGX7sH3VvE8t80PP1b9beJ5u4KCIJfkd3jnS4

' 陳微：從清華女神到護國戰神 ', 商業文化 , Vol. 9, 2020.
https://gb.global.cnki.net/KCMS/detail/detail.aspx?dbcode=CJFD&dbname=CJFDLA
SN2020&filename=DXNB202009020&uniplatform=OVERSEAS_CHS&v=OkyRO4zZ
ul7Mpx48ojvfTyBzNFQrQh5J8EjcxiUaR3BNoNhFVmSyTVUCjBjhCdQ0

' 潛心苦鑽研 十年磨一劍 —— 記我的同窗好友陳薇博士 ', 中國青年科技 , Vol.
12, 2003.
https://gb.global.cnki.net/KCMS/detail/detail.aspx?dbcode=CJFD&dbname=CJFDN
7904&filename=QNKJ200312004&uniplatform=OVERSEAS_CHS&v=Za9fP-KpdN_
ybcCaqXh6e7e7w9FxyhRg_cG5E8iBcRlWzONBfB4_0y6axxYAPzhR

Clarke, Ryan, 'The International Frontier of the CCP's Bioweapons Program: Wuhan
Institute of Virology, Chinese Academy of Medical Sciences, and the Pakistan Army's
Defence Science and Technology Organization', The Klaxon, 14 April 2022.
https://static1.squarespace.com/static/5de08d699f40c13aa68de2ee/t/6257ac00eb8d8d
7ccddc5eba/1649912833748/The+Emerging+Frontier+of+the+CCP+Bioweapons+Pr
ogram+-+Dr+Ryan+Clarke.+14+April+2020.pdf

Clarke, Ryan, Lam, Peng Er, and Lin, Xiaoxu, 'High-Risk Virology Research at the
Chinese Academy of Medical Sciences and Peking Union Medical College', EAI
Background Brief No. 1642, 24 March 2022.

Clarke, Ryan, 'Emerging Global Pandemic Risks Come from Engineered Viruses in
Chinese Labs, Not the Jungle or Bat Caves', Epoch Times, 4 September 2021.
https://www.theepochtimes.com/emerging-pandemic-risks-come-from-engineered-
viruses-in-chinese-labs-not-the-jungle-or-bat-caves_3980204.html

Clarke, Ryan and Lam, Peng Er, 'Coronavirus Research Networks in China: Origins,
International Linkages and Consequences', Center for Non-Traditional Security
Studies, May 2021, Singapore.
https://rsis-ntsasia.org/wp-content/uploads/2021/06/NTS-Asia-Monograph-
Coronavirus-Research-in-China-by-Ryan-Clarke-and-Lam-Peng-Er-May2021-1.pdf

Clarke, Ryan, 'Is China Converting COVID-19 Into a Strategic Opportunity?', EAI
Background Brief No. 1545, 9 July 2020.

Cohen, Jon, 'China's vaccine gambit', Science, Vol. 370, Iss. 6522, 11 December 2020.
https://www.science.org/doi/10.1126/science.370.6522.1263

'Committed Grants: Institute of Medical Biology, Chinese Academy of Medical Sciences', Bill & Melinda Gates Foundation, November 2015 and April 2012. https://www.gatesfoundation.org/about/committed-grants/2015/11/opp1130833 and https://www.gatesfoundation.org/about/committed-grants/2012/04/opp1049425

'Coronavirus Timeline', Hudson Institute, 13 August 2021. https://www.hudson.org/features/coronavirus
'Coronavirus: Trump stands by China lab origin theory for virus', BBC, 1 May 2020. https://www.bbc.com/news/world-us-canada-52496098

'COVID-19 vaccine reaches phase-2 trials in China', Xinhua, 22 June 2020. http://english.nmpa.gov.cn/2020-06/22/c_502093.htm

Croddy, Eric, 'China's Role in the Chemical and Biological Disarmament Regimes', *The Nonproliferation Review*. Spring 2002.

Crowe, Kelly, 'Saudi coronavirus work stymied at Canadian lab', CBC News, 29 May 2013.

Cui, Jie, Li, Fang, and Shi Zhengli, 'Origin and evolution of pathogenic coronaviruses', *Nature Reviews Microbiology*, Vol. 17, December 2018.

Curtis, Kristopher, Yount, Boyd, and Baric, Ralph, United States Patent, Patent No: US 7,279,327 B2, Date of Application: 19 April 2022, Date of Patent Grant: 9 October 2007. https://patentimages.storage.googleapis.com/a8/c0/6a/0584dd67435ef2/US7279327.pdf

Daszak, Peter, Mazet, Jonna, Shi, Zhengli, et. al., 'Joint China-US Call for Employing a Transdisciplinary Approach to Emerging Infectious Diseases', *Ecohealth*, Vol. 12, No. 4, 2015.

Daszak, Peter, et. al., 'Global hotspots and correlates of emerging zoonotic diseases', *Nature Communications*, Vol. 8, No.1124, 24 October 2017.

Daszak, Peter, et. al., 'A strategy to prevent future epidemics similar to the 2019-nCoV outbreak', *Biosafety and Health*, Vol. 2, No. 1, March 2020.

Daszak, Peter, 'Ignore the conspiracy theories: scientists know Covid-19 wasn't created in a lab', The Guardian, 9 June 2020.

Dazsak, Peter, Epstein, Jonathan, et. al., 'Understanding One Health through biological and behavioral risk surveillance in Liberia: a cross-sectional study', *The Lancet*, Global

Health, Meeting Abstracts, Volume 10, Special Issue 22, 1 March 2022.

Daszak, Peter, 'Understanding the Risk of Bat Coronavirus Emergence', NIH Grant Database.
https://grantome.com/grant/NIH/R01-AI110964-06

Demaneuf, Giles, 'BSL-4 laboratories in China: Kunming, Wuhan, Harbin', Medium, 27 April 2022.
https://gillesdemaneuf.medium.com/bsl-4-laboratories-in-china-kunming-wuhan-harbin-109c01d71537

'Designing Quad-Core Loongson-3 Processor', Institute of Computing Technology, Chinese Academy of Sciences, 10 September 2009.
http://english.ict.cas.cn/rh/rps/200909/t20090910_36875.html

'Director of IPB', IPB, CAMS & PUMC.
http://www.mgc.ac.cn/IPB_en/index.html

Division of Infectious Diseases Research, Department of Research Promotion, Japan Agency for Medical Research and Development, 'Research Activities of Japan Initiative for Global Research Network on Infectious Diseases (J-GRID)', July 2018.

'Doctor ZHONG Nanshan', Peking University, 12 September 2019.
https://news.pku.edu.cn/bdrw/f09c73a1063a43b0a02132aff3d51f6a.htm

Dong, Tao, et. al, 'Clinical and epidemiological features of COVID-19 family clusters in Beijing, China', Journal of Infection, Vol. 81, Issue 2, 1 August 2020.

Dong, Tao, et. al., 'Interferon-Induced Transmembrane Protein 3 Genetic Variant rs12252-C Associated With Disease Severity in Coronavirus Disease 2019', The Journal of Infectious Diseases, Vol. 222, Issue 1, 1 July 2020.

Dou, Eva and Kuo, Lily, 'A scientist adventurer and China's 'Bat Woman' are under scrutiny as coronavirus lab-leak theory gets another look', Washington Post, 3 June 2021.
https://www.washingtonpost.com/world/asia_pacific/coronavirus-bats-china-wuhan/2021/06/02/772ef984-beb2-11eb-922a-c40c9774bc48_story.html

Dovih, Pilot, Shi, Zhengli, et. al., 'Filovirus-reactive antibodies in humans and bats in Northeast India imply zoonotic spillover', PLOS Neglected Tropical Diseases, Vol. 13, No. 10, 31 October 2019.

'Dr Tang Fei-fan: The 'Louis Pasteur' of the East', Nspirement, https://www.nspirement.com/2016/12/02/dr-tang-fei-fan-the-louis-pasteur-of-the-east.html

'EcoHealth Alliance Scientists Discover the Deadly Zaire Ebola Virus in West African Bat', EcoHealth Alliance, 24 January 2019.
https://www.ecohealthalliance.org/2019/01/ecohealth-alliance-scientists-discover-the-deadly-zaire-ebola-virus-in-west-african-bat

'Editorial Team', Journal of Thoracic Disease, AME Publishing Company, Hong Kong.
https://jtd.amegroups.com/about/editorialTeam

'Emerging Disease Hotspots – Program Info', EcoHealth Alliance.
https://www.ecohealthalliance.org/program/emerging-disease-hotspots

Enserink, Martin, 'Flu Researcher Ron Fouchier Loses Legal Fight Over H5N1 Studies', *American Association for the Advancement of Science (ScienceMag)*, 25 September 2013.
https://www.science.org/content/article/flu-researcher-ron-fouchier-loses-legal-fight-over-h5n1-studies

Enerink, Martin, 'Scientists Brace for Media Storm Around Controversial Flu Studies', Science, 23 November 2011.
https://www.science.org/content/article/scientists-brace-media-storm-around-controversial-flu-studies

Enserink, Martin, 'Single Gene Swap Helps Bird Flu Virus Switch Hosts', *Science*, 2 May 2013.
https://www.sciencemag.org/news/2013/05/single-gene-swap-helps-bird-flu-virus-switch-hosts

Esposito, Anthony, 'Mexico to start late-stage clinical trial for China's mRNA COVID-19 vaccine', Reuters, 11 May 2021.
https://www.reuters.com/business/healthcare-pharmaceuticals/mexico-start-phase-iii-clinical-trials-chinas-walvax-covid-vaccine-2021-05-11/

Everington, Keoni, 'Video shows Wuhan lab scientists admit to being bitten by bats', Taiwan News, 15 January 2021.
https://www.taiwannews.com.tw/en/news/4102619

'Exchanges - Wuhan Institute of Virology', Wuhan Institute of Virology (WIV).
http://english.whiov.cas.cn/Exchange2016/

'Experts of public health from 10 African countries visited WIV, CAS', Wuhan Institute of Virology (WIV), 21 November 2018.

http://english.whiov.cas.cn/Exchange2016/Foreign_Visits/201811/
t20181121_201447.html

'Faculty', Institute of Pathogen Biology, Chinese Academy of Medical Sciences.
http://www.mgc.ac.cn/IPB_en/faculty.html

Feng, Xiao, et al., 'Development of a chimeric Zika vaccine using a licensed live-attenuated flavivirus vaccine as backbone', *Nature Communications*, Vol. 9, No. 673, 2018.

Ferguson, John Wayne, 'Galveston bio lab explains connections to Wuhan', The Daily News, 22 April 2020.
https://www.galvnews.com/news/free/article_daafd290-4015-5e83-aeb2-c038036da0d9.html

Fernández-Aguilar, Xavier, et. al., 'Novel Henipa-like Virus, Mojiang Paramyxovirus, in Rats, China, 2012', *Emerging Infectious Diseases*, Vol. 20, No. 6, June 2014.
Ferraris, Olivier, et. al., 'The NS Segment of H1N1pdm09 Enhances H5N1 Pathogenicity in a Mouse Model of Influenza Virus Infections', Viruses, Vol. 10, No. 504, September 2018.

Fouchier, Ron, et. al., 'Airborne transmission of influenza A/H5N1 virus between ferrets', *Science*, Vol. 22, No. 336:6088, June 2012.

Fouchier, Ron, et. al., 'The Potential for Respiratory Droplet–Transmissible A/H5N1 Influenza Virus to Evolve in a Mammalian Host', Science, Vol. 22, No. 336:6088, June 2012.

Fouchier, Ron, et. al., 'Gain-of-Function Experiments on H7N9', Science, 3 August 2013.
https://www.science.org/doi/full/10.1126/science.1243325

Fife, Robert and Chase, Steven, 'Chinese PLA general collaborated with fired scientist at Canada's top infectious disease lab', The Globe and Mail, 16 September 2021.
https://www.theglobeandmail.com/politics/article-chinese-pla-general-collaborated-with-fired-scientist-at-canadas-top/

'Foreign Visits', Wuhan Institute of Virology (WIV)
http://english.whiov.cas.cn/Exchange2016/Foreign_Visits/index_1.html

'GABRIEL Network', Merieux Foundation,
https://www.fondation-merieux.org/en/what-we-do/enhancing-research-capabilities/gabriel-network/

'Galveston National Lab Director LeDuc Provided Early Contact Between the NIAID and the Wuhan Lab; Fauci Invited by LeDuc to 'Informal Discussions' with a Dozen Senior Chinese Scientists', Mining Awareness, 24 October 2021. https://miningawareness.wordpress.com/2021/10/24/galveston-national-lab-director-leduc-provided-early-contact-between-the-niaid-and-the-wuhan-lab-fauci-invited-by-leduc-to-informal-discussions-with-a-dozen-senior-chinese-scientist/

'Gao Fu', Chinese Academy of Sciences (CAS), http://people.ucas.ac.cn/~GeorgeGao

Gao, George, Mazet, Joanna, Daszak, Peter, et. al., 'The Global Virome Project', Science, Vol. 359, No. 6378, 23 February 2018.

Gao, George, 'For a better world: Biosafety strategies to protect global health', *Biosafety and Health*, Vol. 1, No. 1, June 2019.

Gardy, Jennifer, 'Leadership – Global Virome Project', Global Virome Project. http://www.globalviromeproject.org/who-we-are/leadership/jennifer-gardy

Gardy, Jennifer 'What We Do – Malaria', Bill and Melinda Gates Foundation. https://www.gatesfoundation.org/What-We-Do/Global-Health/Malaria/Strategy-Leadership/Jennifer-Gardy

'Gates Foundation Honors Director of Africa CDC With 2020 Global Goalkeeper Award', Bill and Melinda Gates Foundation, 21 September 2020. https://www.gatesfoundation.org/ideas/media-center/press-releases/2020/09/gates-foundation-honors-director-of-africa-cdc-with-2020-global-goalkeeper-award

'George F. Gao', Chinese Center for Disease Control and Prevention. https://www.chinacdc.cn/en/aboutus/leadership/201603/t20160324_128015.html

Gewirtz, Julian, 'The Futurists of Beijing: Alvin Toffler, Zhao Ziyang, and China's 'New Technological Revolution,' 1979–1991', *The Journal of Asian Studies*, Vol. 78, No. 1, February 2019.

Gu, Hongjing, et. al. 'Adaptation of SARS-CoV-2 in BALB/c mice for testing vaccine efficacy', *Science*, Vol. 369, No. 6511, 25 September 2020. https://www.ncbi.nlm.nih.gov/pmc/articles/PMC7574913/

'廣州呼吸健康研究院簡介', Guangzhou Institute of Respiratory Health. http://www.gird.cn/show_list.php?id=11

'熱烈祝賀我院李時悅教授當選廣東省醫學會呼吸病學分會第九屆主任委員', Guangzhou Institute of Respiratory Health, 9 July 2020.

http://www.gird.cn/show.php?id=459

' 創先锋立品牌，不忘使命爲民服務 —— 記廣州醫科大學附屬第一醫院呼研所
第一黨支部先進事迹 ', Guangzhou Institute of Respiratory Health, 5 June 2019.
http://www.gird.cn/show.php?id=62

' 國際合作交流 ', Guangzhou Institute of Respiratory Health.
http://www.sklrd.cn/show_list.php?id=47;%20http://www.sklrd.cn/show.
php?id=1858

' 陳榮昌 ', Guangzhou Medical University, 5 January 2022.
https://ygc.gzhmu.edu.cn/info/1121/1632.htm

' 鄭勁平 ', Guangzhou Medical University.
https://www.gzhmu.edu.cn/10021716

'Harvard, Guangzhou Institute to Share $115 Million Coronavirus Grant', Philanthropy
News Digest, 25 February 2020.
https://philanthropynewsdigest.org/news/harvard-guangzhou-institute-to-share-115-
million-coronavirus-grant

'Homepage, Institute of Medical Biology – Chinese Academy of Medical Sciences',
https://www.imbcams.ac.cn/en

Horvat, Branka, et. al., 'Reprogrammed Pteropus Bat Stem Cells as A Model to Study
Host-Pathogen Interaction during *Henipavirus* Infection', *Microorganisms*, Vol. 9, No.
12, December 2021.

' 侯建國 (Hou Jianguo; Hou Jian Guo)', Chinese Academy of Sciences (CAS).
https://www.cas.cn/houjianguo/

Hu, Yuan-Yuan, et. al., 'Role of three tick species in the maintenance and transmission
of Severe Fever with Thrombocytopenia Syndrome Virus', *PLOS Neglected Tropical
Diseases*, Vol. 14, No. 6, 10 June 2020.

Huang, Xiaoliang, 'Revisit the oath of joining the party,' Guangzhou Institute of
Respiratory Disease institute news, 20 June 2012, archived at https://web.archive.org/
web/20120827072216/http://www.gird.cn/girdweb/Article-816.aspx

'Hundreds of Thai medical workers infected despite Sinovac vaccinations', Reuters, 11
July 2021.
https://www.reuters.com/world/asia-pacific/hundreds-thai-medical-workers-
infected-despite-sinovac-vaccinations-2021-07-11/

'Inauguration of the Institut Pasteur of Shanghai – Chinese Academy of Sciences', Shanghai, Institut Pasteur-Chinese Academy of Sciences (IPS), 10 October 2004. https://www.pasteur.fr/en/inauguration-institut-pasteur-shanghai-chinese-academy-sciences

'Indoor air quality survey and respiratory disease,' Sina, 20 Aug. 2014. http://jiaju.sina.com.cn/news/20140820/375596_2.shtml

'關於我們', Institute of Medical Biology, Chinese Academy of Medical Sciences. https://www.imbcams.ac.cn/

'科學研究', Institute of Medical Biology, Chinese Academy of Medical Sciences. https://www.imbcams.ac.cn/kxyj/kydw

'Institute of Pathogenic Biology, Chinese Academy of Medical Sciences 2022 Recruitment Notice', Institute of Pathogen Biology, Chinese Academy of Medical Sciences, 20 May 2022. http://www.gaoxiaojob.com/zhaopin/zhuanti/zgyxkxybyswxyjs2019/index.html

'Interview: China-aided Africa CDC project running smoothly with "full force," says expert', Xinhua, 6 June 2021. http://www.xinhuanet.com/english/africa/2021-06/06/c_139992119_2.htm

'Introduction', State Key Laboratory of Respiratory Diseases. http://www.sklrd.cn/show_list.php?id=10

'中國科學院簡介 (Introduction to Chinese Academy of Sciences; Zhong Guo Ke Xue Yuan Jian Jie)', Chinese Academy of Sciences, 20 December 2020. https://www.cas.cn/zz/yk/201410/t20141016_4225142.shtml

'Investigation visit to Zhengzhou campus', Henan University News, 12 April 2021, https://news.henu.edu.cn/info/1083/113389.htm

Jie, Liu, Wang Pan and Xiao Sisi, 'Profile: Zhong Nanshan: outspoken doctor awarded China's top honor', Xinhua, 8 September 2020. http://www.xinhuanet.com/english/2020-09/08/c_139352929.htm
JIN Qi's profile on X-MOL. https://www.x-mol.com/university/faculty/210903

'蘭溪籍科學家陳薇榮獲'浙江驕傲'年度致敬人物', Jinhua.gov.cn, 25 January 2021. http://swb.jinhua.gov.cn/art/2021/1/25/art_1229168153_58839064.html

'Joint Research Units', Wuhan Institute of Virology (WIV) http://english.whiov.cas.cn/International_Cooperation2016/Joint_Institutes2016/

Joske, Alex, Picking Flowers, Making Honey: The Chinese Military's Collaboration with Foreign Universities, Policy Brief Report No. 10, Australian Strategic Policy Institute, 30 October 2018. https://ad-aspi.s3.ap-southeast-2.amazonaws.com/2018-10/Picking%20 flowers%2C%20making%20honey_0.pdf?VersionId=H5sGNaWXqMgTG_2F2yZTQw Dw6OyNfH.u

'Journal Editor-in-Chief', Website of the *Journal of Thoracic Disease*, https://jtd. amegroups.com/about/editorInChief

Kaiser, Jocelyn, 'EXCLUSIVE: Controversial experiments that could make bird flu more risky poised to resume: Two 'gain of function' projects halted more than 4 years ago have passed new U.S. review process', *Science*, 8 February 2019. https://www.science.org/content/article/exclusive-controversial-experiments-make-bird-flu-more-risky-poised-resume

Kania, Elsa and Vorndick, Wilson, 'Weaponizing Biotech: How China's Military Is Preparing for a 'New Domain of Warfare'', Defense One, 14 August 2019.

Kawaoka, Yoshihiro, et. al., 'Syrian hamsters as a small animal model for SARS-CoV-2 infection and countermeasure development', PNAS, Vol. 117, No. 28, 14 July 2020.

Kerlin, Kat, '$85M to Develop a One Health Workforce for the Next Generation - USAID Award Supports New Project Led by UC Davis One Health Institute', University of California at Davis, 9 October 2019.

Kupferschmidt, Kai, 'As Outbreak Continues, Confusion Reigns Over Virus Patents', *American Association for the Advancement of Science (ScienceMag)*, 28 May 2013.

'Kuwaitis praise traditional Chinese medicine for treating COVID-19', Xinhua, 4 March 2021, http://www.xinhuanet.com/english/2021-03/04/c_139781331.htm

Lau, Susanna, et. al., 'Differential Tropism of SARS-CoV and SARS-CoV-2 in Bat Cells', *Emerging Infectious Diseases*, Vol. 26, No. 12, December 2020.

'Leadership', Chinese Center for Disease Control and Prevention. https://www.chinacdc.cn/en/aboutus/leadership/

'Leadership – Chinese Academy of Agricultural Sciences', Chinese Academy of Agricultural Sciences (CAAS).

http://www.caas.cn/en/administration/Leadership/index.html

LeDuc, James, National Biocontainment Training Center, Award Number: W81XWH-11-2-0148, US Army Medical Research and Materiel Command, Fort Detrick, Maryland 21702-5012, October 2016.
https://apps.dtic.mil/sti/pdfs/AD1022067.pdf

LeDuc, James and Ksiazek, Thomas, National Biocontainment Training Center, Annual Report, Grant Number: W81XWH-09-2-0053, US Army Medical Research and Materiel Command, Fort Detrick, Maryland 21702-5012, June 2014.
https://careersdocbox.com/87871061-Nursing/Prepared-for-u-s-army-medical-research-and-materiel-command-fort-detrick-maryland.html

Lei, Li, 'Visiting the mobile P3 lab that contributed to curbing COVID-19 in Beijing', Global Times, 12 July 2020.
https://www.globaltimes.cn/page/202007/1194237.shtml

Letko, Michael, et. al., 'Bat-borne virus diversity, spillover, and emergence', Nature Reviews Microbiology, Vol. 18, 2020.
Li, Fang, Wang, Linfa, Shi, Zheng-Li, et. al, 'Angiotensin-converting enzyme 2 (ACE2) proteins of different bat species confer variable susceptibility to SARS-CoV entry', Archive of Virology, Vol. 155, 22 June 2010.

Li, Heng, et. al., 'Self-Assembling Nanoparticle Vaccines Displaying the Receptor Binding Domain of SARS-CoV-2 Elicit Robust Protective Immune Responses in Rhesus Monkeys', Bioconjugate Chemistry, Vol. 32, 2021.

Li, W., Shi, Z. Yu, M., Ren, W., Smith, C., Epstein, J.H., Wang, H., Crameri, G., Hu, Z., Zhang, H., Zhang, J., McEachern, J., Field, H., Daszak, P., Eaton, B.T., Zhang, S., Wang, L. 'Bats Are Natural Reservoirs of SARS-Like Coronaviruses', Science, 2005.
Lin, Christina, 'Why US outsourced bat virus research to Wuhan', Asia Times, 22 April 2020.
https://asiatimes.com/2020/04/why-us-outsourced-bat-virus-research-to-wuhan/

Lin Lin, 'The Eighth Chinese Young Women in Science Awards', All-China Women's Federation, 12 January 2012.
https://web.archive.org/web/20200416155646/http://www.womenofchina.cn/html/people/Crowd/137083-7.htm

Lin, Wan, 'Anthrax human immunoglobulin enters trials, important to China's defense against biological and chemical attacks' Global Times, 6 June 2020.
https://www.globaltimes.cn/page/202006/1190749.shtml

Lin, Wan, 'China passes first biosafety law following COVID-19 epidemic, raises level to national security', Global Times, 18 October 2020. https://www.globaltimes.cn/page/202010/1203840.shtml

Ling, Justin, 'A brilliant scientist was mysteriously fired from a Winnipeg virus lab. No one knows why', Maclean's, 15 February 2022. https://www.macleans.ca/longforms/winnipeg-virus-lab-scientist/

Liu, Li-Teh, et. al., 'Isolation and Identification of a Rare Spike Gene Double-Deletion SARS-CoV-2 Variant From the Patient With High Cycle Threshold Value', Frontiers in Medicine, 6 January 2022.

'Liu Youning personal website', Medcon Conference platform, https://www.sciconf.cn/cn/person-detail/50?user_id=wUtevF5lLL4MV9lBh8geRQ_d_d

Liu, Roxanne and Lee, Se Young, 'Chinese military researchers move a new COVID vaccine candidate into human trial', Reuters, 25 June 2020. https://www.reuters.com/article/us-health-coronavirus-china-vaccine-idUSKBN23V2QO

Luby, Stephen, et. al., 'Assessing the feasibility of Nipah vaccine efficacy trials based on previous outbreaks in Bangladesh', Vaccine, Vol. 39, Iss. 39, 15 September 2021.

Luby, Stephen, et. al., 'Nipah Virus Transmission from Bats to Humans Associated with Drinking Traditional Liquor Made from Date Palm Sap, Bangladesh, 2011–2014', EID Journal, Vol. 22, No. 4, April 2016.

Ma, Josephine, 'Domestic clinical trials planned for China's mRNA Covid-19 vaccine', South China Morning Post, 22 July 2021. https://www.scmp.com/news/china/science/article/3142084/domestic-clinical-trials-planned-chinas-mrna-covid-19-vaccine

Ma, Liping, et. al., 'Rapid and specific detection of all known Nipah virus strains' sequences with reverse transcription-loop-mediated isothermal amplification'. Frontiers in Microbiology, Volume 10, Article 418, March 2019

Ma, Qiuyue, et. al., 'Global Percentage of Asymptomatic SARS-CoV-2 Infections Among the Tested Population and Individuals With Confirmed COVID-19 Diagnosis: A Systematic Review and Meta-analysis', JAMA Network Open, Vol. 4, No. 12, 14 December 2021.

Ma, Zhongliang and Li, Yanli, 'Dr Wu Lien Teh, plague fighter and father of the Chinese public health system', Protein Cell, Vol. 7, No. 3, March 2016.

'Management' page, Zhong Nanshan Medical Foundation of Guangdong Province, http://www.znsmf.org/zjwrh/

Mancheri, Nabeel and Rammohan, Viswesh, 'China's 'leapfrogging' in high performance computing', The Strategist, 15 November 2013. https://www.aspistrategist.org.au/chinas-leapfrogging-in-high-performance-computing/

Markson, Sharri, *What Really Happened In Wuhan: A Virus Like No Other, Countless Infections, Millions of Deaths*, HarperCollins, October 2021.
Marzetta, C.A., et. al., 'The potential global market size and public health value of an HIV-1 vaccine in a complex global market', Vaccine, 14 May 2010.

Mazet, Joanna, Dazsak, Peter, Shi, Zheng-Li, et. al., 'Isolation and characterization of a bat SARS-like coronavirus that uses the ACE2 receptor', *Nature*, Vol. 503, No. 28, November 2013.

McKay, Hollie, 'Prominent university bio lab urged to reveal extent of relationship with Wuhan lab at center of coronavirus outbreak', Fox News, 1 May 2020.

Menachery, Vineet, et. al., 'SARS-like cluster of circulating bat coronavirus pose threat for human emergence', Nature Medicine, Vol. 21, No. 12, December 2015.

'Mid-term report meeting of Lianhua Qingwen', State Key Laboratory of Respiratory Disease News, 2 Mar. 2018, http://www.sklrd.cn/show.php?id=702

'Monitoring the Deadly Nipah Virus – Program Info', EcoHealth Alliance. https://www.ecohealthalliance.org/program/monitoring-the-deadly-nipah-virus

'National Key Disciplines', China Academic Degrees and Graduate Education Development Center, PRC Ministry of Education, http://www.cdgdc.edu.cn/xwyyjsjyxx/zlpj/zdxkps/zdxk/

'打疫苗，還是'吸'疫苗？陳薇院士團隊又傳來好消息……', New.qq.com, 10 August 2021. https://new.qq.com/rain/a/20210810a081vz00

'New Vaccine Industrial Base Project in Kunming High-tech Industrial Development Zone', Yunnan Investment Promotion, 21 January 2022. https://invest.yn.gov.cn/ENArticleInfo.aspx?id=19069

'Nipah Virus International Conference Proceedings', Coalition for Epidemic Preparedness Innovations, National Institute of Allergy and Infectious Diseases, and

Duke-NUS Graduate School of Medicine, Singapore, 9-10 December 2019.
https://cepi.net/wp-content/uploads/2020/06/2019-Nipah-Conference-Proceedings.
pdf

Nowotny, N and Kolodziejek, J, 'Middle East respiratory syndrome coronavirus
(MERS-CoV) in dromedary camels, Oman, 2013', Euro Surveillance, Vol. 19, No. 16,
24 April 2014.
https://www.eurosurveillance.org/content/10.2807/1560-7917.ES2014.19.16.20781

'Number of college and university students from China in the United States from
academic year 2008/09 to 2018/19', Statista.
https://www.statista.com/statistics/372900/number-of-chinese-students-that-study-
in-the-us/

Nyabiage, Jevans, 'How the US lost Africa to China over new disease control centre in
Addis Ababa', South China Morning Post, 13 August 2022.
https://www.scmp.com/news/china/diplomacy/article/3188010/how-us-lost-africa-
china-over-new-disease-control-centre-addis

Nyabiage, Jevans, 'Why China is building gleaming new government facilities in
Africa', South China Morning Post, 23 May 2021.
https://www.scmp.com/news/china/diplomacy/article/3134224/why-china-building-
gleaming-new-government-facilities-africa?module=inline&pgtype=article

O'Keefe, Kate, 'U.S. Probes University of Texas Links to Chinese Lab Scrutinized Over
Coronavirus', The Wall Street Journal, 1 May 2020.
https://www.wsj.com/articles/u-s-probes-university-of-texas-links-to-chinese-lab-
scrutinized-over-coronavirus-11588325401

Oran, Daniel and Topol, Eric, 'Prevalence of Asymptomatic SARS-CoV-2 Infection',
Annals of Internal Medicine, 1 September 2020.

'Our Goals', Global Virome Project.
https://www.globalviromeproject.org/our-goals

Owen, Glen, 'Wuhan virus lab was signed off by EU Brexit chief Michel Barnier in
2004 – despite French intelligence warnings that China's poor bio-security reputation
could lead to a catastrophic leak', The Guardian, 23 May 2020.
https://www.dailymail.co.uk/news/article-8351113/Wuhan-virus-lab-signed-Michel-
Barnier-2004-despite-French-intelligence-warnings.html

'籃壇50傑之李少芬：女籃首批健將 鐘南山賢伉儷', 163.com, 27 September
2015.

https://www.163.com/sports/article/AVH5TGT800052UUC.html
'Partnerships - Wuhan Institute of Virology', Wuhan Institute of Virology (WIV).
http://english.whiov.cas.cn/International_Cooperation2016/Partnerships/

'Party Committee – Wuhan Institute of Virology, Chinese Academy of Sciences',
Wuhan Institute of Virology (WIV).
http://www.whiov.cas.cn

'Past leaders', Guangzhou Medical University School Profile, archived at https://web.
archive.org/web/20220330042623/https://www.gzhmu.edu.cn/10009021

'Party branch work,' Guangzhou Institute of Respiratory Disease, archived at https://
web.archive.org/web/20120825030253/http://www.gird.cn/girdweb/List-50.aspx

Pauls, Karen, 'Canadian government scientist under investigation trained staff at Level
4 lab in China', CBC News, 3 October 2019.
https://www.cbc.ca/news/canada/manitoba/national-microbiology-lab-scientist-
investigation-china-1.5307424

Pauls, Karen, 'Canadian scientist sent deadly viruses to Wuhan lab months before
RCMP asked to investigate', CBC News, 14 June 2020.
https://www.cbc.ca/news/canada/manitoba/canadian-scientist-sent-deadly-viruses-
to-wuhan-lab-months-before-rcmp-asked-to-investigate-1.5609582

Pauls, Karen, "Wake-up call for Canada': Security experts say case of 2 fired scientists
could point to espionage', CBC News, 10 June 2021.
https://www.cbc.ca/news/canada/manitoba/winnipeg-lab-security-experts-1.6059097

' 醫者鐘南山 ', Peking University, 12 September 2019.
https://news.pku.edu.cn/bdrw/f09c73a1063a43b0a02132aff3d51f6a.htm

'Peking Hospital Takes Back Pre-1949 Name', *New York Times*, 9 June 1985.
https://www.nytimes.com/1985/06/09/world/peking-hospital-takes-back-pre-1949-
name.html

' 鐘南山受聘深圳市人民醫院 任呼吸疾病研究所榮譽所長 ', People.Cn. 29 July
2021.
http://sz.people.com.cn/n2/2021/0729/c202846-34842681.html

Pérez-Núñez, Daniel, et. al., 'CD2v Interacts with Adaptor Protein AP-1 during African
Swine Fever Infection', PLOS ONE, 27 April 2015.

'Perspectives for Reinforcing Scientific Cooperations', Ecole Normale Superieure Lyon,

30 September 2019.
http://www.ens-lyon.fr/en/article/research/perspectives-reinforcing-scientific-cooperations

Petrovsky, Nikolai, et. al., 'In silico comparison of SARS-CoV-2 spike protein-ACE2 binding affinities across species and implications for virus origin', *Scientific Reports*, Vol. 11, 24 June 2021.

Power, John, 'Exclusive | '0 per cent' chance: former French official who oversaw safety standards at Wuhan lab dismissed leak theory', South China Morning Post, 11 June 2021.
https://www.scmp.com/week-asia/health-environment/article/3136833/0-cent-chance-french-official-who-oversaw-safety

'President He Jianxing', Current Leadership, First Affiliated Hospital of Guangzhou Medical University, archived at https://web.archive.org/web/20180209005808/http://www.gyfyy.com/cn/list-170-745.html

'President's Working Group on Financial Markets: Report on Protecting United States Investors from Significant Risks from Chinese Companies', US Department of Treasury, 24 July 2020.
https://home.treasury.gov/system/files/136/PWG-Report-on-Protecting-United-States-Investors-from-Significant-Risks-from-Chinese-Companies.pdf

'Principal Investigators 2016: Jie CUI', Institut Pasteur of Shanghai – Chinese Academy of Sciences.
http://sourcedb.shanghaipasteur.cas.cn/yw/Talent2016/PI2016/202106/t20210624_6116681.html

'Principal Investigators in Oxford', Chinese Academy of Medical Sciences Oxford Institute,
https://www.camsoxford.ox.ac.uk/PIs/principal-investigators-oxford

'Professor Branka HORVAT in French National Institute of Health and Medical Research visited WIV', Wuhan Institute of Virology, 1 August 2016.
http://english.whiov.cas.cn/Exchange2016/Seminars/201712/t20171212_187686.html

' 简 浩 然 教 授 (Professor Jian Haoran; Jian Hao Ran Jiao Shou)', Institute of Microbiology, Guangdong Academy of Sciences, 26 August 2013.
http://www.gdim.cn/jggk/lrld/201308/t20130826_121604.html

'Professor Luo Yuanming of SKLRD honored as Fellow of the Royal College of Physicians', State Key Laboratory of Respiratory Disease News Information, 9 Feb.

2021, http://www.sklrd.cn/en/show.php?id=858

'Prof. Jianxing He: ones with more motive power and willpower, a better traveler he is', *Journal of Thoracic Disease*, Vol. 10, No. 6, June 2018.

'Professor Zheng Jinping of Guangzhou Medical University presided over drafting of the country's first guidelines for pulmonary function testing', Work News, Guangzhou Medical University, archived at https://webcache.googleusercontent.com/search?q=cache:unQHjbDx598J:https://tzb.gzhmu.edu.cn/info/1039/1114.htm+&cd=1&hl=en&ct=clnk&gl=sg

'Profile Chen Wang: new President of CAMS and PUMC', *The Lancet*, Vol. 391, 16 June 2018.

'Promoting global public health security, U.S. CDC and China CDC conduct a national assessment', United States Centers for Disease Control and Prevention, 6 October 2017. https://www.cdc.gov/globalhealth/countries/china/stories/health-security.htm

'Project Deep Forest – Program Info', EcoHealth Alliance. https://www.ecohealthalliance.org/program/project-deep-forest

'Publication', Chinese Center for Disease Control and Prevention. https://www.chinacdc.cn/en/publication/fms/

Qi, Chen, et. al., 'SARS-CoV-2 infection in the mouse olfactory system', *Cell Discovery*, Vol. 7, No. 9, 2021.

Qi, Chen, at. al., 'The recombinant pseudorabies virus expressing African swine fever virus CD2v protein is safe and effective in mice', *Virology Journal*, Vol. 17, No. 180, 16 November 2020.

Qi, Chen, Chao Shan, Shi Peiyong, et. al., 'Treatment of Human Glioblastoma with a Live Attenuated Zika Virus Vaccine Candidate', mBio, Vol. 9. Iss. 5, September/October 2018.

Qi, Chen, et. al., 'Pathogenicity and pathogenesis of a United States porcine deltacoronavirus cell culture isolate in 5-day-old neonatal piglets', Virology, Vol. 482, August 2015.

Qiu, Xiangguo and Chen Wei, 'Potent neutralizing monoclonal antibodies against Ebola virus isolated from vaccinated donors', *MABS*, Vol. 12, No. 1, 2020.

Qiu, Xiangguo, et. al., 'Equine-Origin Immunoglobulin Fragments Protect Nonhuman Primates from Ebola Virus Disease', *Journal of Virology*, Vol. 93, No. 5, March 2019.

Qiu, Xiangguo, Chen Wei, et. al., 'An Adenovirus Vaccine Expressing Ebola Virus Variant Makona Glycoprotein Is Efficacious in Guinea Pigs and Nonhuman Primates', *The Journal of Infectious Diseases*, Vol. 214 (Suppl 3), 2016.

Qu, Tracy, 'The Bill & Melinda Gates Foundation is spending millions in China, a fraction of its total funding', South China Morning Post, 6 May 2021. https://www.scmp.com/tech/big-tech/article/3132384/bill-melinda-gates-foundation-spending-millions-china-fraction-its

Quay, Steven, 'A Bayesian analysis concludes beyond a reasonable doubt that SARS-CoV-2 is not a natural zoonosis but instead is laboratory derived', *Zenodo*, 29 January 2021.

Quay, Steven, et. al., 'Contamination or Vaccine Research? RNA Sequencing data of early COVID-19 patient samples show abnormal presence of vectorized H7N9 hemagglutinin segment', *Zenodo*, 3 July 2021.

Quay, Steven and Dalgleish, Angus, *The Origin of the Virus: The hidden truths behind the microbe that killed millions of people*, Clinical Press Ltd., September 2021.

Quay, Steven and Muller, Richard, 'The Science Suggests a Wuhan Lab Leak: The Covid-19 pathogen has a genetic footprint that has never been observed in a natural coronavirus', Wall Street Journal, 6 June 2021. https://www.wsj.com/amp/articles/the-science-suggests-a-wuhan-lab-leak-11622995184

Quay, Steven, Zhang, Daoyu, et. al., 'Nipah virus vector sequences in COVID-19 patient samples sequenced by the Wuhan Institute of Virology', *arXiv*, q-bio, 19 September 2021.

Quay, Steven, Zhang, Daoyu, et. al., 'Vector sequences in early WIV SRA sequencing data of SARS-CoV-2 inform on a potential large-scale security breach at the beginning of the COVID-19 pandemic', *Zenodo*, 19 September 2021.

Raska, Michael, 'Scientific Innovation and China's Military Modernization', The Diplomat, 3 September 2013. https://thediplomat.com/2013/09/scientific-innovation-and-chinas-military-modernization/,

'Report on the Outline of the Tenth Five-Year Plan for National Economic and Social Development (2001)', National People's Congress of the People's Republic of China, 2001.

'Report on the Outline of the 11th Five-Year Plan for National Economic and Social Development (2006)', National People's Congress of the People's Republic of China, 2006.

'Respiratory disease expert wins alumni award', University of Edinburgh, 16 April 2020.
https://www.ed.ac.uk/news/2020/respiratory-disease-expert-wins-alumni-award

Reusken, Chantal B E M, et. al., 'Middle East respiratory syndrome coronavirus neutralizing serum antibodies in dromedary camels: a comparative serological study', Lancet Infectious Diseases, Vol. 13, No. 10, October 2013.
https://www.thelancet.com/journals/laninf/article/PIIS1473-3099(13)70164-6/fulltext

Rey, Felix, Schwartz, Olivier, and Wain-Hobson, Simon, 'Gain-of-function research: unknown risks', Science, Vol. 342, No. 6156:311, 18 October 2013.

Riordan, Primrose, Li, Gloria, Chan, Ho-him and Lockett, Hudson, 'China Covid-19 tsar pushed treatments without revealing business ties', Financial Times, 25 April 2022.
https://www.ft.com/content/fcac2cbc-4bff-44f5-81bf-66db32b99fca

Rogin, Josh, 'State Department cables warned of safety issues at Wuhan lab studying bat coronaviruses', New York Times, 14 April 2020.
https://www.washingtonpost.com/opinions/2020/04/14/state-department-cables-warned-safety-issues-wuhan-lab-studying-bat-coronaviruses/

Roos, Robert, 'Fouchier study reveals changes enabling airborne spread of H5N1', Center for Infectious Disease Research and Policy, University of Minnesota, 21 June 2012.
https://www.cidrap.umn.edu/news-perspective/2012/06/fouchier-study-reveals-changes-enabling-airborne-spread-h5n1

Rowlands, Rebecca, et. al., 'The CD2v protein enhances African swine fever virus replication in the tick vector, Ornithodoros erraticus', Virology, Vol. 393, Iss. 2, October 2009.

'SARS-CoV-2 mRNA vaccine', DrugBank Online.
https://go.drugbank.com/drugs/DB15855

'SARS Technology is declaring war against you', Chinese Academy of Sciences, 2 May 2003.
https://www.cas.cn/zt/kjzt/fdgx/ggqy/200305/t20030502_1709485.shtml

Search page for ' 陈 薇 ' on the Chinese language website of the All-China Women's Federation (中華全國婦女聯合會), https://www.women.org.cn/jsearch/search.do? pagemode=result&appid=1&webid=1&style=1&pos=title%2Ccontent&pg=10&ck=o&t mp_od=0&q=%E9%99%88%E8%96%87&query=%E9%99%88%E8%96%87&radiobutton =1&Submit=%E6%90%9C%E7%B4%A2

'Senior Management - Institut Pasteur of Shanghai', Institut Pasteur-Chinese Academy of Sciences (IPS).
http://english.shanghaipasteur.cas.cn/Overview2016/ms2016/sm2016/

Shajan Perappadan, Bindu, 'Study on bats and bat hunters in Nagaland to be probed', The Hindu, 3 February 2020.
https://www.thehindu.com/news/national/study-on-bats-and-bat-hunters-of-nagaland-come-under-the-scanner/article61635549.ece

Shan, Chao, et. al., 'An Infectious cDNA Clone of Zika Virus to Study Viral Virulence, Mosquito Transmission, and Antiviral Inhibitors', Cell Host Microbe, Vol. 19, No. 6, 8 June 2016.
Shan, Chao, et. al., 'A Zika virus envelope mutation preceding the 2015 epidemic enhances virulence and fitness for transmission', PNAS, Vol. 117, No. 33., 18 August 2020.
She, Jingwei, 'Expert: Chinese medicine Lianhua Qingwen capsule proven effective for COVID-19', CGTN, 5 May 2020, https://news.cgtn.com/news/2020-05-05/Expert-Lianhua-Qingwen-capsule-proven-effective-for-COVID-19-QeXiCOf18A/index.html
' 深圳市東陽光實業發展有限公司 - 2015 年度报告 ', Shenzhen Dongguan Industrial Development Co., Ltd.
http://file.finance.sina.com.cn/211.154.219.97:9494/MRGG/BOND/2018/2018-12/2018-12-12/9576048.PDF

' 鐘南山的妻子是女籃 5 号 ', Sina, 16 June 2003.
http://news.sina.com.cn/c/2003-06-16/02521173575.shtml

Shi, Pei-Yong, 'Spike mutation D614G alters SARS-CoV-2 fitness', Nature, Vol. 592, 26 October 2020.

Shi, Zhengli, Dazsak, Peter, et. al., 'Bat Severe Acute Respiratory Syndrome-Like Coronavirus WIV1 Encodes an Extra Accessory Protein, ORFX, Involved in Modulation of the Host Immune Response', Journal of Virology, Vol. 90, No. 14, July 2016.

Shi, Zhengli, Daszak, Peter, et. al., 'Discovery of a rich gene pool of bat SARS-related coronaviruses provides new insights into the origin of SARS coronavirus', PLOS Pathogens, 30 November 2017.

Shi, Zhengli, Peng, Zhou, Daszak, Peter, et. al., 'Fatal swine acute diarrhoea syndrome caused by an HKU2-related coronavirus of bat origin', *Nature*, Vol. 556, No. 7700, April 2018.

Shi, Zheng-Li, Hu, Ben, et. al., 'Genetic Mutation of SARS-CoV-2 during Consecutive Passages in Permissive Cells', *Virologica Sinica*, Vol. 26, 2021.

Shi Zhengli, 'Inter-nation collaboration Sino-French NiV taskforce 2019', Nipah Virus International Conference, 9-10 December, Singapore. https://cepi.net/wp-content/uploads/2020/06/2019-Nipah-Conference-Proceedings.pdf

Shi, Zheng-Li, Zheng, Yufei, et. al., 'SARS-CoV-2 rapidly adapts in aged BALB/c mice and induces typical pneumonia', *Journal of Virology*, Volume 95, Iss. 11, June 2021.

Shi, Zheng-Li, Baric, Ralph et. al., 'A SARS-like cluster of circulating bat coronaviruses shows potential for human emergence', *Nature Medicine*, Vol. 21, No. 12, December 2015.

'Shiyue LI 李時悅', Chinese University of Hong Kong, 4 July 2019. https://www.surgery.cuhk.edu.hk/atccs2019/Shiyue%20LI.pdf

Shoham, Dany, 'Report: China and Viruses: The Case of Dr Xiangguo Qiu', Begin-Sadat Center for Strategic Studies, 2020.

Shoham, Dany, 'China's Biological Warfare Programme: An Integrative Study with Special
Reference to Biological Weapons Capabilities', *Journal of Defence Studies*, Vol. 9, No. 2, April-June 2015.

Shu, Yuelong, Cox, Nancy, et. al., 'A ten-year China-US laboratory collaboration: improving response to influenza threats in China and the world, 2004-2014', *BMC Public Health*, Vol. 19, No. 520, 10 May 2019.

Smith, Charles, 'Why the Coronavirus Slipped Past Disease Detectives', *Scientific American*, 3 April 2020.

'官方最新回應：鐘南山院士是曹雪濤等論文調查複核專家組組長', Sohu, 3 February 2021. https://www.sohu.com/a/448494013_100226214

'第十三屆全國人民代表大會代表名單（2980名 吉林省64名）', Sohu, 25 February 2015. http://news.sohu.com/20130227/n367313787.shtml

Sørensen, Birger, Susrud, Andres, and Dalgleish, Angus, 'Biovacc-19: A Candidate Vaccine for Covid-19 (SARS-CoV-2) Developed from Analysis of its General Method of Action for Infectivity', *QRB Discovery*, Volume 1, 29 May 2020.

'Spillover: Visual Risk Ranking', Global Virome Project. https://www.globalviromeproject.org/spillover

'廣東省十一屆人民代表大會代表', Standing Committee of Guangdong Provincial People's Congress, 11 February 2009. http://www.gdrd.cn/rdgzxgnr_4349/rddbmd/syjrddb/202006/t20200601_172252. html

'碩士研究生導師', State Key Laboratory of Respiratory Disease. http://www.sklrd.cn/show.php?id=1027

'全體研究人员', State Key Laboratory of Respiratory Disease. http://www.sklrd.cn/show.php?id=357

Subbaraman, Nidhi, 'Heinous!': Coronavirus researcher shut down for Wuhan-lab link slams new funding restrictions', *Nature*, 21 August 2020.

Subbarao, Kanta, Chen, Hualan, et. al., 'Generation and characterization of a cold-adapted influenza A H9N2 reassortant as a live pandemic influenza virus vaccine candidate', *Virology*, Vol. 305, Iss. 1, 5 January 2003.

Subbarao, Kanta, Chen, Hualan, et. al., 'Evaluation of a Genetically Modified Reassortant H5N1 Influenza A Virus Vaccine Candidate Generated by Plasmid-Based Reverse Genetics', *Virology*, Vol. 305, Iss. 1, February 2003.

Subbarao, Kanta, Chen, Hualan, et. al., 'Generation and Characterization of an H9N2 Cold-Adapted Reassortant as a *Vaccine* Candidate', Avian Diseases, Vol. 47, No. s3, September 2003.

Subbarao, Kanta, Chen, Hualan, et. al, 'Generation and characterization of a cold-adapted influenza A H9N2 reassortant as a live pandemic influenza virus vaccine candidate', Vaccine, Vol. 21, November 2003.

Subbarao, Kanta, Chen, Hualan, et. al., 'Lack of transmission of H5N1 avian– human reassortant influenza viruses in a ferret model', *PNAS*, Vol. 103, No. 32, 8 August 2006.

Sun Bangyao, et. al., 'Phylogeography, Transmission, and Viral Proteins of Nipah Virus', *Virologica Sinica*, Vol. 33, No. 5, 2018.

Tan, Kevin, 'The Plague Fighter: Dr Wu Lien-Teh and His Work', National Library, Singapore, 1 July 2020.
https://biblioasia.nlb.gov.sg/vol-16/issue-2/jul-sep-2020/plague

Terry, Mark, 'China Has Big Presence in Top 10 Biotech IPOs this Year', *BioSpace*, 17 July 2019.
https://www.biospace.com/article/top-10-biopharma-ipos-in-the-first-half-of-2019/

'Testimonials', Journal of Thoracic Disease, AME Publishing Company, Hong Kong.
https://jtd.amegroups.com/pages/view/testimonials

'The Fifty Superstars of China's Basketball Hall of Fame: ZHONG Nanshan's wife in the first cohort of female basketball in China', 163.com, 27 September 2015.
https://www.163.com/sports/article/AVH5TGT800052UUC.html

'The French Ambassador to China bestowed medals on Two Scientists in Wuhan Institute of Virology', WIV Newsletter, No. 11, July 2016.

'The French Ambassador to China bestowed medals on Professor Zhiming Yuan and Professor Zhengli Shi in Wuhan Institute of Virology', Wuhan Institute of Virology (WIV), 1 August 2016.
http://english.whiov.cas.cn/Exchange2016/Foreign_Visits/201712/t20171215_187978.html

'The history of the Huyan Institute', Guangzhou Institute of Respiratory Disease Institute Overview, 24 Aug. 2011, archived at https://web.archive.org/web/20120825030305/http://www.gird.cn/girdweb/Article-565.aspx

'The P4 Jean Merieux-Inserm Laboratory expands making it one of the largest facilities in the world', Merieux Foundation, 18 May 2015.
https://www.fondation-merieux.org/en/news/the-p4-jean-merieux-inserm-laboratory-expands-making-it-one-of-the-largest-facilities-in-the-world/

'The research team of Wuhan Institute of Virology/ Biosafety Science Center and the Academy of Military Sciences found that calcium channel inhibitors can treat fever with thrombocytopenia syndrome (SFTS)', Wuhan Institute of Virology (WIV) and the Center for Biosafety Mega-Science (CAS), 30 August 2019.

'The Risk Exposure of U.S. Investors Holding Chinese Sovereign Bonds', RWR Advisory Group, 28 October 2020.
https://www.rwradvisory.com/wp-content/uploads/2020/11/RWR-China-Sovereign-Bond-Report.pdf

The Science of Military Strategy 2017, National Defense University, People's Liberation Army, Beijing, 2017.

'Three Generations of Medical Professionals: Listening to the story of their family's heritage told by ZHONG Nanshan's son', Xinhua, 19 August 2020. http://www.xinhuanet.com/2020-08/19/c_1126386735.htm

' 趙洪 ', Tsinghua University, 16 May 2021. https://www.arts.tsinghua.edu.cn/info/1109/1549.htm

'U-M Chinese Alumni – Huang Jiasi', University of Michigan, https://sites.lsa.umich.edu/chinese-alumni/huang-jiasi-%E9%BB%84%E5%AE%B6%E9%A9%B7/

United States Centers for Disease Control and Prevention, Biosafety in Microbiological and Biomedical Laboratories – fifth Edition, Atlanta, December 2009. 'USAID PREDICT Semi-Annual 2019 Report', United States Agency for International Development. https://ohi.sf.ucdavis.edu/sites/g/files/dgvnsk5251/files/files/page/SAR2019-draft-final-compressed.pdf

'U.S China Dialogue and Workshop on the Challenges of Emerging Infections, Laboratory Safety, Global Health Security and Responsible Conduct in the Use of Gene Editing in Viral Disease Research', Draft Version 4, Harbin Veterinary Research Institute – Chinese Academy of Agricultural Sciences, 8-10 January 2019. This document was obtained via a Freedom of Information request from the University of Texas System.

'US Fort Detrick biolab becomes hot topic on Chinese social media', Global Times, 22 January 2021. https://www.globaltimes.cn/page/202101/1213588.shtml

Wadman, Meredith, 'NIH imposes 'outrageous' conditions on resuming coronavirus grant targeted by Trump', *Science*, 19 August 2020.

Wang, Bei, Zhang, Chongyang, Lei, Xiaobo, Ren, Lili, Zhao, Zhendong and He Huang, 'Construction of Non-infectious SARS-CoV-2 Replicons and Their Application in Drug Evaluation', *Virologica Sinica*, Vol. 36, No. 5, October 2021.

Wang, Hualei, Qiu, Xiangguo, et. al., 'Equine-Origin Immunoglobulin Fragments Protect Nonhuman Primates from Ebola Virus Disease', *Journal of Virology*, Vol. 93, No. 5, March 2019.

Wang, Linfa, et. al., 'Evidence of Henipavirus Infection in West African Fruit Bats',

PLOS ONE, 23 July 2008.

Wang, Linfa, Wei, Liu, et. al, 'A Zoonotic Henipavirus in Febrile Patients in China', New England Journal of Medicine, Vol. 387, 4 August 2022.
  - Supplementary Appendix to Wang, Linfa, Wei, Liu, et. al, 'A Zoonotic Henipavirus in Febrile Patients in China', *New England Journal of Medicine*, Vol. 387, 4 August 2022.

Wang, Ning, Daszak, Peter, Shi, Zhengli, et. al. 'Serological Evidence of Bat SARS-Related Coronavirus Infection in Humans, China', *Virologica Sinica*, 2 March 2018.

Wang, (YY), Shu, (HB), et. al., 'A20 is a potent inhibitor of TLR3- and Sendai virus-induced activation of NF-kappa B and ISRE and IFN-beta promoter', FEBS Letters, Vol. 576, No. 1-2, 8 October 2004.

Wang, (YY), Shu, (HB), et. al., 'VISA is an adapter protein required for virus-triggered IFN-beta signalling', Molecular Cell, Vol. 19, No. 6, 16 September 2005.

Wei, William, 'China's Brain Drain to the United States: Views of Overseas Chinese Students and Scholars in the 1990s', *China Review International*, Vol. 4, No. 1, 1997.

Whittaker, Zack, 'FBI and DHS accuse Chinese hackers of targeting US COVID-19 research', Tech Crunch, 13 May 2020.
 https://techcrunch.com/2020/05/13/fbi-dhs-china-coronavirus/

WHO Consultative Meeting on High/Maximum Containment (Biosafety Level 4) Laboratories Networking, Meeting Report, Lyon, France, 13-15 December 2017.
 https://www.who.int/publications/i/item/who-consultative-meeting-high-maximum-containment-(-biosafety-level-4)-laboratories-networking-venue

'Why GVP is Needed', Global Virome Project.
 https://www.globalviromeproject.org/our-approach

Williams, Shawna, 'NIH Cancels Funding for Bat Coronavirus Research Project', The Scientist, 28 April 2020.

Woodward, Aylin, 'A 2019 video shows scientists from the Wuhan CDC collecting samples in bat caves — but the agency hasn't revealed any findings', Business Insider, 9 June 2021.
 https://www.businessinsider.com/chinese-scientists-bat-caves-video-2021-6

' 中國科協第十屆全國委員會副主席人選公布 喬杰、向巧、陳薇三位女性當選', Women.org.cn, 31 May 2021.

https://www.women.org.cn/art/2021/5/31/art_23_166394.html

'陳薇：'除了勝利，別無選擇！', Women.org,cn, 16 November 2020.
https://www.women.org.cn/art/2020/11/16/art_24_165256.html

'與新冠病毒賽跑的女英雄——'人民英雄'陳薇談新冠疫苗研制心路歷程',
Women.org.cn, 14 August 2020.
https://www.women.org.cn/art/2020/8/14/art_24_164868.html

'戰鬥在抗疫一線女院士陳薇：以最充分方案做最長期奮戰', Women.org.cn, 3
February 2020.
https://www.women.org.cn/art/2020/2/3/art_24_163679.html

'中國婦女兒童博物館大型融媒體項目'家風故事匯'上綫', Women.org.cn, 28
December 2020.
https://www.women.org.cn/art/2020/12/28/art_19_165462.html

'十三屆全國政協女委員 440 名！女委員比例再提升！', Women.org.cn, 25
January 2018.
https://www.women.org.cn/art/2018/1/25/art_19_154197.html

Wong, Teresa, 'Covid: Is China's vaccine success waning in Asia?', BBC, 19 July 2021.
https://www.bbc.com/news/world-asia-57845644

Wright, Guowei, 'Lin Qiaozhi: The Steady Pulse of a Quiet Faith' in Carol Lee Hamrin,
ed., with Stacey Bieler, *Salt and Light: Lives of Faith that Shaped Modern China*, Eugene,
OR., Wipf and Stock Publishers, Pickwick Publications, 2008.

'武漢市志 - 第八卷 社會人物大事記：高尚蔭' (Wuhan City Chronicles-Volume 8
Memorabilia of Social Figures: Gao Shangyin; Wu Han Shi Zhi – Di Ba Juan She Hui
Ren Wu Da Shi Ji: Gao Shang Yin), Wuhan Digital Local Chronicles Museum.
http://szfzg.wuhan.gov.cn/book/dfz/bookread/id/273/category_id/58160.html

'中國科學院武漢病毒研究所喜迎建所五十周年華誕 (Wuhan Institute of
Virology, Chinese Academy of Sciences celebrates its 50th anniversary; Zhong Guo
Ke Xue Yuan Wu Han Bing Du Yan Jiu Suo Xi Yin Jian Suo Wu Shi Zhou Nian Hua
Dan)', Wuhan Institute of Virology (WIV), 11 January 2006.
http://www.whiov.cas.cn/xwdt_160278/zhxw2019/201911/t20191111_5428884.html

Wu, Qianhui, et. al, 'Evaluation of the safety profile of COVID-19 vaccines: a rapid
review', *BMC Medicine*, Vol. 19, Issue 173, 2021.

Wu, Yu-lin, *Memories of Dr Wu Lien-teh, Plague Fighter*, World Scientific, 1995.

Vernick, Michael and Thompson, Marta, 'Prominent Chinese Academy of Military Medical Sciences is Added to Export Control Blacklist', Akin Gump, 28 December 2021.
https://www.akingump.com/en/experience/industries/education/ag-study-guide/prominent-chinese-academy-of-military-medical-sciences-is-added-to-export-control-blacklist.html

Vogel, Ezra (ed), *Living with China: U.S./China Relations in the Twenty-first Century*, W.W. Norton: 1997.

Vogel, Ezra, *Deng Xiaoping and the Transformation of China*, Belknap Press: 2011.

'Xi Focus: Xi signs order to award 4 persons for outstanding contribution in COVID-19 fight', Xinhua, 11 August 2020.
http://www.xinhuanet.com/english/2020-08/11/c_139282926.htm

'Xi Focus – Quotable Quotes: Xi Jinping on work, production resumption', XinhuaNet, 22 April 2020.
http://www.news.cn/english/2020-05/13/c_139053247.htm

'Xinlin Stories of SHEN Jieping: Going through the adversities and growing up out of struggles', YCWB, 17 July 2021.
http://news.ycwb.com/2021-07/17/content_40145876.htm

' 一門 ' 醫三代 ' 聽鐘南山之子親述祖孫三代傳承故事 ', Xinhua, 19 August 2020.
http://www.xinhuanet.com/2020-08/19/c_1126386735.htm

'Xin Lu'. Chinese Academy of Medical Sciences Oxford Institute,
https://www.camsoxford.ox.ac.uk/team/xin-lu

' 陈榮昌 ', X-MOL.
https://www.x-mol.com/university/faculty/96389

Yao, Yanfeng, et. al., 'An Animal Model of MERS Produced by Infection of Rhesus Macaques With MERS Coronavirus', *Journal of Infectious Diseases*, Vol. 209, No. 2, 15 January 2014.

' 杏林往事 | 沈皆平: 在激流中磨礪, 在奮鬥中成長 ', YCWB, 17 July 2021.
http://news.ycwb.com/2021-07/17/content_40145876.htm

Yong, Michael, 'People who got Sinovac vaccine nearly 5 times more likely to develop severe COVID-19 than Pfizer: Singapore study', ChannelNewsAsia, 14 April 2022.
https://www.channelnewsasia.com/singapore/covid-19-vaccines-sinovac-pfizer-

moderna-singapore-study-2625511

Yuan, Ling, et. al., 'A single mutation in the prM protein of Zika virus contributes to fetal microcephaly', *Science*, Vol. 17, No. 358, 17 November 2017.

Yuan, Ping, 'The Chinese Society of Animal Husbandry and Veterinary Medicine held an academic annual meeting to show the appearance of experts. Animal husbandry and veterinary experts highlight the role of science and technology to promote animal husbandry. Experts at the meeting wish Chen Lingfeng 90th birthday', *China Animal Husbandry*, Vol. 19, 2003.

Yuan, Zhiming, 'Current status and future challenges of high-level biosafety laboratories in China', *Journal of Biosafety and Biosecurity*, Vol. 1, Issue 2, September 2019.

Zaugg, Julie, 'The virus hunters who search bat caves to predict the next pandemic', CNN, 27 April 2020.

'ZHAN Qimin', Shenzhen Bay Laboratory, http://www.szbl.ac.cn/en/scientificresearch/researchteam/371.html

Zhao, Frank, 'ACWF Executive Committee Member Chen Wei Promoted to Major General', All-China Women's Federation, 21 July 2015. https://web.archive.org/web/20200416163956/http://www.womenofchina.cn/html/news/china/15071648-1.htm

Zhang, Chi, 'A Novel Scoring System for Prediction of Disease Severity in COVID-19', *Frontiers in Cellular and Infection Microbiology*, Vol. 10, Issue 318, June 2020.

Zhang, Daoyu, et. al., 'Unexpected novel Merbecovirus discoveries in agricultural sequencing datasets from Wuhan, China', *ArXiv* 6 June 2021.

Zhang Leiliang's profile on the website of Shandong First Medical University. https://stic.sdfmu.edu.cn/info/1012/1196.htm#

Zhang, Phoebe, 'Top-grade biosafety lab building spree planned in southern China', South China Morning Post, 25 May 2020. https://www.scmp.com/news/china/science/article/3085977/top-grade-biosafety-lab-building-spree-planned-southern-china

Zhang, Yabin and Ma, Xiaoqing, '65 Years of Study Abroad History: From Soviet Union to the US, From Paid by Government to Paid by Family', Edited by Xiaoyi Wang, Data.163, 28 September 2014.

'Zheng Jinping', Guangzhou Medical University.
https://www.gzhmu.edu.cn/10021716

'Zheng Jinping, the Member of the City's Committee of the Chinese People's Political Consultative Conference (CPPCC): Suggesting building an extra Infectious Disease Unit for Guangzhou National Respiratory Health Medical Center', Guangzhou Institute of Respiratory Health, 5 June 2019.
http://www.gird.cn/show.php?id=458

Zheng, Lei-Ping, Daszak, Peter, Shi, Zhengli, et. al. 'Bat Severe Acute Respiratory Syndrome-Like Coronavirus WIV1 Encodes an Extra Accessory Protein, ORFX, Involved in Modulation of the Host Immune Response', *Journal of Virology*, Vol. 90, No. 14, July 2016.

Zhi, Qiang and Pearson, Margaret, 'China's Hybrid Adaptive Bureaucracy: The Case of the 863 Program for Science and Technology', *Governance: An International Journal of Policy, Administration, and Institutions*, Vol. 30, No. 3, July 2017.

Zhou, Peng, Shi, Zhengli, et. al., 'IFNAR2-dependent gene expression profile induced by IFN-alpha in Pteropus alecto bat cells and impact of IFNAR2 knockout on virus infection', *PLOS ONE*, 17 January 2018.

Zhuang, Pinghui, 'Coronavirus: Indonesia, Mexico approve late-stage trials of Chinese mRNA vaccine hopeful', South China Morning Post, 1 September 2021.
https://www.scmp.com/news/china/science/article/3147168/coronavirus-indonesia-mexico-approve-late-stage-trials-chinese

'鐘南山：智慧、熱血與擔當'('Zhong Nanshan: Wisdom, passion, and responsibility') in 中國高新科技 12 January 2021.
http://www.zggxkjw.com/content-18-9320-1.html

'ZHONG Nanshan', Chinese Academy of Engineering, 7 March 2017.
https://web.archive.org/web/20170306224833/http:/www.cae.cn/cae/jsp/introduction.jsp?oid=20111231115352671145511

'ZHONG Nanshan is hired by People's Hospital of Shenzhen, as an Honorary Director for the Guangzhou Institute of Respiratory Health', People.Cn. 29 July 2021.
http://sz.people.com.cn/n2/2021/0729/c202846-34842681.html

'Zhong Nanshan: outspoken doctor awarded China's top honour', *Xinhua*, 8 September 2020. http://www.xinhuanet.com/english/2020-09/08/c_139352929.htm

'Zhong Nanshan: Wisdom, passion, and responsibility' in *Zhongguo Gaoxin Keji* (Chinese

Emerging High Technology), 12 January 2021.
http://www.zggxkjw.com/content-18-9320-1.html

'ZHONG Nanshan's wife wears the number Five in China's Female National Basketball Team', *Sina*, 16 June 2003.
http://news.sina.com.cn/c/2003-06-16/02521173575.shtml

Zhou, Peng, Shi Zhengli, et. al., 'A pneumonia outbreak associated with a new coronavirus of probable bat origin', *Nature*, Vol. 579, 12 March 2020.